Psychology Revivals

Becoming a Profession

Britain was the first country to recognise art therapy as a profession in the state health service. How did this come about? Can the British experience serve as a model for other countries?

Originally published in 1991 *Becoming a Profession* is the first comprehensive history of art therapists in Britain and of their struggle for professional recognition. Diane Waller discusses the work of the founding art therapists of the 1940s and 1950s and assesses their contribution in detail. She also puts art therapy in a political context, showing how the British Association for Art Therapists worked closely with the trade union movement in its campaigns to get professional recognition.

Becoming a Profession
The history of art therapy in Britain 1940-82

Diane Waller

LONDON AND NEW YORK

First published in 1991
by Routledge

This edition first published in 2013 by Routledge
27 Church Road, Hove, BN3 2FA

Simultaneously published in the USA and Canada
by Routledge
711 Third Avenue, New York, NY 10017

Routledge is an imprint of the Taylor & Francis Group, an informa business

© 1991 Diane Waller

All rights reserved. No part of this book may be reprinted or reproduced or utilised in any form or by any electronic, mechanical, or other means, now known or hereafter invented, including photocopying and recording, or in any information storage or retrieval system, without permission in writing from the publishers.

Publisher's Note
The publisher has gone to great lengths to ensure the quality of this reprint but points out that some imperfections in the original copies may be apparent.

Disclaimer
The publisher has made every effort to trace copyright holders and welcomes correspondence from those they have been unable to contact.

A Library of Congress record exists under ISBN: 0415025818

ISBN: 978-0-415-84473-4 (hbk)
ISBN: 978-0-203-75020-9 (ebk)

Becoming a profession

Britain was the first country to recognise art therapy as a profession in the state health service, and the British example continues to serve as a model for other countries wishing to develop on similar lines. *Becoming a Profession* is the first comprehensive historical account of the way in which art therapists achieved recognition and the strategies they employed to establish their training. It covers the period from 1940, when the term was first used in Britain, to 1982, when the Whitley Council granted art therapy its own career and salary structure.

Diane Waller draws on a vast amount of previously unpublished material to show how the disciplines of art education, psychiatry and psychoanalysis were influential in giving rise to notions of 'art as healing' and 'art as expression'. She includes interviews with some of the founder art therapists of the 1940s and 1950s, and assesses their contribution in detail. She also describes the work of the British Association of Art Therapists (BAAT), and in particular the campaigns for recognition mounted by BAAT in co-operation with the trade union movement.

Fascinating reading for all practising art therapists, art therapy teachers and students, *Becoming a Profession* will also be relevant to anyone interested in the formation and development of professions.

Diane Waller is head of the Art Psychotherapy Unit at Goldsmiths' College, University of London. In 1989 she was appointed the first adviser in art therapy to the Department of Health.

Becoming a profession
The history of art therapy in Britain
1940–82

Diane Waller

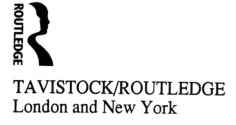

TAVISTOCK/ROUTLEDGE
London and New York

First published in 1991
by Routledge
11 New Fetter Lane, London EC4P 4EE

Simultaneously published in the USA and Canada
by Routledge
a division of Routledge, Chapman and Hall Inc.
29 West 35th Street, New York, NY 10001

©1991 Diane Waller

Typeset by Michael Mepham, Frome, Somerset
Printed and bound in Great Britain by
Mackays of Chatham PLC, Chatham, Kent

All rights reserved. No part of this book may be reprinted or
reproduced or utilized in any form or by any electronic,
mechanical, or other means, now known or hereafter invented,
including photocopying and recording, or in any information
storage or retrieval system, without permission in writing from
the publishers.

British Library Cataloguing in Publication Data
Waller, Diane, *1943–*
  Becoming a profession: the history of art therapy
  in Britain, 1940–82.
  1. Great Britain. Art Therapy, history
  I. Title
  615.851560941

Library of Congress Cataloging in Publication Data
Waller, Diane, 1943–
  Becoming a profession: the history of art therapy
  in Britain, 1940–82 / Diane Waller.
  p.   cm.
  Includes bibliographical references.
  1. Art therapy—Great Britain—History. I. Title.
  RC489.A7W36 1991
  615. 8'5156'0941—dc20   91-8570
                                                               CIP

    ISBN 0–415–02581–8
       0–415–05820–1 (pbk)

Contents

Foreword		viii
Roland Littlewood		
Acknowledgements		x
Introduction		xi

Part I   Background to art therapy

1	Some views of art therapy	3
2	Art therapy's roots in art education	16
3	Psychiatry and art	25

Part II   The role of individual artists and psychotherapists in the development of art therapy from the 1940s to the formation of BAAT

	Introduction	35
4	The context of the visual arts and health care provision in the 1940s	38
5	Adrian Hill	45
6	Edward Adamson and Rita Simon: moving from commercial art to art therapy	52
7	The Withymead Centre: the role of Gilbert and Irene Champernowne in promoting the theory and practice of art therapy	60
8	The influence of psychoanalysts on the intellectual development of art therapy	73
9	Reflections on being a pioneer art therapist	80

v

Becoming a profession

Part III Beginning of organised activity: the first working parties in art therapy

Introduction   93

10 Art therapy in the witness box   94

11 A struggle for ownership   100

12 Moves towards organised activity: the idea of forming a professional association   106

13 The inaugural meeting of BAAT: aims and objects established   113

14 Some of the main issues influencing BAAT's decision to become a Central Association of the NUT   119

15 The campaign organised by BAAT and the NUT to gain comparable status with adult education lecturers   129

16 Some problems and contradictions within the campaign for employment under the LEAs   146

17 First moves towards the Health Service   151

18 Struggles for control of art therapy in the context of a Whitley Council initiative   162

Part IV The campaign to establish art therapy in the NHS

Introduction   181

19 BAAT and ASTMS: joint negotiations for a place on the Whitley Council for art therapists   183

20 The DHSS Consultative Document on art, music, drama, etc., therapy and the subsequent campaign by BAAT and ASTMS to change its recommendations   197

21 The Clegg Commission   206

Part V Training in art therapy

Introduction   219

22 Some contextual background and early views on training   221

23 Art therapy training within an educational framework   229

Contents

24 The BAAT Registration and Training Sub-Committee
and its contribution to the debate on art therapy training
during the 1970s   242

25 Attempts at training which failed to materialise   253

Part VI   Concluding thoughts

26 After 1982: fresh challenges for art therapists   261

Appendix: BAAT Registration Advisory Committee:
report and recommendations   267

References   273

Name index   280

Subject index   284

Foreword

Humankind has devised a rich variety of practical therapies and forms of healing. Many employ a biomedical and thus western idiom while others are closely aligned to popular everyday ways of alleviating physical and psychological distress, to patterns of resolution which accept the individual as deriving his/her identity through a matrix of locally accepted values, through religious, ethical, political or kin relationships.

Among this vast array of world-wide practices, both professional and popular, art therapy has a distinctive status. Nearly all therapies work through a formal relationship between the cause of sickness and its treatment: alleviation of distress is achieved simply through the therapist counter-acting or reversing the cause of the illness for the patient. Penicillin counters the bacterium, exorcism the spirit intrusion, behaviour therapy the faulty conditioning. The theories of causation and resolution are simple mirror images of each other.

Art therapy, by contrast, is distinctive in its emphasis on the patient as an active searching agent: no longer a passive being through whom practitioners simply represent their clinical systems, but a unique individual capable of self-healing and capable of self-determination. Its symbols are not the paraphernalia of the physician or the shaman but the vital creations of the patient.

The healing potential of visual imagery has been recognised in all societies I know. In the West, there is a long-standing recognition that 'art' can be an active response to personal trauma, a reframing of the problem and its working through. As Diane Waller shows here in her account of the differences between the supporters of *L'Art Brut* and the nascent art therapists, there were problems of value here. Do we privilege the spontaneous art works of those who are in a state of profound personal crisis or psychiatric illness, allocating to them a special 'outsider' status which guarantees their authenticity? Or, do we abandon our perspectives of art criticism to focus on the meaning of the art work within the

Foreword

immediate context of the individual's life? Are these two approaches compatible?

Art therapy takes, of course, the second position one closer to the healing traditions of small-scale 'tribal' societies than to the arid connoisseurship of 'fine art'. The tensions within what was to become art therapy are well developed in Diane Waller's account which continually show the interplay between the personal motivations of the pioneers and the social framework within which they developed. Was art therapy to be a recreation? Was it art? A diagnostic aid? A type of occupational therapy? Was it dynamic psychotherapy? Or even, as some argued, a sort of remedial art teaching? Was it a skill to be acquired by any health professional, or was it to be a distinctive disipline in itself? When does a profession become a profession?

Students of art therapy now know what happened, but the results were by no means foreordained. When we become members of a profession, with all the expectations of what Max Weber argued 'a profession' should conventionally constitute – its particular expertise and training, accreditation, membership of a body of appropriately qualified colleagues, ethics committees, journals, conferences, and so on – it is easy to forget the personalities and politics, the contingencies and sheer happenstance which comprise the history of any practice.

For art therapy students, then, here is their history written by one actively engaged in the events which she chronicles. For the social historian, an absorbing account of the recognition of a new profession which has developed a distinct body of theoretical and practical knowledge with, at the same time, a concern for the quality of life and status of its practitioners. We learn of the conflicts between the pragmatic demands for trade union representation and a type of understanding rooted in image and metaphor; between art as a spontaneous exercise and art as a process of guided healing.

When a disipline comes of age, its history comes to be written (and indeed the two processes are not necessarily distinct). From charisma to routine; so Weber put it, from the visions of pioneers to an accepted social role. As written here, it is evident that the 'routine' of art therapy will never become one of dull complacency but can only continue its active searching. The tension between its two poles, between art and therapy, between the spontaneous and the healing, constitute its vigour and its excitement.

Roland Littlewood
Reader in Psychiatry and Anthropology,
University College,
London

Acknowledgements

This book has taken a long time to write and I have often felt daunted by the task. Being a historical account of the way that art therapy has developed during the past five decades, it has involved discussion and debate with a very large number of people, all of whom have played a part in its evolution. A simple acknowledgement is really inadequate as an appreciation of their help, as it is for the art therapists who gave the interviews and contributed valuable written material, and I can only hope that I have done justice to them in the text. I am sad that Ralph Pickford and Elizabeth Wills died before the book could be finished.

The material for the book was prepared in the first place for a DPhil of the University of Sussex. Over the period of preparation I had four supervisors – Mary and Martin Lewis, Peter Kutnik, and, in the past three year, Barry Cooper. I am indebted to all of them for their patience for supporting an area of study which was unfamiliar. I owe special thanks to Barry Cooper for introducing me to the literature on the sociology of professions and for his constructive criticism and encouragement, especially during particularly difficult periods of writing up.

I am grateful to the Council of the British Association of Art Therapists for giving permission to use archive material, and to my friends, colleagues, and students for being prepared to debate many of the issues raised in the book.

Finally, I should like to try to express my gratitude to Dan Lumley, who has been a solid source of support throughout my involvement with 'art therapy matters' and has patiently read through and commented on the drafts and put up with much evil temper and despair combined with moments of extreme elation as the book took shape. I hope he will feel the effort is worthwhile!

Introduction

This book will describe the struggle of art therapists to gain recognition and validation for their work within the British National Health Service and higher education.

I began my research for a DPhil thesis (and also for this book) 'officially' in 1981, the year in which the Department of Health acknowledged the necessity for art therapists to be trained in the 'therapeutic application of their art'. From being closely involved in the negotiations leading to the DHSS's acknowledgement, both as an officer of the British Association of Art Therapists and as an initiator of art therapy training, I had the idea that art therapy was a term that had been used loosely to cover a variety of elements, some harmonious, some conflicting, but held together by a conviction on the part of the practitioners that there was a special and positive value in using visual art imagery in the treatment of a wide range of emotional disorders and handicaps. In order to continue to be involved in this work, and to make sense of my own role within it, I needed to stand back a little, to understand more about the historical and political factors which had caused art therapy to develop in a certain way in Britain. I realised how specific this development was when I began to work in other European countries, where art therapy is emerging from medical and paramedical roots rather than from the arts. Such a historical analysis, partial though it will obviously be, and even painful to come to terms with in some areas, seems to me essential if the art therapy movement is to continue to flourish both in theory and practice, as a radical form of psychotherapy.

Part I: Background

I decided to limit this historical account of art therapy to the period between 1938 and 1982 approximately, that is from the time that the term was first used by Adrian Hill for the work he was carrying out in sanatoriums, to the point where art therapy was assimilated to the Whitley Council in 1982. I have, however, presented some introductory material

Becoming a profession

concerning the pre-Second World War context in which the notions of 'art as healing' and 'art as expression' began to emerge. Some definitions of art therapy, from the 1940s to the present, are included to show both the convergence and divergence of opinion among practitioners. As many of the founder art therapists were art teachers and purport to have been influenced by the 'child centred' approach to art education, I shall draw attention to the main aspects of this approach and some of its historical antecedents. Equally important is the contribution of psychiatrists, as far back as the mid-nineteenth century, who were fascinated by the so-called 'art of the insane' and who encouraged artists to work with their patients. Many artists were equally fascinated by patients' art work and in some cases this led them to work as art therapists. I shall discuss the work of doctors and psychiatrists who influenced artists and vice versa, concluding with a descriptive account of Arthur Segal's painting school in Hampstead, where he aimed to bring together doctors, artists, and psychiatric patients as his pupils.

Part II: Individual contributions

The work of several individuals who have made long-lasting contributions to art therapy is explored in the context of wartime and post-war Britain, the formation of the National Health Service, and the position of the visual arts at that time. In drawing attention to particular individuals, it is important to bear in mind that such a selection is intended, not to negate the contributions of others not mentioned or mentioned only briefly, but simply to give an illustration of the kinds of backgrounds and motivating forces which drove the pioneers of art therapy to continue their work in the face of many difficulties.

Part III: First organised activity

In this section I shall discuss, first, the working parties on art therapy which were sponsored by the National Association for Mental Health from the late 1940s through the 1950s, and, second, the events leading up to the formation of the British Association of Art Therapists in 1964.

Many of the individuals mentioned in Part II actively participated, and attempted to clarify their ideas about art therapy as a process. In the course of these meetings, they sowed the seeds for the emergence of a new occupational group called art therapists.

At the same time, they prompted art therapy in hospitals by lecturing, broadcasting, publishing, and holding exhibitions, and by practising themselves either in the NHS or privately. The years 1964 to 1977 marked a period when collective work predominated, co-ordinated by the British

Introduction

Association of Art Therapists in liaison with the National Union of Teachers. It was characterised by identification with art education and art education lecturers, who served as comparators for art therapists. The early association of BAAT with the NUT was important in establishing the trade union function of BAAT which has remained strong ever since. The aims and objectives of BAAT will be discussed, together with the strategies employed to put them into practice – particularly the campaign to have art therapists employed by local education authorities.

Part IV: Moves towards the NHS: BAAT links with ASTMS

The change of strategy necessitated by developments in the art therapy movement itself, in higher education and in government policy on adult education led BAAT to sever its association with the NUT and thus lose its identification with 'education'. The mid-1970s marked a period of search for a new strategy and new identity, and a long-term campaign for a career and salary structure within the NHS. The link with the health service union, the Association of Scientific, Technical and Managerial Staff, proved vital in achieving this goal.

Part V: Training

Although discussions about appropriate training for art therapy had been going on since the late 1940s, the major developments took place from 1965 onwards. One of BAAT's aims was to promote training courses, and initially these were conceived of as taking place within an art education framework. With the advent of a course which, although situated in an art college, was identified more closely with the health service, and with the changes of strategy for regulating the employment of art therapists being evolved by BAAT, the policy changed towards promoting art therapy training as separate from that of art teachers. The entry requirements, i. e. a degree or equivalent in art or design plus working experience, were maintained and generally adhered to in principle by the three training courses which grew up during the 1970s.

BAAT became the body which regulated training through the provision of 'core course requirements', and, as well as drawing attention to those courses which became 'recognised', I shall briefly discuss those which did not, suggesting some of the reasons for their demise.

Part VI: Conclusion

It will be apparent from the material discussed in the book that the concept of art therapy in Britain has emerged from many and varied roots,

Becoming a profession

influenced by people and institutions as seemingly far apart as Carl Jung and the British Red Cross Movement, the Beveridge Report which led to the National Health Service and the Coldstream Report concerning the structure of art education. Its practitioners are mainly artists, working in a medical environment, albeit with a training in 'therapy'. It now has training courses at diploma and master's level, in two universities and a college of higher education, and its own adviser to the DHSS. Art therapy seems to straddle the arts and the sciences. It does not fit neatly into any system. Its early practitioners rejected more 'traditional' ways of earning a living through their art in favour of the unknown path of art therapy. Hundreds of graduates apply each year for the sixty or so places available on courses. Art therapy, as an occupation and perhaps as a profession, exists, despite many attempts to subsume it under other labels.

The conclusion will serve as a summary of the patterns which have emerged throughout the period under discussion, and will draw attention to issues which may need to be further researched or at least debated within the profession in the interests of maintaining a dynamic approach to patient care.

My approach to writing the book

When I started gathering material for this book, I held the view that a profession was like a person and went through the same stages of development. Being 'acknowledged' by the DHSS could have been seen to represent a step towards 'maturity' as far as art therapy was concerned. I played with this concept in 'Art therapy in adolescence' 1987, subtitled 'A metaphorical view of a profession in progress', in which I suggested that many of the features of the profession at that time could be likened to the human adolescent stage. But I was not very happy to continue with this model because the logical outcome would be the death of the profession, or a kind of fossilised 'maturity'. So I subsequently began to explore other models of profession which would present a less pessimistic outcome. This exploration took me into the area of the sociology of professions and eventually to the work of Bucher and Strauss (1961), two American sociologists who present a 'process' model of professions, focusing on diversity and conflicts of interests which give rise to 'missions' within a profession, and on the implications of these processes for development and change. In this model, a profession is seen in terms of segments, missions, and evolution, and in relationship to the political and economic fluctuations of a given society. It takes into account the fact that there are bound to be conflicts, or at least differences of opinion, within any profession, out of which new movements or segments may develop.

Segments develop distinct identities, a sense of the past and goals for the future, and they organize activities which will secure an institutional

Introduction

position and implement their distinctive missions. The competition and conflict of segments in movement cause the organisation of the profession to shift. Through reference to this model, it is possible to show how conflicts within the art therapy movement, which were experienced at the time by all sides as potentially destructive, were eventually resolved, enabling the group to move to a different stage.

Such a 'process' model is far more in keeping with how I personally see art therapy: that is, as providing the opportunity for a recipient to experience their own conflicts through the combination of image-making and a close relationship with the therapist, and thus to have the possibility of resolving them and gaining the power to change – and moreover, to continue to be able to do so. This is opposed to a view of therapy which suggests a 'once and for all' cure. I have been fortunate in being able to draw on a large archive of material held by BAAT and containing original documents, letters, minutes of meetings, constitutions, agreements, memoranda, etc., and the archive of the late Irene Champernowne in which she had stored notes of the early art therapy working party meetings, together with material about the formation of the Withymead Centre.

Most important, though, and, from my point of view, rewarding, has been the material gained from the interviews I conducted with a range of practising art therapists, including people who were practising in the 1940s and who became founder members of BAAT. Their memories and impressions have provided a 'living' element in the book. The books and articles written by British art therapists from the 1940s onwards have also served as valuable material in the preparation of this history.

I have also drawn on my own experience as a member of BAAT for twenty years and an officer during the period of negotiations with the DHSS. There are obviously problems inherent in trying to write a history of a profession while being actively involved in the processes that have shaped that profession. It is inevitable that the account will have a bias, and in my case that is revealed through the emphasis on the organised activity of the professional association, BAAT, especially in its trade union function. Although not claiming to be a sociologist, I have certainly drawn on sociological models to help me to order the material. I have been alerted to the problem of masquerading as an analyst or interpreter while actually being prescriptive through studying Colin Lacey's account of *The Socialisation of Teachers* in which he draws attention to the distinction between 'prescriptive' and 'analytical' psychology. Lacey says:

> As Hansen (1967) points out, the dangers of not distinguishing these studies are obvious. Personal prejudice masquerading as analysis is one, and Hansen enumerates a number of others.... Sociologists will continue to present their work as analytical even though it contains

xv

Becoming a profession

large prescriptive elements. It will require the critical appraisal of colleagues and others to locate and identify the prescriptive bias.

(Lacey 1977: 25–9)

Such appraisal will surely serve to modify my account, and lead to further histories of art therapy which will focus on other elements of the discipline. For the time being, though, I offer the following account in the hope of providing some insight into how, as art therapists, we have arrived at our current state.

Part I

Background to art therapy

Chapter one

Some views of art therapy

I have stated in the preamble that I consider art therapy to be a term used to describe a collection of diverse practices, held together by their practitioners' belief in the healing value of image-making. In this chapter, I shall draw attention to the way that art therapy has been defined by many art therapists, mainly from Britain but also from the USA where the definitions appear to have influenced the practice in Britain.

This chapter will also serve to map out areas of intellectual dispute. Of necessity, it will contain several quotes, showing how each author constructs their image of art therapy.

The current definition of an art therapist

The currently accepted public definition of an art therapist in use by the Department of Health is as follows:

> A person who is responsible for organising appropriate programmes of art activities of a therapeutic application with patients, individually or in groups, and possesses a degree or equivalent for entry to an accepted post-graduate training course, and also a qualification in art therapy following the completion of an accepted course at a recognised institution of further or higher education.
>
> (DHSS: Personnel Memorandum, 6 March 1981)

There is, however, no definition of 'art therapy' in any document of the DHSS. The most current 'official' definition is that agreed by BAAT and used in a document entitled *Artists and Art Therapists: a brief discussion of their roles within hospitals, clinics, special schools and in the community*:

> The focus of art therapy is the image, and the process involves a transaction between the creator (the patient), the artefact and the therapist. As in all therapy, bringing unconscious feelings to a conscious level and therafter exploring them holds true for Art Therapy,

3

but here the richness of artistic symbol and metaphor illuminate the process.

Art therapists have a considerable understanding of art processes, are proficient in the area of non-verbal and symbolic communication, and aim to provide an environment in which patients feel safe enough to express strong emotions.

Aesthetic standards are of little importance in the context of Art Therapy – rather the expression and condensation of unconscious feelings that art-making engenders are at the heart of the therapeutic transaction.

(BAAT 1989)

This document was prepared for circulation to all health and social services departments and to teachers of children with special needs and advisers. We can see that there is a difference between the two statements, in that the first focuses on seemingly practical 'activities' and the second on 'processes involving the unconscious'. This difference of perception has led to ongoing problems, as I shall try to show in later chapters.

Different things to different people

It has become very clear to art therapists in encountering NHS and other professionals, and also members of the public, that the term 'art therapy' means very different things to different people. Sometimes nurses, occupational therapists, art students, and volunteers believe they are 'doing art therapy' when they offer art materials to patients, encourage them to paint murals, try to analyse their drawings, set art and craft exercises, encourage the making of Christmas cards and decoration of wards.

To test out public understanding of art therapy, a small project was undertaken by a postgraduate art therapy student, in which a cross-section of the general public from Deptford, Hampstead, and Preston was invited to comment on what they thought art therapy to be about. The nearest guesses were that it 'had something to do with psychiatry'. Others felt it was 'about making artists feel better', but many had 'no idea' (Setlogelo 1987).

Considering that the occupational group has existed in some form or other since the 1940s, it is interesting that there is such a level of confusion, not only among the public but also among professional colleagues. Myths and misperceptions abound. (See Waller and Gilroy 1986 for further discussion.)

It is necessary, then, to explore some of the ways in which practitioners have defined what they do, and to see if and how this has changed over the years.

Some views of art therapy

Margaret Naumburg

Margaret Naumburg is considered to have been one of the founders, if not *the* founder of art therapy in the USA. She was a psychologist by background, later becoming a psychoanalyst. Her sister was Florence Cane, a well-known art educator, and Margaret too was a keen artist.

In her first published monograph, *Studies of the Free Art Expression of Behaviour Disturbed Children as a Means of Diagnosis and Therapy* (1947), she draws on case histories compiled between 1943 and 1945, referring to 'free art expression' rather than art therapy, and seeming to view the art activity and art objects as concrete versions of a dream. She offers the following comment on the value of this process:

> When emphasis is placed on the release of the patient's personality through his art, and not on any technical proficiency attained, it serves a different therapeutic purpose (from occupational therapy). For the patient it helps to release unexpected capacities which bring confidence and provide satisfaction; and to the psychiatrist it offers a revealing projective technique for both diagnosis and therapy. When the patient has been helped to overcome his inhibitions and is able to express his deepest fears, wishes and fantasies on paper or in clay, he is tapping the unconscious in the symbolic language of images, which will often bring to the surface what he dare not say in words.
>
> (Naumburg 1947)

Later, in *Art Therapy: Its Scope and Function* (1958), Naumburg offered the following definition:

> The process of art therapy is based on the recognition that man's most fundamental thoughts and feelings, derived from the unconscious, reach expression in images rather than in words.
>
> (Naumburg 1958: 511)

and

> The techniques of art therapy are based on the knowledge that every individual, whether trained or untrained in art, has a latent capacity to project his inner conflicts into visual form. As patients picture such inner experiences, it frequently happens that they become more verbally articulate.
>
> (Naumburg 1958: 511)

The emphasis, then, is on the images which arise from the patient's unconscious and which contain conflicts. Once these conflicts are made concrete, they can be understood, which in turn would assist in their resolution. Image-making, because it taps pre-verbal feelings, is more able to produce this resolution than words.

Background to art therapy

In her later books, Naumburg developed a 'dynamic' model of art therapy, which made use of the transference relationship between patient and therapist, suggesting that art or spontaneous image-making was a means to furthering therapeutic communication. (See *Dynamically Oriented Art Therapy: Its Principles and Practices*, 1966.)

Both Margaret Naumburg and her sister Florence were influenced by the 'child art' movement in art education, which stressed the importance to the child of allowing spontaneous image-making to take place. Both believed that everyone had the capacity to become an artist, or at least to be visually creative. Eleanor Ulman, writing in the *American Journal of Art Therapy* in 1983, following the death of Naumburg aged 93, commented:

> It was Numburg who was responsible – almost single-handed – for the emergence of art therapy as a profession. In the 1950s she initiated the first art therapy training courses and she strove mightily in the 1960s for the development of full scale graduate training for art therapists.
>
> (Ulman 1983: 122–3)

Ulman mentions that Naumburg's views eventually departed from those of her sister, so that, by 1958, she was convinced that her work 'had its roots in the transference relationship between patient and therapist' (Naumburg 1958). She also believed that, if an art therapist was well versed in psychotherapy, then art therapy could function as an independent treatment method or an alternative form of psychoanalysis to the verbal mode.

Edith Kramer

Edith Kramer was a contemporary of Naumburg's and an art teacher by background. She is considered by some to be the founder of art therapy, or at least as essential to its development as Naumburg. Kramer still teaches on courses in New York and elsewhere.

Kramer considered that it was the art activity itself that had inherent 'healing' properties, and this gave the opportunity to externalise, re-experience, and resolve conflicting feelings:

> Art is a means of widening the range of human experiences by creating an equivalent for such experiences. It is an area wherein experiences can be chosen, varied, repeated at will. In the creative act, conflict is re-experienced, resolved and integrated.
>
> (Kramer 1958)

Some views of art therapy

Unlike Naumburg, Kramer did not work with the transference, but preferred to focus on the art object as a 'container of emotions' and she related to the patient through their art.

She herself was influenced by Freudian psychoanalysis, believing that art could be a means of sublimating feelings, but she felt this to be positive, in that, for example, out of destructive and aggressive feelings could emerge an object (drawing, painting, model, etc.) which would symbolise these feelings and thus prevent them being acted out.

Both Naumburg and Kramer were practising in the USA during the 1940s at the same time as Adrian Hill and others were introducing the concept of art therapy to British hospitals and sanatoriums. We shall see from the comments made by these early art therapists that the same divergence was emerging in Britain between those who placed emphasis on the image-*making* as therapeutic in itself (Hill *et al.*) and those who saw the art object as both integrative and healing, and also as an aspect of the transference relationship between the therapist and patient (Champernowne *et al.*)

Adrian Hill

In 1945, Hill's book *Art Versus Illness* was published. His work will be fully discussed later on, but it is interesting to note how he considered painting to be helpful to patients:

> To redress the injuries of a morbid introspection, the bitterness and resentment may have to be released by encouraging the sufferers to express their exacerbation in pictorial form, while anxiety and distress in another case may well be deflected and a more hopeful mental attitude established by inciting the very opposite type of picture making and that in the form of a sequence of paintings... never invite a recital of their physical disabilities and forebodings, but concentrate their attention on ways and means for their immediate mental emancipation.
>
> (Hill 1945: 33)

Here we see a basic agreement with Naumburg and Kramer that feelings can be externalised through painting, but the emphasis is on distracting the patient from those feelings, or 'morbid introspection' as Hill puts it.

Marie Petrie

Petrie's book, *Art and Regeneration*, was published in 1946, based on work she had done in the early 1940s. In the context of writing about occupational therapy, she comments:

Background to art therapy

The time has come to enlarge the field even further and to include the practice of the visual arts, more especially in the media employed by occupational therapists, or, better still, to form a distinct new branch, art therapy, requiring a separate training... the indirect remedial and diversional use of the crafts could be supplemented by the vitalising effect of the more spontaneous and personal use of colour, form and rhythm in painting and by the close contact with the earthy materials of sculpture and its laws of space, weight and balance.

(Petrie 1946: 87)

Petrie had much in common with both Kramer and Hill in focusing on the 'healing' and 'integrative' aspects of art. She left Britain for the USA shortly after her book was published and is best known there as an educator with a strong interest in art therapy.

Winston Churchill

Art as therapy received indirect support in the 1940s from Winston Churchill, the Prime Minister of Britain during the Second World War. He shared views similar to those of Hill about the restorative value of painting:

Many remedies are suggested for the avoidance of worry and over-strain by persons, who, over prolonged periods, have to bear exceptional responsibilities and discharge duties upon a very large scale... some advise exercise, and others, repose. Some counsel travel, and others, retreat.... No doubt all these may play their part according to the individual temperament. But the element which is constant and common in all of them is Change.... I consider myself very lucky that late in life I have been able to develop this new taste (for sketching and painting).... Painting came to my rescue in a most trying time and I shall venture in the pages that follow to express the gratitude I feel.

(Churchill 1948: 7–13)

Here we have the suggestion that painting, as a hobby, can provide release from the burdens of responsibility and an escape from worries. We can see the beginnings of the idea that art *is* therapy – if therapy is taken to mean diversion and relaxation, a way of taking one's mind away from conflict and difficult emotions. On the other hand, Naumburg and, to some extent, Kramer, believe it is important to *focus* on these emotions through the art work and try to resolve them with the help of an interested other (the therapist).

Some views of art therapy

Irene Champernowne

As Champernowne said on many occasions, she admired and was influenced by Naumburg's work and had a great respect for it. However, the major influence on Champernowne was C. G. Jung. In her article 'Art therapy in the Withymead Centre', published in the *American Bulletin of Art Therapy* in 1963, she wrote:

> More than 25 years ago I became acutely aware of the fact that words, particularly in prose, were an extremely difficult medium through which to convey our deepest experiences of life. It was clear that the mind was filled with visual, aural and bodily images which were suitable containers for emotions and ideas that were otherwise inexpressible. The experience of these images was not only a means of communication between one human being and another, though that is something we experience here most strongly, but it is also a way of communication from the unconscious levels of experience to a more conscious understanding in the individual himself.
>
> (Champernowne 1963: 97)

She goes on to refer to Jung's use of art media with patients, in which he hoped that his patients would experiment 'with their own nature, a state of fluidity, change and growth where nothing is eternally fixed and hopelessly petrified.' (cited in Champernowne 1963: 98)

Champernowne believed that the therapist, whether art therapist or psychotherapist, needed to 'enter the process with the patient or student and live through it' (1971: 141). She felt in this way the consciousness of both the creator of the image (the patient) and the therapist came together and they could thus understand the message that the image conveyed.

Edward Adamson

Adamson, who was employed as a full-time artist at Netherne Hospital in 1946, felt that art activity in itself was a positive benefit for patients:

> At its simplest it confers the benefits of an occupational activity: it detaches the patient from the deleterious effects of idleness and self-absorption; it imposes a discipline involving concentration and decision-making, and co-operation with and reaction to the limitations of the artistic medium. Finally, it gives the patient satisfaction in the fact that he has created something.
>
> (Adamson 1970: 153)

Adamson cautioned that, when patients were encouraged by psychotherapists to produce paintings, the results often demonstrated the patient's

Background to art therapy

wish to please, which might result in Freudian phallic symbols, or Jungian signs, as the case may be. He felt that the psychotherapist might unconsciously stimulate such manifestations without being aware of the true content of the products.

Although Adamson wrote the above in the late 1960s, he seems not to have changed his views much since the 1940s when he first became involved in art therapy. He stayed firmly in the role of 'artist' believing in the curative value of art. He saw the therapist as a 'catalyst', providing a welcome for the patient's images, whatever form these may take, and encouraging communication (Adamson and Freudenberg 1968: 11).

E. Cunningham Dax

Cunningham Dax, as medical superintendent at the Netherne, believed it was important for the art therapist to remain first and foremost in the role of 'artist'. The artist was responsible for encouraging the patients to paint and for creating

> an atmosphere sympathetic to self-expression and persuasive to production. The fact that he is an artist, a professional and not an amateur, that he can speak with knowledge and authority and that he is in charge of the studio, is important.
>
> (Cunningham Dax 1953)

Later writers do not seem to differ much in their understanding of art therapy from the authors already quoted. Some place emphasis on the healing, change-provoking nature of image-making, others on the relationship between patient and therapist, with the art object forming an important element in the transference.

E. M. Lyddiatt

Lyddiatt was a friend and colleague of Champernowne, and had undergone Jungian analysis. In 1971 she published *Spontaneous Painting and Modelling*, the first British book to be devoted entirely to the practice of art therapy, although it is not titled as such.

Lyddiatt refers to Hill coining the term 'art therapy' in 1938 and points to the rather vague use of the term to cover 'all that goes on under the name of art in hospitals'. Lyddiatt felt that work produced in art therapy sessions should never be viewed as art, and that an ability to draw and paint could actually hinder spontaneous expression. She believed that the fundamental purpose of art therapy was 'to make contact with what is unknown' (1971: 2–3).

Some views of art therapy

Her book was reviewed in *The Times* (3 March 71) under the title 'Art as psychiatric therapy – bridging the gap between the disturbed mind and the doctor'. The anonymous reviewer, 'Our Medical Correspondent', referred to the book as 'one of the most promising empirical approaches to the management of mental illness'. He/she pointed out that 'Spontaneous painting and modelling has to be carefully distinguished from art therapy in the *conventional sense of the term*' (my emphasis). He understands the latter to be about giving patients an interest in life, something to do which was well within their physical capacity and which might develop the patient's individuality and personality. He thought that it was a form of occupational therapy. Here we see a public acknowledgement of two different approaches to art therapy which had emerged from Hill's and Champernowne/Naumburg's approaches. The reviewer concluded that 'Spontaneous painting is not a universal remedy but it is clear that it is a form of psychotherapy that should be practised much more widely than it is.'

Ralph Pickford

At the same time as Lyddiatt was preparing her book, Ralph Pickford, Professor of Psychology at Glasgow University, published *Studies in Psychiatric Art*. Pickford defines art therapy in a chapter entitled 'Principles and problems: notes on art therapy'.

> Art therapy is a mode of expression by which the patient may be said to communicate his problems and conflicts to himself... a constructive link between the unconscious and the conscious... a form of communication between the patient and other people.
>
> (Pickford 1967: 24)

Pickford believed that the art productions of both patients and non-patients could help them to express and utilise unconscious aggression and sexuality and to sublimate them. The art objects could enable a patient to integrate previously fragmented aspects of their personality, which could lead to restoration of 'unity and harmony within the artist's ego' (1967: 25).

As Pickford himself was ready to acknowledge, his approach to art therapy was strongly influenced by his own Freudian analysis, although he does not focus exclusively on a Freudian model in his book.

Joyce Laing

Joyce Laing was a founder member of BAAT, published many articles and pamphlets on art therapy, and made films of her work in Scotland.

Background to art therapy

While art therapist at the Ross Clinic, Aberdeen, Laing published a paper in which she compared the paintings of patients suffering from tuberculosis with those of Expressionist artists. Laing suggested that by externalising inner conflicts through art, patients with a predisposition towards certain physical diseases might be prevented from developing the disease. Adrian Hill's work with TB patients ws carried out after they had developed the disease and while they were recuperating. Laing suggests that art therapy might be used as a form of 'preventive medicine' as well as in 'rehabilitation'. (This notion has received more attention in recent years but is still not well developed.)

In summary then, looking back over the ways in which art therapists and those close to them construed art therapy, it appears that it should have the following characteristics:

1. it should be a means of communicating innermost feelings (Champernowne, Naumburg, Kramer, etc.);
2. it should provide access to a wide range of mark-making and plastic materials (paint, clay, collage, etc.) (Lyddiatt, Kramer, Petrie, etc.);
3. it should take place in a special environment, such as a studio in a hospital (Adamson, Cunningham Dax, Champernowne, etc);
4. it should consist of patient, therapist and art work (Naumburg, Champernowne, Adamson);
5. the approach of the therapist might vary, in that they may (Hill, Petrie, Pickford) or may not (Lyddiatt) regard the product of the session as 'art'. They would tend not to offer instruction or technical assistance except in the interests of the patient trying to realise an image or form necessary to their communication.

Art therapy in the 1980s: the current position

The issue of the transference relationship between the patient and the art therapist was taken up again by British art therapists only in the 1980s. During the 1970s there was a dearth of publications in Britain. There were many articles, but, after Lyddiatt's book, no major works on art therapy until the 1980s. *Inscape*, the journal of the British Association of Art Therapists, had been founded in 1969 and was published twice a year, but all editors experienced difficulty in getting art therapists to contribute. One reason for this may have been that the energy of the small movement was taken up with trying to establish itself in the NHS: in other words, with organisational matters. Some research was going on in the training establishments, notably at Birmingham Polytechnic, but in comparison with the USA, few books had been produced.

Some views of art therapy

Art as Therapy

In 1984, *Art as Therapy* was published. This was a collection of essays by fifteen British art therapists or psychotherapists involved with art therapy. Most focused on practice with specific client groups, and there were chapters on training and on the history and philosophy of art therapy.

The book's editor Tessa Dalley takes up the issue of transference:

> As with any therapeutic endeavour, the relationship between the therapist and client is of central importance. Art is used as a medium through which this relationship develops. Although the art production becomes the focus of the relationship, the strong feelings that develop between patient and therapist are usually concerned with transference.
>
> (Dalley 1984: xxii)

Dalley goes on to point out that the dynamics of transference and countertransference are complex. Sometimes, psychoanalysts consider that focusing on an art production detracts from the 'real work' between therapist and patient. Dalley suggests that, whereas transference is the main tool of a psychotherapist, art is the central therapeutic agent for an art therapist, even though transference develops and is a powerful phenomenon within an art therapy relationship. This view of art therapy is not far from that of Naumburg, writing back in the 1950s.

In a chapter on 'Art therapy as a form of psychotherapy', John Birtchnell, a psychiatrist at the Institute of Psychiatry and a long-time active member of the art therapy movement, criticised the notion that art is 'healing':

> There are still others who believe that it is sufficient to make the aesthetic statement in order to resolve the conflict which led to it. They speak of the therapeutic value of art and consider that patients can paint their way back to health without the assistance of a therapist. It is my belief that various forms of aesthetic pursuit, while being satisfying in themselves, do not bring emotions and conflicts near enough to the surface; or if they do we do not hold onto them long enough to work with them.
>
> (Birtchnell 1984: 37)

Birtchnell is concerned that some art therapists may be caught up in attitudes common during the 1940s in large psychiatric hospitals: 'There are unfortunately still those who use the pictures painted in art therapy sessions as aids to diagnosis and such people may not appreciate that mad pictures are not necessarily painted by mad patients' (1984: 39).

There is little evidence to show that art therapists do work in this way, but Birtchnell may be aiming his criticism more at psychiatrists. He has

13

Background to art therapy

persistently challenged the view that art therapists should be art graduates before training, fearing that such graduates will be too absorbed with the aesthetic value of art work. He shares this anxiety with the late Irene Champernowne, who tackled the issue in her article 'Art and therapy: an uneasy partnership' in 1971.

Art Therapy for Groups: a handbook of themes, games, and structures

This is another collective work, edited by Marion Liebmann and produced out of her MA research at Birmingham Polytechnic. It has a very different focus from *Art as Therapy* (in which Liebmann wrote a chapter entitled 'Art games and group structures') in that it offers practical suggestions for running art groups, which are designed to be used by art therapists or other workers. The book came into a lot of criticism for its emphasis on setting themes and possibly giving other NHS and social services staff the means to run 'art therapy' groups.

Other art therapists influenced by group work, and especially by group analytic art therapy, are Gerry McNeilly (1985, 1986) and myself (1983, 1984a) and there are now an increasing number of art therapists trained as group psychotherapists (Joan Woddis, Sally Skaife, Val Huet, etc.) and combining the models.

Images of Art Therapy

Yet another book by several authors, this one was written by seven female art therapists (Dalley *et al.* 1987) and reflects new developments in theory and practice. For example, the influence of the British object-relations school, and especially Klein and Winnicott, is evident, as is the interest in group dynamics as applied to a profession (Waller) and work with children (Case, Halliday). The issue of transference is taken up again by Schaverien. There is no evidence in this book to compound Birtchnell's anxieties, even though the writers all come from a strong art background and have worked in many different clinical situations.

Summary

From the discussion of various definitions and approaches put forward by practitioners of art therapy from the 1940s to the present, we can see how there was initially a difference in the way that art therapy was perceived by Adrian Hill and Margaret Naumburg/Irene Champernowne. Hill placed emphasis on the making of art as a therapeutic occupation, the others on the making of images as part of a therapeutic transaction between patient and therapist. In more recent years, the views of

Some views of art therapy

Naumburg and Champernowne have tended to dominate in British art therapy (according to the literature and to the syllabuses of training courses) and Adrian Hill's view has become split off into a segment now more accurately subsumed under the 'Hospital Arts' movement.

This brief sketch, of necessity excluding many contributors to the literature, provides a background from which we may proceed to examine the development of art therapy towards organising itself as a profession.

Chapter two

Art therapy's roots in art education

Many of the founder art therapists were art teachers and were influenced, either consciously or unconsciously, by their own art education, which in the 1940s and 1950s tended towards the 'child-centred' approach. This approach had developed in the period between the two major world wars, a time of economic stringency and apprehension.

For many years, an art teaching qualification formed part of the membership requirements of the professional association, which was for ten years a central association of the National Union of Teachers. From my understanding of the way in which art therapy is developing in other European countries, I have come to the conclusion that the strong link with art education is peculiar to the development of art therapy in Britain and in the USA and some exploration of this fact is required.

Historical links

MacDonald makes the following observation about the state of art in the late nineteenth century:

> The downfall of academic High Art at the end of the 19th century and the rise of the colourful post Impressionist work shortly afterwards, made possible for the first time a comparison between child and adult art. Child art, primitive art, tribal art and Western Asiatic art were no longer regarded as crude, but rather as sensitive and expressive forms of art.
>
> (MacDonald 1970: 329)

During that period, the term 'Child Art' was coined by Franz Cizek, and the movement was to become widespread throughout Europe.

Cizek was born in 1865 at Leitmeritz, in Bohemia. He entered the Academy of Fine Arts in Vienna at the age of 20 and was in close contact with the founders of the Secession movement. This movement, founded by Gustav Klimt, was a revolt by artists against what they regarded as traditional 'academic' art. The movement owed much to writers active in

Art therapy's roots in art education

left-wing politics as well as to artists, and its aims were to break with previous classical art movements, to make a critical assault on bourgeois culture, and to seek a refuge from the pressures of the external world. There seem to be similarities with the 'Art as Regeneration' movement which inspired both Adrian Hill and Marie Petrie, for fundamental to both was a belief that the arts could promote change and liven up a jaded culture, in the case of post-Empire and post-war depression.

Shorske described Austria at that time as 'a hothouse with political crisis providing the heat'. He maintained that:

> Almost simultaneously in one area after another, that city's intelligentsia produced innovations that became identified throughout the European cultural sphere as Vienna 'schools' – notably in psychology, art history and music. But even in fields where an international awareness of Austrian achievement dawned more slowly – in literature, architecture, painting and politics, for example, the Austrians engaged in critical reformations or subversive transformations of their traditions that their own society perceived as radically new if not indeed revolutionary.
>
> (Shorske 1981: xxvi)

Cizek was associated with the Secession from its beginning and in his rejection of traditional art-teaching methods, became one of Austria's most progressive art teachers. Cizek believed that every child had the potential for creative expression, and those who came to his studio were encouraged to engage in 'free expression', with Cizek providing the materials and the support for their efforts.

Wilhelm Viola, one of Cizek's biographers and a staunch disciple, introduced these concepts to Britain through his books and his lectures to teachers throughout the country. Viola reported that Cizek believed the teacher's function was to create an atmosphere conducive to creative work, to gain rapport with the children and take them seriously, and to provide love, security, and significance (1942: 35–6).

Cizek's personal friends were significant figures in the arts – Klimt, Olbrich, Moser, Otto Wagner – and they were excited and impressed by Cizek's ideas. With their encouragement, Cizek submitted a proposal to the Vienna Schoolboard for a new school, the aims of which he stated as: 'To let the children grow, develop and mature.' The Board considered such aims inadequate and turned down the proposal, but later, in 1897, Cizek got permission to open a juvenile art class – an experiment which proved so successful that he was offered rooms in the state art school.

Viola considered that the minimum of state support that Cizek received was a blessing, because it prevented interference in his innovative work. Later, we shall see that there are parallels in this attitude between Cizek

Background to art therapy

and Champernowne, in her relations with the NHS while at the Withymead Centre.

In 1908, a public exhibition entitled the 'Kunstschau' was mounted, presided over by Gustav Klimt. A special feature of the Kunstschau was a garden designed by William Morris, eminent art educator and founder of the Arts and Crafts Movement in Britain. The whole event had a strongly anti-bourgeois flavour. Cizek was given pride of place there for an exhibition of children's art: The Art of the Child. At that time he was head of the department of education in the Arts and Crafts School, where Oscar Kokoschka was studying to be an art teacher. According to Shorske, this would have been considered a suitable occupation, considering that he came from the 'artisan' class. Had he aspired to the less secure but more prestigious career as a painter, he would have gone to the Academy of Fine Arts. Such attitudes reflected the snobbishness of the art world towards art teaching – an attitude which is not confined to nineteenth-century Vienna.

In Cizek's teaching philosophy, there is, I suggest, a clear parallel with the basic principles of non-directive art therapy practiced in Britain throughout the 1950s and up to the present day, some of which were illustrated in Chapter 1. By this I mean that the therapist provides a room, materials, and a non-judgmental attitude, assuming that each patient has the potential to create images and to develop him or herself through this creative act. The therapist follows the patient's image-making and avoids directing it.

Did Cizek follow his own rules in practice, though? One of the founder members of BAAT, who worked as an art therapist in a large psychiatric hospital from the 1950s, was a pupil of Cizek's and attended his Saturday morning classes. She was eight at the time (1920s) and the school was well established. In her interview she said:

> Cizek was tall and had a goatee beard, frock coat, striped trousers. He appeared awe-inspiring and was dominating. One could do what one liked.... I can't remember how I started.... The great moment came in the second or third year when he saw a little drawing and he said...'You may do this one big...'. If you did a figure the head had to reach to the top and fill the whole page... it was one of the rules. There were set rules, not laid down, but understood.... You were not allowed to be late. It was taken very ill if you missed a session. It was to be absolutely serious. There was no noise in the room.

As in 'non-directive therapy' or in 'spontaneous painting' (Lyddiatt), there were no rules and boundaries but within this structure the pupil was expected to produce images from the imagination, with the minimum of technical assistance.

18

Art therapy's roots in art education

In 'Art teaching and art therapy' (1984) I have pointed out that the theories of art education which were prevalent in the 1930s continued in modified forms well into the 1960s under the influence of authors like Herbert Read (*Education Through Art*, 1943) and Viktor Lowenfeld (*Creative and Mental Growth*, 1947). Art was a means for developing a seeing, thinking, feeling, and creative human being, a logical development of the ideas of the early-twentieth-century American educational philosopher John Dewey and an ideal well suited to a world war and post-war period when the children, at least, could have their freedom. But there is a weakness in a theory of art as development which stressed 'natural' development and seemed to pay scant attention to the fact that a child or adult could be positively as well as negatively influenced by social and cultural factors.

Cizek was passionate in his belief in 'child art'. In a lecture to teachers in 1924, he said:

> Child art is sacred. If it is destroyed, external values are destroyed. And if it is covered by foreign layers, the natural growth of the child is made impossible. The task is to let the child grow naturally, but not arbitrarily.
>
> (Viola 1942: 45)

Such a strong belief may have arisen partly as a result of the work of G. Stanley Hall, the leading American psychologist of education at the turn of the nineteenth century, who received the first doctorate in psychology of Harvard University in 1878. Hall's major work on *Adolescence* (1904) advanced a concept, developed earlier by Rousseau and continued by Pestalozzi and Froebel, that the mind of the child was qualitatively different from that of an adult, and the teacher's task was to facilitate its 'natural development'. Hall wrote that a child's personal development was 'a recapitulation of the human race'. He felt that by studying the child, one could obtain an understanding of how the race came to be what it is. Hall's views, and those of his chief disciple, A. F. Chamberlain, are frankly racist, but at the time they were acceptable as part of the imperialist culture, when 'primitive people' (especially Blacks) were regarded as the 'children of the race'.

Gould (1981: 114–15) gives an account of the recapitulation theory and its domination of several professions. It served as a general theory of biological determinism, where all 'inferior' groups – races, sexes, and classes – were compared with the children of white males.

Gould suggests that recapitulation spilled over from biology to influence other disciplines in crucial ways, including psychology and medicine, with Freud and Jung being no exceptions. It appears that art education did not escape, as a result of the work of Hall and his followers. In Britain, James Sully, an eminent psychologist, compared the aesthetic

Background to art therapy

senses of children and 'savages' but gave the edge to children (1895: 386). His appallingly racist statements, now seeming blatantly crude and simplistic in postulating, among other things, that both children and 'savages' share a delight in 'bright, glistening things and gay colours, and the use of feathers', are unfortunately not so unconnected with problems that ethnic groups experience in modern Britain. Littlewood and Lipsedge (1982) have discussed this issue in terms of the problems that these groups experience in obtaining psychotherapy because of the assumptions that are made about their capacity to symbolise or 'have insight'.

Eisner (1972), putting aside the racist elements in Hall's work, considered that it had a profound significance to art education in that it gave rise to the idea of using the curriculum to meet the child's needs rather than the teacher's. 'Progressive' educators, influenced by Cizek, Hall, and also by John Dewey, felt it was important for the child to initiate image-making in art classes, whereas previously the teacher had set examples to copy or put up still-lifes or set tasks. (I was reminded of the impact of the child art movement in Britain after a visit to Bulgaria in the late 1970s. The available text books for art were full of exercises to copy and there was still much emphasis on perspective drawing, and overall much more focus on art history than on practical art sessions. This made me aware of how many of the concepts put forward by art therapists concerning non-directive approaches to art-making have come from art education in Britain and the USA.)

The excitement that the child art movement generated throughout the art education world is evident in the literature of the 1930s and 1940s (Rosalind and Arthur Eccott, Evelyn Gibb, John Dewey, Herbert Read, etc.). Tomlinson and Mills (1966) note that hundreds of British teachers visited Cizek in Vienna, but the major impact of his work came after his exhibition of children's work in London in 1934–5.

However, it was not until another exhibition had been organised in 1938, by Marion Richardson, that most teachers could be convinced that a new approach to art teaching was desirable.

Richardson was perhaps the most famous exponent of child art in Britain. She had been dissatisfied with her own art school training, and, after starting to teach, was influenced by the headmaster of the Birmingham Art School, Catterson-Smith, who had developed a style of drawing known as the 'shut-eye' technique. He suggested that children should draw with their eyes closed, which he felt would put them more in touch with their 'inner world' and encourage spontaneous expression. Richardson encouraged the children to paint freely, which did not endear her to the staff of a London school where she went for an interview for a new job. Undeterred by her rejection, she went to see an exhibition of children's art at the Omega Gallery, where she met the art critic, Roger Fry.

20

Art therapy's roots in art education

She showed Fry her portfolio of children's work, and he was sufficiently impressed to include them in the exhibition.

Richardson had previously worked at the Birmingham prison, taking embroidery and handicraft classes. She reported one old warder saying: 'I am sorry you are going away... we like your coming... it has stopped all that sobbing in the cells' (1948: 39). Perhaps this was actually the first art therapy, Adrian Hill style.

Mary Hodgkins, one time head of art at a large girls' school in London, was a personal friend of Richardson, and was much influenced by her. Apparently, when Richardson became an inspector, she was as passionate as Cizek in promoting the cause of child art. Mary Hodgkins remembers attending Richardson's classes for teachers, where they were given a wide range of materials and encouraged to work spontaneously. This was very strange to the teachers but they found it great fun. Those who had no art background found it easier to adjust to the approach than the artists, as they were not afraid of losing their art skills.

R. Tomlinson, who was for twenty-five years Senior Inspector of Art and Art Adviser to the London County Council, discussed the change of the teacher's attitude towards the child in the art class:

> The teacher's attitude towards the child has changed. Instead of impressing upon the child pre-conceived ideas of his own, relating to technical attainment and adult standards, the teacher encourages him to express fearlessly his own creative and imaginative impulses. Efforts are made by some to release the sub-conscious mind by letting the child draw and paint patterns and colours which he sees in his mind's eye. It is believed that morbid fears and fancies are thus released.
>
> (Tomlinson 1934: 37)

Marie Petrie echoed this:

> The only thing that the adult in charge of children has to do now is to place the right material within the reach of the child at the right time, even at the right moment, so that the great experience the child is having, the picture before its inner eye, can be fixed at once, somehow or other, and can thus cause a wholesome release after tension and can provide happiness through communication.
>
> (Petrie 1946: 63–4)

This sounds very similar to some of the definitions of art therapy discussed in Chapter 1, and we find that, in the 1940s, the notion that visual expression could be an essential tool in the child's emotional development was well established.

Eisner reminds us that this approach could have pitfalls, and that the approach of 'some progressives' could lead to 'a type of neo-Rousseauism

21

Background to art therapy

in which the naivete of the child is to be maintained in the name of fresh vision' and that

> The view of the child's development, and of the teacher's role within it, is based on the assumption that the child develops best from the inside out rather than from the outside in... it is reminiscent of Plato's belief that the task of education is to turn the individual's attention to the content of his soul: the educational problem for Plato was one of recollection.
>
> (Eisner 1972: 51)

There were criticisms from the practitioners of child art themselves, as they saw the movement degenerate into a rather woolly, lazy attitude on the part of the teachers, a misinterpretation of the aims of the movement. For example, in 1938, the honourary vice-president of the Progressive Education Association criticised the tendency to 'superstitious reverence for childhood' and the spirit of anti-intellectualism which was reflected in the reliance on 'improvising instead of long-term organisation' (Bode 1938: 9).

Comparisons between 'child art', 'primitive art', and 'insane art'

We have seen that there was a tendency to link children's art with that of the 'primitive' in the late nineteenth and late early twentieth century. The comparison was carried a stage further when the 'art of the insane' was added. It seems that underlying these comparisons was the assumption that the child, the 'primitive' (or 'savage'), and the 'lunatic' were all somehow removed from 'culture'. It was a view which perpetuated the notion of the 'noble savage' and I suggest it was a way of projecting both innocent and impotent feelings on to those who were in no position to reply. These groups were not allowed a historical or cultural context for their art, which could thus be viewed as aesthetically outside the main-stream of art, frozen in time. In imperialist thinking, the subject people, i.e. the 'primitives', were excluded, like children, from decision-making processes and from the autonomous world of the adult. Their art, too, was relegated to a pre-adult level and could thus be admired using the same aesthetic criteria as for 'child-art'.

The fact that children grew up and ceased to make 'child-art' was regretted by Cizek and some of his followers. A commonly held view was that, at the time of puberty, the child loses his or her spontaneity in image-making in the attempt to make 'realistic' images. MacDonald, perhaps, puts it most succinctly:

Art therapy's roots in art education

By nine years of age, the modern child is working from nature to a limited extent and by 11 years the realisation that his favourite symbols are non-realistic causes him to abandon them. Creativity is usually terminated in the frustrations of attempted realism.

(MacDonald 1970: 329)

The growth of interest among the public and art critics in art forms which were outside the mainstream and outside western 'high art' traditions, together with the movement known as 'modern art', led to a spate of exhibitions of 'insane art' and to comparisons being made between these 'outsider' groups. Not all reviewers agreed that there were similarities between 'modern art' and 'insane art', however, and the reviewer of an exhibition of patients' art from Bethlem Hospital offers a challenge:

We must remember that the lunatic is judged to be one because of his conduct, not because of his art. Max Nordau tried to prove that nearly all modern artists were mad, by reason of certain symptoms of insanity which he professed to find in their art. If madness and sanity mean anything, we ought rather to conclude that an art which seems to us mad is perfectly sane if we find no symptoms of insanity in the conduct of the artist.

(*The Times*, 14 August 1913)

There were many reviewers who were convinced of the link, however. For example, an article by an anonymous reviewer, entitled 'The line of lunacy: modern art as a form of dementia praecox', appeared in 1921. It concerned an exhibition of art work by psychiatric patients which had been collected by Dr Hans Prinzhorn at the University of Heidelberg. Most of the patients had been suffering from 'dementia praecox' (later associated with schizophrenia). The reviewer considered that:

The specimens of their work shown to the German public revealed an uncanny, sometimes incredible likeness to those of the artists of the so-called 'expressionist' school of our own day. Others were indistinguishable from the work of mere children. An important class of these exhibits may have been dug up from the ruins of ancient and extinct civilisations.

(*Current Opinion* 71 (1921): 81–2)

It is important to bear in mind the excitement which prevailed at the beginning of this century – and indeed the outrage – concerning art forms which had apparently broken free from academic traditions. Critics of 'modern art' made comparisons with 'insane art' as a way of abusing the work, relegating it to the status of 'mad' painting, or having the importance 'only of children's scribbles'.

Background to art therapy

On the other hand, some artists actively sought out the art work of psychiatric patients and identified with it. The most notable example is Jean Dubuffet, who spent his life collecting works from the so-called 'outsider' artists, which he called 'Art Brut'. This collection is now permanently housed in Lausanne, and parts of it have been exhibited internationally, including at the Hayward Gallery in London.

John MacGregor says of Dubuffet:

> In seeking for an artistic language that might be truly his own and at the same time relevant to other human beings whose vision is not totally clouded with traditional delusions of 'art and beauty', Dubuffet has tried to free himself of the burden of culture. Unlike the artists whose work he admires, he is neither a madman nor an innocent. One might well ask whether it is possible for a man as deeply knowledgeable and sophisticated as Dubuffet to break out of the culture and the pictorial tradition within which he developed.
>
> (MacGregor 1978: 687)

The Art Brut collection, and 'Outsider Art', have been extensively discussed by MacGregor (1978), Cardinal (1972), Thevoz (1976), Musgrave and Cardinal (1979). It provides a link between the child art movement in art education and the art of the insane, and exerted a considerable influence on many founder art therapists. I shall therefore examine this phenomenon in more depth in the following chapter, which will be concerned with the links between medicine and art which developed in the late nineteenth and early twentieth centuries.

Chapter three

Psychiatry and art

As far back as the mid to late nineteenth century, psychiatrists had been interested in the visual imagery of mental patients: in particular Charcot and Richer (1887), Simon (1888), Tardieu (1872), Prinzhorn (1922, 1923, 1926, 1932), Pfister (1923), Morgenthaler (1918, 1921); more recently, Fairbairn (1938), Kris (1932, 1933, 1952, 1953), Baynes (1940), Reitman (1950), Cunningham Dax (1953), and Pickford (1967); and in the present day, Birtchnell (1984). The relationship between psychiatrists and artists and the growth of interest in the art of psychiatric patients has been thoroughly investigated and described by MacGregor (1978) in his thesis 'The discovery of the art of the insane', which contains a comprehensive bibliography. It is not my intention to re-examine this field, but simply to draw attention to certain aspects of it and to some of the people who are relevant to art therapy because of their influence both on founder art therapists and on the development of concepts out of which art therapy gradually emerged.

Dubuffet and Art Brut

In the previous chapter I drew attention to comparisons which had been made between the art of children, 'primitives', and the 'insane', and to the fascination that this work had for some artists and art critics.

Jean Dubuffet made it his life's work to collect so-called 'outsider' art. He had been intrigued by the pictures in Hans Prinzhorn's book *Artistry of the Mentally Ill*, published in 1922. It was not until 1945, however, that he had the idea of doing some research into the art work of the mentally ill, with the aim of forming a collection which could be exhibited in Paris. He spent three weeks in Switzerland, touring psychiatric hospitals, encountering en route Dr Morgenthaler, who had encouraged one of his patients, Adolf Wolffli, to paint. (Wolffli has since achieved some fame as an 'outsider' artist.)

Apparently Swiss psychiatrists were very helpful to Dubuffet's aims, parting readily with their patients' paintings, and in 1948 he founded the

25

Background to art therapy

Compagnie de l'Art Brut with several other artists and two doctors. Dubuffet paid most of the costs of the organisation, which was always in financial difficulties. In 1958, when the money ran out, the collection went to America. It later returned to Paris, and is now in Lausanne. Dubuffet's activity as a collector and writer on Art Brut was entwined with his own work as an artist. He identified with the 'outsider' artists, especially with what he felt to be their desire to escape from cultural conditioning in art.

In the days when Dubuffet was forming his collection in Europe, there were no art therapists working with the patients whose art works he acquired. One of the biographers of Art Brut, Michel Thevoz, felt this was a good thing: he considered that the advent of art therapy had caused a 'drying up of springs of creativity' because over the years from the 1950s onwards patients were usually encouraged to draw and paint, often with a therapist.

> Instead of thwarting their patients' efforts to express themselves, as they usually did in the past, they now encourage them. They are even disposed to attribute a therapeutic value to the practice of drawing and modelling. There is hardly a psychiatric hospital today that doesn't have its studio or workshop, and hardly one that fails to organise exhibitions periodically.
>
> (Thevoz 1976: 13)

Thevoz is complaining that the images to be found in modern psychiatric hospitals somehow lack the power and interest of former times – i.e. when patients had neither chemotherapy nor art therapists to 'interfere' with the creative process. Such attitudes are still to be found among some artists today, who maintain a 'Romantic' view of the relationship between creativity and madness. There is, though, no evidence to show that patients in a deeply disturbed or psychotic state are more 'creative' than others – indeed, the experience of art therapists would suggest the opposite.

Dubuffet's collection, and his own art work, inspired many art students who later became art therapists. From the interviews, it emerged that many were somewhat discontented with their art school experiences, and rejected the dominant 'fashions' in art, looking for a more 'individual' mode of expression. Some were drawn to 'outsider' art, and to the art work of psychiatric patients, as a stimulus to their own work. This attitude often caused them problems with their art school tutors, who usually misunderstood art therapy as being about interpreting paintings or being a second-rate kind of teaching. An art therapist who was working in the early 1960s said about his first impressions of art therapy:

> I thought it was just a matter of going into a studio in the hospital, smoking my pipe and looking wise, and that patients would turn out marvellous, dramatic pictures like those I had seen in exhibitions of

26

Psychiatry and art

psychotic art. I soon found out that it wasn't like that and most people had to be encouraged just to put a bit of paint on the paper.

Another said:

I got interested in eccentric art. I found out about Stanley Spencer, how weird he was – the drawings no one had ever seen, hidden away. I read a few books about psychedelic art, and about Ed Burra and his funny brand of Surrealism. Bacon's favourite involvement, the drug scene, all seemed very interesting. One of my liberal studies tutors said, if you are really interested, go and look at psychiatric hospitals. I went to a hospital which had a little art department in occupational therapy. It was quite embarrassing as I didn't know what I wanted to look at. They showed me some fascinating things, nothing like I had seen at college. Then somebody told me something about the Adamson Collection. I got into art therapy at that stage, in 1967. But I really didn't know what it was.

The same art therapist notes that from being interested in psychiatric art he started to wonder about the people who produced it, and found his way into art therapy instead of training as a teacher.

This was quite a common way into art therapy during the 1960s, given that there was no formal training, and many founder art therapists found their route through an initial fascination with the paintings of psychiatric patients which they had seen in the various exhibitions of the late 1950s and early 1960s. It was not only artists, though, who were intrigued by this work, but many doctors and psychiatrists too, for a variety of personal and professional reasons.

Medical contributions to the growth of art therapy

Erich Guttmann and Walter Maclay

These two doctors were working at the Maudsley Hospital during the 1930s. Guttmann had trained in Germany as a doctor and pharmacologist, later specialising in neurology and psychiatry. He and his colleague Walter Mayer-Gross emigrated to Britain as a result of Nazi persecution – along with many other intellectuals, in a migration which ws crucially important to the development of medicine and psychoanalysis in Britain and the USA.

Guttmann and Mayer-Gross joined the staff of the Department of Clinical Research at the Maudsley, where they stayed until the late 1930s. It was here that they met a Scottish psychiatrist, Walter Maclay.

Background to art therapy

Guttmann and Maclay collaborated on several research projects in the general area of neuro-psychiatry. In particular, they investigated 'depersonalisation' and 'manic depressive psychosis'.

Guttmann had begun to conduct experiments using mescaline intoxication on depressive patients. He had used the drug himself, in order to study its effects first hand. Mescaline induces hallucinations which could be described verbally, but Guttmann was becoming more interested in the visual descriptions made by the 'normal' subjects studied in the research.

As a result of the studies into the effects of mescaline intoxication on perception, and following on from their studies of 'depersonalisation', Guttmann and Maclay began to study the art work of schizophrenic patients, which they found in the hospital's collections. Most of the work had been done by artists while in a psychotic state, rather than by 'ordinary' patients, so the two doctors started to collect examples of art made by patients diagnosed as schizophrenic in order to make a comparison with the artists' work before and after they became psychotic. Perhaps one of the most famous of these artists was Louis Wain, a commercial artist who is known for his cat paintings and drawings. Guttmann and Maclay's notes on Wain link the apparently fragmented quality of his later paintings to the schizophrenic condition. They observed that his colours became brighter and more intense as his illness developed, whereas in the work of another mentally ill artist, Richard Dadd, his work was characterised by lack of colour.

To take the research further, and to try to establish a method of interpreting and evaluating the art work of patients, they needed to acquire more material, from both schizophrenic patients and 'normal' control groups. It was thus fortunate for them that the *Evening Standard* mounted a competition in 1938, offering a prize for the most 'outstanding doodle submitted', and the services of an 'expert psychologist' to inform the readers about the personality of the doodler.

As a result of a visit to the editor, Guttmann and Maclay acquired over 9000 examples of doodles, each labelled with the profession, sex and occupation of the doodler at time of doodling.

The advantage of doodles, as the doctors saw it, was that the doodler would have no preconceived idea of how the finished product would look. It was not likely that they would have been influenced by fashion and taste in art. A disadvantage was, that as a prize was offered, the doodle might be contrived to look impressive. Also, 'pornographic' doodles had been excluded, so the doodle might be unrepresentative of a person's usual work.

They made a classification of doodles according to the maker's profession, sex, and occupation, discovering that the largest percentage came from people in the 'creative' professions. But in an attempt to subdivide and categorize the doodles, they soon realised that there was neither

28

Psychiatry and art

appropriate descriptive terminology nor any adequate comparison for characterising the material. They were, nevertheless, impressed by their collection, and began to conceive of the therapeutic value of doodling, in that it gave a chance to release the censor of the conscious mind, and to relax – which to creative people was indispensable to production (Guttmann *et al.* 1938).

Francis Reitman joins Guttmann and Maclay

Reitman arrived at the Maudsley from Hungary in the summer of 1938. He was familiar with the work of Prinzhorn in Heidelberg, and with his collection of psychiatric paintings. He quickly joined Guttmann and Maclay's research into the effects of mescaline.

Professional artists were invited to participate in the experiments, but there was little response until Guttmann managed to enlist the help of Lionel Penrose, the psychologist employed by the *Evening Standard*, whose brother, Roland, was an eminent writer and critic of the Surrealist movement.

Guttmann was attracted to the Surrealist artists, seeing them as sharing his own interests in the unconscious and irrational, and in Freud's work. The catalogue notes of an exhibition entitled 'Realism and Surrealism', May 1938, Guildhall, stated that Roland Penrose, Julian Cant, and Julian Trevelyan had been engaged in research into the effects of mescaline on vision at the Maudsley Hospital. A paper describing the work, 'Hallucinations in artists', was published in 1941 by Guttmann and Maclay (see Roman 1986: 15–23 for further discussion of this work).

Reitman at Netherne Hospital

In 1945, Reitman was appointed Head of Clinical Research at the Netherne Hospital, Surrey, by Dr E. Cunningham Dax. He was free to devote his time to research into the effects of pre-frontal leucotomy. This operation, also known as lobotomy, was described by Sargant thus:

> Leucotomy is reserved for patients suffering from severe and persisting states of anxiety and tension, produced in some cases by real and unpleasant facts, and in others by hallucinations or delusions; but in either case resisting dispersion by non-surgical treatments. The operation, especially in its recently improved and modified form, can greatly diminish the tension, while not always eradicating the thoughts that created it.
>
> (Sargant 1957: 69)

Background to art therapy

Sargant noted that at the time of writing some 15,000 patients had been operated on in Britain alone.

There were problems about the effects of leucotomy, though, and Sargant was obliged to point these out. Apparently, patients became 'more ordinary members of a group, open to suggestion and persuasion without stubborn resistance', but given too extensive an operation on the frontal lobes, 'religious feeling might be destroyed' (1957: 70–1).

When Reitman joined the Netherne team in 1946, 179 leucotomies had been performed there already that year. He discovered that after the operation symptoms appeared which he described as extroversion, increased motor activity, and euphoria. These were similar to states of mind that Guttmann and Maclay had identified as conducive to free spontaneous drawing. Reitman subsequently became interested in creative activity in schizophrenia, this time in relation to pre-frontal leucotomy (see Roman 1986 for elaboration).

The arrival of Reitman at Netherne also coincided with new developments in the treatment of servicemen being rehabilitated at the Northfield Military Hospital in Birmingham. It was there that the term 'therapeutic community' was coined by Dr Tom Main. Cunningham Dax visited Northfield with Dr Sybil Yates and Mrs S. Bach (a member of an early art therapy working party), and all three were very impressed by what they saw – including a painting group conducted by an army sergeant with an interest in art. They decided to introduce such a group to Netherne, and sought for a suitable person to run it.

The principles and conditions of Edward Adamson's subsequent appointment as a full-time artist at Netherne are described by Cunningham Dax (1951). Adamson's work will be discussed in detail in Chapter 6, as he played a prominent role in the early development of art therapy in Britain through his lectures and collection of patients' work.

The prevailing attitudes towards the treatment of mental illness in the 1940s, which consisted of physical treatments like electro-convulsive therapy and leucotomy for severe anxiety and depression, and more 'socially orientated' therapies for the rehabilitiation of servicemen, gave rise to the idea of appointing an artist at the Netherne, not as an art *therapist*, but as someone who could assist the medical team in obtaining paintings for their researches. The person appointed had to have the right kind of temperament to participate in the rigorously ordered research of both Reitman and Cunningham Dax. They could not be of a psychoanalytic persuasion, as Reitman was highly critical of this approach (1950: 137).

Reitman seems to have solved the problem of Adamson's role in the experiments by defining him as a 'catalyst who should remain passive and unbiased, an artist and not a psychotherapist' (1950: 72). We shall see that Adamson himself went along with this definition, but as the nature of the

30

Psychiatry and art

medical research changed, and the art work was not required for strictly regulated projects, conditions became less constricting for him.

Arthur Segal

Having discussed both artists and doctors who were fascinated by psychiatric patients' art, and used it in their work, it is time to mention Arthur Segal, who attempted to bridge what he saw as a gap between artists and doctors.

Segal was a Romanian, who, like the doctors mentioned above, had fled from the Nazis to London in 1936. He had studied art in Berlin, at a time when the art academies were under the influence both of the Vienna Secession movement and German Expressionism. He had no formal psychological training, although he had become interested as a result of his membership of an intellectual circle which contained many psychoanalysts, including Ernst Simmel, a pupil of Freud. On arrival in London, he sought permission to start an art school, which proved no easy task, but eventually he acquired a studio in England's Lane, Hampstead, and started to give classes. On the studio wall hangs a letter from Freud, warmly approving Segal's aim of bringing together doctors, artists, and patients in his art classes.

Segal was convinced that painting was a therapeutic activity – and painting was the only medium employed at the school. His ideas about art and its value in diagnosis are described in a pamphlet *Art as a Test for Normality and its Application for Therapeutical Purposes* (1939). Its curative values are expounded in *Art as Psychotherapy* (1942). He went so far as to suggest that certain painting styles went with certain disorders: for example, 'inferiority complexes' expressed themselves through widely varying forms of instability, through fear of decision or precipitate decision. This affected tonal qualities, the colours were undifferentiated, and the brushwork tentative and vague.

These seemed to be the kind of observations that Reitman and Cunningham Dax were seeking in their work at the Netherne, that is, to note if there was a link between certain qualities of style and approach to painting and certain states of mind or illness. There is no evidence, however, that either of them used Segal's theories, although they were familiar with each other's work.

Segal's work is little known about in the history of art therapy, perhaps because he wrote only the two pamphlets mentioned above, which were not widely circulated. He was a quiet man, preferring to teach rather than to engage in public relations, and there is no evidence that he wished to be known in any role other than artist/teacher.

31

Background to art therapy

It was through Irene Champernowne that I first came across Segal's work, which was continued in England's Lane after his death by his daughter.

In the studio, all Segal's pupils were treated the same, be they doctors or patients. He believed in setting subjects to study and paint, rather than encouraging free expression. In a talk to an art and music therapy conference (1949), a pupil of Segal, Elsie Davies said:

> He (Segal) came to the conclusion that the way to teach has to be as impersonal as possible without the subjective influence of the teacher or a style or the work of any other artist, and he built up a method meant to be a guide for everybody, for professional as well as non-professional.
>
> (Davies 1949: 18)

It is probable that Reitman and Segal encountered each other, as they were both refugees, and Reitman was keen on drawing and painting himself. During the War, Segal's school was evacuated to Banbury Road, Oxford, a short distance from the Radcliffe Infirmary where Guttmann and Maclay were then posted.

Throughout the first half of the twentieth century, then, ideas from the prevailing art education models of the 1930s and 1940s, and especially the child art movement, began to merge with those from psychiatry which saw art as a possible diagnostic or therapeutic agent in the treatment of the mentally ill. By the early 1940s, the link between art and medicine was firmly established and set to continue through the work of the pioneers who will be discussed in the next section.

Part II

The role of individual artists and psychotherapists in the development of art therapy from the 1940s to the formation of BAAT

Introduction

The period in question is marked by a number of contributions by artists, art teachers, psychotherapists, and psychologists to the practice of 'art therapy', a term which was used to cover quite different approaches, the common factor being a belief in art as a process which could help to heal troubled minds. The period is also characterised by the formation of working parties on art therapy which focused on how the activity could be regulated and who should practice it, leading eventually to the establishment of the British Association of Art Therapists in 1963.

In the chapters which follow, I shall discuss the work of many founder art therapists, noting their background and the way in which they entered the field and their relationship (or not) to each other. This will lead us on to the period of the first 'organised' activities in which many of these founders participated between 1940 and 1963 when BAAT was formed.

Dissemination of ideas

In their article 'Social factors in the origins of a new science: the case of psychology', Ben-David and Collins ask how it happens that at a certain time the 'transmission and diffusion of ideas relating to a given field become strikingly increased in effectiveness' (1966: 452).

They suggest that the ideas necessary to create a new discipline are usually available over a relatively prolonged period of time and in several places; that only a few of these potential beginnings lead to further growth; and such growth occurs when and where persons become interested in the new idea, not only in its intellectual content but as a means of establishing a new identity and, in particular, a new occupational role.

We have seen that the idea of art or image-making as an aid to the treatment of patients suffering from emotional disturbances had been about in the USA (Naumburg *et al.*) during the 1930s and even earlier in Vienna, in the late nineteenth century (Cizek), and in Switzerland in the 1920s (Jung). Several doctors had become interested in their patients' art

The role of individual artists and psychotherapists

work for its diagnostic potential and Jungian analysts in particular had encouraged their patients to bring paintings into the therapeutic session. Art educators, influenced by the 'child art' movement, valued children's art work as an essential element in their overall development and had moved towards a 'non-directive' stance in their teaching. However, the concept of an 'art therapist' seems to have been born in the early 1940s in Britain, after Hill used the term 'art therapy' to describe his work at the King Edward VII sanatorium. The title 'art therapist' began to be applied to artists who were working with patients even though they were actually performing the task of 'non-directive' art teachers, having no medical or psychological training to undertake psychotherapy.

Forerunners, founders, followers, and pioneers

In their exploration of the way that psychology developed as a discipline, Ben-David and Collins make an operational distinction among three categories of persons: forerunners, founders, and followers:

> The first two are distinguished by whether or not they had students who became psychologists... those who were not themselves the students of psychologists but who trained their own disciples as psychologists are the founders of the new discipline of psychology. Their disciples are the followers. The latter two classes can be considered psychologists proper.
>
> (Ben-David and Collins 1966: 454)

Whereas Ben-David and Collins drew on five histories of psychology to arrive at their categories, this has not been possible in the case of art therapy as there is no previous historical account of its development as an occupational group. It is, nevertheless, useful to bear these categories in mind when discussing individuals' contributions, as it has helped to establish their relationship to the ideas, concepts, and practices mentioned in the introductory chapters of the book.

All the people whose work will be described considered themselves 'founders' or 'pioneers' of art therapy, whether they used the label 'art therapist' for themselves or not, and have been seen as such by those who studied under them as their 'disciples'. In the final part of the book which concerns training, the perceptions of the 'followers' will be particularly illuminating in building up a 'live' history of the discipline.

I have tended to use the terms 'founder' and 'pioneer' interchangeably, even though the latter term conveys a more 'heroic' status, as these early art therapists were at times struggling against considerable odds in having their own ideas recognised.

Before discussing the individuals, however, I think it is important to take a look at the position of the arts and of medicine at the time, as many

36

Introduction

of them came from a visual art or art education background. The majority worked in hospitals or sanatoriums, and in the late 1940s found themselves employees of the National Health Service. To enable us to consider the position of the founder members in these contexts, the next chapter will consist of a brief overview of the position of the visual arts and of health care provision during the 1940s.

Chapter four

The context of the visual arts and health care provision in the 1940s

The position of the visual arts

A useful source of information is a report sponsored by the Dartington Hall Trustees entitled *The Visual Arts*. This report was published on behalf of the Arts Enquiry by the independent Political and Economic Planning Organisation in 1946. (The Dartington Hall Trustees were later to play a significant role in the fortunes of the Withymead Centre established by the Champernownes in 1942, through acting as its main financial source.) There were actually four reports, on visual arts, music, drama, and factual film, in a series designed to give an account of the place of these arts in British life, their economic and administrative background, their social importance and value in education. The Trustees felt that the arts should have a recognised place in post-war planing (1946: 5).

The enquiry was initiated in 1941 by the Minister of Education and the Reconstruction Secretariat (later the office for the Ministry of Reconstruction) which agreed to receive the report when it was completed. At the outset the committee consisted of a number of eminent art educators and some civil servants. It was chaired by Dr Julian Huxley. Mrs Dorothy Elmhirst, a trustee of Dartington Hall and later of Withymead, also served on the committee.

The information for the report was collected from interviews and published material, and most of the material refers to 1944. It identified four categories of art school: those for which the Ministry of Education was responsible and those administered by local education authorities; university art schools such as the Slade and Goldsmiths', and Ruskin in Oxford; the Royal Academy Schools; and private schools such as the Heatherley. Out of these, the RA Schools, the Royal College of Art, the Slade, and the Central were regarded as the senior art teaching institutions. (At one time as many as 80 per cent of RCA students were intending to be teachers. After 1936 it was no longer necessary to take a one-year course after gaining the ARCA to qualify as a teacher but 'some students

38

Visual arts and health care in the 1940s

have been given continuation scholarships for one year teacher training courses at Goldsmiths' College, the London Institute, etc'.)

The majority of art school teachers were drawn from the RCA or the Slade, with a few with the Art Teacher's Diploma being accepted from provincial schools. Salaries depended on length of service and under the Burnham scale ranged from £300 per annum to £525 for men and £270 to £470 for women. The report states that

> Art School posts thus provide reasonable remuneration as compared with the precarious livelihood offered by the fine arts or industrial design. But enterprising artists usually avoid full-time teaching posts in order to concentrate on their own work.
>
> (Dartington Hall Trustees 1946: 94)

Another career option open to art graduates was that of 'commercial art' or illustration and we shall see that some founder art therapists (Adamson and Simon, for example) started their working life thus.

The report suggests, however, that the commercial artist and illustrator differed from the 'pure' painter or sculptor since their work was intended to be seen only in reproduction and to express the ideas of others; that there was little satisfaction in the type of work required for most popular advertising and illustration intended as it was to arouse sentimental interest by realistic means (p.59).

The report further suggests that work requiring a 'purely illustrative technique' was mostly left to 'third-rate artists' and that commercial artists did not think of themselves as creative artists but rather as craftsmen, their pay and conditions being like office clerks (p.63).

When considering the role of the founder art therapists, it is worth bearing in mind that art therapy may have been an attractive alternative to art teaching at a time when part-time lecturing posts had become scarce, as it would seem to leave time and opportunity for practising one's own art work.

The opportunities for art graduates, as outlined in this report and in the several career guides of the time, seem to have been few and far between. They either had to decide to stake everything on becoming a professional artist, painting full time or supplementing their work by part-time art school teaching, or they went into teaching or commercial art. It seems that art therapy as it appeared in the 1940s may have proved an interesting alternative, offering challenge, a chance to work 'with people', and pay and conditions which were no worse than those of a commercial artist and at best equal to art college teaching.

One further possibility of using art training suggested by the report was in youth and adult education classes, which fell into two strictly separate categories: 'appreciation' and 'practical art work'. Adult education tutors giving these classes were paid nearly as well as art school tutors. Some of

The role of individual artists and psychotherapists

the schemes mentioned in the report (e.g. the Ashington Group, which consisted of miners – also see Heard 1986) sounded rather like art therapy as defined by Hill (1946) and gave models from which art therapists could later develop their approach to work in hospitals (paid by the Ministry of Education as opposed to the Ministry of Health).

The report maintained that the then current theories of art education could not be studied in isolation but were intimately bound up with

> psychological theory and modern developments in general educational practice, it being assumed 'by exponents of the modern movement in education that creative ability is natural to all children to be drawn out and developed by the teacher' and further more that 'free methods of painting require very special qualifications from the teacher'.
>
> (Dartington Hall Trustees 1946: 151)

The material in the report is useful when considering the contributions of the founder art therapists, coming as they did from backgrounds in art education or the commercial arts. With such limited possibilities for using their art training and talents in satisfying careers (unless exceptionally talented and dedicated to full-time pursuit of their own art work or decided on teaching) it is likely that 'art therapy' would appeal, especially if it could be paid on a similar scale to that of art school tutors, the most acceptable option to a career as an artist (also see Madge and Weinberger 1973, for a useful discussion on the aspirations of art graduates post-college).

Art therapy would seem to satisfy a need to use art skills in an obviously socially useful way, while at the same time giving scope for preserving an identity as an artist.

The early days of the National Health Service and its effects on art therapy

The work of the first 'art therapists' began in the early 1940s before the National Health Service was introduced, in 1946. During the 1940s, there had been considerable parliamentary debate over whether or not such a service could provide free cover for the whole population or only for roughly 90 per cent. Elston (1977) suggested that the British Medical Association favoured the option of limited cover, so that there would always be a need for private medicine and that the issue was eventually resolved by allowing consultants the right to be employed full or part time by the NHS and to supplement their income from private practice.

Opposition to the NHS by the medical profession was considerable and there were many divisions within it. Certain sections of work were seen as meriting special payments, e.g. acute physical illness and maternity where the majority of prestigious consultants worked at that time. General

Visual arts and health care in the 1940s

practitioners were also reluctant to serve the NHS and could be persuaded to join only by a promise from the Minister of Health that they would not be salaried (see Elston 1977; Barnard and Lee 1977; Gray 1974).

The aim of the Act of Parliament based on the report by William Beveridge and passed in 1946 was to make health care available to all, regardless of financial circumstances. The hope and expectation was that a free service would help to defeat illness arising from neglect and poverty, leading to an all-round improvement in the population's health, which in turn would decrease demand on the Service. However, as the past forty years have shown, the aim of reducing demand has not been realised. On the contrary, it has increased due to sophisticated medical technology and treatment methods, innovative medical research and possibilities, such as lung and heart transplants, once undreamed of. There are also expectations for longer and healthier lives, and for cures to be found for fatal diseases, such as Aids.

Treatment of mental illness

The 1930s had seen the introduction of physical treatments in the form of insulin coma therapy, electro-convulsive therapy (ECT) and neurosurgery (see Sargant and Slater 1940: 51; Sargant 1957; Sargant and Craske 1941 for a full account of these developments).

Roberts (1967) suggests that such physical treatments were helpful in making psychiatry more valid and scientific in the eyes of the medical profession, in that they probably helped to establish the medical superintendent of a psychiatric hospital as a 'real doctor', rather than 'a man who practised a more or less humane hotel keeping behind locked doors' (1967: 16).

Psychiatry was not, and still is not, generally viewed as a prestigious area of medicine and mental health has not been well funded. In the early 1940s, the mental health services were split off from those of physical health, until a White Paper of 1944 suggested that the distinction should be reduced. Little detailed consideration was devoted to the specific needs of psychiatric patients and there was general fear and ignorance among the general public about their condition. There was a paucity of medical research on mental health, and the chemotherapy 'revolution' had not yet happened. Psychotherapy could hardly be said to exist outside private consulting rooms.

Roberts suggests that there were two main factors in the development of mental health care from 1930s on: one stemmed from the teachings of Freud, whose 'disciples' were found chiefly in the psychiatric departments of general hospitals, treating psychoneurotic and psychosomatic

The role of individual artists and psychotherapists

cases; the second was the result of mass unemployment and the economic depression of 1930s Britain:

> Men, out of work through no lack of intelligence, energy or general capability, queued for jobs in mental hospitals. They may have been untrained and lacking formal qualifications – games players and those proficient on a musical instrument were favoured, which in itself tells us something about the hospitals of that period – but experience shows that a great many of them were eminently trainable.
>
> (Roberts 1967: 19)

Many of these men (and women) became occupational therapists or craft instructors, and programmes of rehabilitation became a regular feature of hospital life.

Liberal ideas concerning the role of the mental hospital – i.e. that it was a 'hospital' rather than a custodial centre – spread throughout the late 1930s and early 1940s, but the Second World War drained resources and staff into the armed services or industry, and the needs of the mentally ill came low in terms of national priorities.

Attitude of founder art therapists towards the NHS

From the discussion of the role of the Withymead Centre in Chapter 7, it will be clear that Irene and Gilbert Champernowne regarded the advent of the NHS with much ambivalence. They did not wish to see Withymead become part of it, fearing that the needs of the patients and community would be subsumed in the service of a bureaucracy. They feared control by a medical hierarchy in which patients would take a dependent role and where professions would have strictly regulated tasks – unlike at Withymead where boundaries were often crossed. Irene Champernowne felt that the treatment programmes would be determined by agreements forged in central offices, and would have little relationship to patient and staff needs in each hospital.

Champernowne recognised that Withymead could serve only a small and specific section of the mentally ill population, but she felt that small communities run on similar lines would be the best way of solving the mental health needs of the majority, rather than the large and impersonal psychiatric hospitals, which were the norm. (Recent government recommendations on care in the community have tended to support Champernowne's views, some forty years later.)

Kelly (1984), writing about the development of 'community arts' in Britain, urges a consideration of the role of the State in health care and criticises what he feels have become habits of 'dependent consumerism'. He maintains that the activities of the State require the population to

Visual arts and health care in the 1940s

re-define health needs in such a way that they can be met by 'an increased consumption of quantified professional services' (1984: 72).

Although writing from a different perspective, he appears to have much in common with Champernowne who rejected the idea of Withymead coming under the National Health Service for fear of state intervention and bureaucracy interfering with the needs of the community, its patients and its staff.

Adrian Hill seems to have welcomed the NHS in its provision of free treatment for all (see Chapter 5) and Adamson made no comment but was employed in the NHS from its beginnings, as a full-time artist, actively participating in clinical experiments on the effects of leucotomy and lobotomy at Netherne Hospital.

The limits imposed by the NHS on the powers of the medical superintendents did, however, create some difficulties, as they could no longer employ 'art therapists' at will and pay them with whatever monies were available. They first had to get approval from their Regional Board. Some art therapists regretted this, as the following comments by some of the founder members I interviewed show:

> Medical superintendents were grand old gentlemen in special offices with cream teas, and they did all they could to make you stay. They didn't see you in any way as an auxiliary. You were an artist, sent by God, or whatever, to make people a bit happier. They were fatherly people towards the patients, and willing to pay whatever the going rate was. They would say, I'll pay you as a visiting dentist, or as an OT, or something like that.

> Oh, when the term art therapy started, Adrian told me that the newly formed NHS tried to find out how to pay us. They couldn't pay us unless we became auxiliary medical staff, and he had been very much against the word therapist as many of us have been ever since, but agreed to it because of the question of being paid.... It was important if art therapists were to develop... it would depend on art therapy being used in hospitals where the medical superintendent was willing to find money.

> I had the great luck to work for Dr R. He was a great chap, and Dr M who followed him... the personality to make things go as they wanted to. Things are a bit different now... all controlled by committees. Dr R couldn't have been controlled by anybody!

> I applied to the two big psychiatric hospitals.... But of course these were the NHS hospitals and it was a slightly different ball game. One began to see the red tape and the bureaucracy and there wasn't the freedom I had in the sanatorium.

43

The role of individual artists and psychotherapists

There were problems, though, in the pre-NHS structures, and the positive recollections of those days were not shared by all:

> Art therapists worked very much under a kind of personal psychiatric patronage. If you worked in a hospital where the consultants were interested, it was fine. They would do all sorts of deals for you. If you didn't, it was pretty grim. The present structure irons things out and makes it more consistent.

The main attitude, then, seems to have been of ambivalence towards the formation of the NHS, the main expressed fear being of losing the freedom from pre-set structures which had drawn many towards art therapy in the first place; losing what little control they had over their work, and being subjected to rules made by an impersonal bureaucracy rather than medical staff with whom they could make a direct relationship, for better or worse. The advantages, in terms of fairer distribution of health care and the possibilities of expanding the art therapy service seem to have been perceived. But it seems there was again ambivalence at this time over the fact that the challenge of getting themselves established and sorting out their own conditions of service – even though this limited their movements and put them under a kind of 'medical patronage' – might disappear in the fact of standardized agreements on pay and conditions. This attitude could possibly be affected by the fact that artistic patronage had been the norm, either by individuals or by galleries, so medical patronage was not seen as a problem. As we shall see later on, ambivalence towards the NHS, as representing 'state bureaucracy' has been a feature of the art therapy movement throughout, resulting at times in an underlying mistrust of 'professionalism' (see Waller 1987: 191–5).

Chapter five

Adrian Hill

Background to his work

Adrian Hill claims to have coined the term 'art therapy' to describe his work (*Art Versus Illness* 1945). It seems appropriate, then, to begin with a discussion of his work, and also that of his contemporary, Marie Petrie, an art educator who emigrated to the USA in the early 1950s. In addition to *Art Versus Illness*, he wrote *Painting Out Illness* (1951) and two articles in *Studio Magazine* (1942 and 1947), gave radio broadcasts, and lectured throughout Britain and Holland. Hill was made President of BAAT in the few years before his death in his mid-80s.

Hill is, perhaps, best known for his series of 'How to' art books (eg *How to Paint Watercolours, Seascapes, Trees*, etc.) intended to popularise the visual arts, and for his television *Sketch Club* programmes. He tried to demystify drawing and painting, to make it accessible to the 'man in the street'. Hill was never highly regarded in the world of fine art, possibly because of his populist attitudes, but his own forte was water-colour painting, for which he became well known.

Art therapy at the King Edward VII Sanatorium, Midhurst

In 1938 Hill was convalescing from tuberculosis in this sanatorium. In those days, the treatment of TB required major surgery and usually a period of complete rest in quiet surroundings, preferably with fresh air and sunshine, by the sea or in the mountains. Rehabilitation centres for TB patients tended to be somewhat spartan in concept.

Hill found the lack of visual or other stimulation in the hospital stultifying, so started to draw to pass the time. He found that the problem of how to occupy his mind and emotions for a six-month period had been largely solved as he quickly became involved in his own art work again. At that time he did not think of introducing painting to his fellow patients, and, reflecting upon this in *Art Versus Illness*, said he felt he had to become 'properly fit before he could be of any service to others' (1945: 15).

45

The role of individual artists and psychotherapists

In 1939, Hill became an out-patient and his doctor asked if he would encourage a patient called 'Bert' to sketch. Hill agreed and referred to Bert as his 'first student' (1945: 23). In 1941, as a result of exhibiting a painting made at the sanatorium, Hill received much publicity in the press under captions such as 'Artist Laughs at Death', 'Artist's Triumph over Illness'. In this year, occupational therapy (OT) was introduced to the sanatorium and Hill immediately began to co-operate with the department in teaching drawing and painting as an alternative activity to craft work, and as a useful pastime designed to distract traumatised minds from distressing thoughts. In the publicity received as a result of his exhibited painting we can see the emergence of the idea that, if artists could help to cure themselves through painting, others might also do the same. Hill himself seemed to believe that painting contributed to 'a quick recovery' (1945: 26).

Hill was not afraid to criticise the content and style of the art work, having clear personal preferences: for example, he displayed 'bored indifference' to 'imaginative portraits of beautiful brunettes' (1945: 27), which he found were invariably painted as a contrast to 'horrific war scenes'.

Hill was bemused as to why the act of drawing and painting seemed to help patients to come to terms with their traumas and to speed up the rehabilitation process, and became determined to pursue the work further.

Formalising of the work

On discussing his plans with the Medical Superintendent, it was decided to offer 'art therapy' to convalescing patients. At first the response was poor, but after Hill gave a talk to the patients in which he advised that they should not be put off by the term 'therapy' but take it to mean 'a little of what you fancy does you good' (1945: 30), several patients enrolled for his classes. At this point Hill realised that he would need to individualise his approach and have some idea of the patient's medical history in order to direct them in appropriate ways.

> To redress the injuries of a morbid introspection, the bitterness and resentment may have to be released by encouraging the sufferers to express their exasperation in pictorial form, while anxiety and distress in another case, may well be deflected and a more hopeful mental attitude established by inciting the very opposite type of picture making and that in the form of a sequence of paintings.
>
> (Hill 1945: 33)

(Precedents for this view can be found in Iveson 1938 and Segal 1942.)

Adrian Hill

'Therapeutic art'

Both Hill and Marie Petrie believed that 'art' might have the power to restore lost health, but this could only be a certain kind of art. For example, Hill thought that when a patient's physical resistance was at its lowest, their imaginative powers rose to a high level, only to fall on recovery to a 'pictorial commonplace' (1945: 41). He attributed this to the patient's 'animal ego' being quiescent:

> the spiritual or subliminal essence, hitherto cramped by a humdrum environment, is allowed free play in producing works of considerable imagination, both of an idealistic and necrotic nature.
>
> (Hill 1945: 41)

Marie Petrie similarly felt that art could 'show the way' in the struggle between individual and 'mass' ideals:

> Where mass standards and mob-passions rule, rebirth can only come from the better quality of individual effort, and from the finer differentiation it brings with it. In the poet's or the composer's lonely vigils, in the great painter's or sculptor's agonised struggle to give form to the inner vision... lies salvation. They show the way out of this soulless mechanisation which is threatening to turn men into robots.
>
> (Petrie 1946a: 50)

Petrie was writing from the context of the movement for 'national regeneration' following the Second World War. She felt that art had an essential role to play in 'construction and creation of order' and that it was essential for artists to use their healing powers to 'persuade mankind to put aside fear and hatred' (1946a: 13). Adrian Hill shared this sentiment, applying it to his work in the sanatorium:

> Art in illness as well as in health will together forge a new national characteristic which will in the end learn to venerate the creative artist as it will ridicule and deplore the professional killer.
>
> (Hill 1945: 97)

Art therapy might, then, give artists a chance to find a new, social role. But this could produce problems in that it would mean an end to the 'special position' of the artist:

> The Ivory Tower of the aesthete must be stormed, the citadel of snobs, academicians and vested interests must be invaded in the campaign by the fresh and naïve army of the people.
>
> (Petrie 1946a: 36)

Jones suggests that, while condemning the defenders of 'artistic privilege', Hill and Petrie would

The role of individual artists and psychotherapists

leave a guard on the gate to keep the more unruly members of 'the mob' as she called them (1946: 50) out. The mob were the supposedly passive consumers of the mass media mechanised art products. Commercial, or so called 'popular' art was to be avoided because the consumer was not directly involved in the process of creation.

(Jones 1987: 34–5)

In many respects, then, Hill and Petrie shared a similar approach to 'art therapy' and, had she remained in Britain, Petrie might have made an active contribution to its organisational development. As it was, she left for the USA, where she was better known as a sculptor and an art educator. She greatly admired Hill, referring to him in a review of his book as 'The pioneer of art therapy in this country' (1946b: 137).

Art therapy and cultural imperialism

It is not within the scope of this book to deal adequately with this important issue, but necessary nevertheless to draw attention to the other side of a seemingly liberal and altruistic attitude to 'the arts'.

Kelly criticises attitudes such as those outlined above as examples of 'cultural missionary work', whose prime movers came from religious movements and were the wives of politicians and aristocrats:

The effect of their charity was to stigmatise the very people whom they imagined they were helping (poor girls, prostitutes, slum children, etc). Their approach lives on today in the use of such spurious notions as 'cultural deprivation' with its implications that those people happily playing darts (or push-pin) need to be helped across the road into the opera house. It lives on, too, in the creation of the 'voluntary sector' whose business it is to tend to certain officially approved categories of 'the disadvantaged'.

(Kelly 1984: 88–9)

(A precedent for this critique can be found in Oscar Wilde's essay of 1898, 'The soul of man under socialism', concerning the tyranny of charity.) Bearing in mind that both Hill and Adamson began their hospital work through the British Red Cross, it is interesting to note Kelly's comments on this movement.

The British Red Cross movement selected works of art which upheld the 'Great Tradition' of European art. The 'Great Tradition' is itself an ideological construction of the imperialist climax and is profoundly Eurocentric in its assumptions.

(Kelly 1984: 89)

Adrian Hill

Hill and Petrie and their fellow artists were, then, working within the context of post-imperialist Britain and had absorbed prevailing ideology concerning the 'great traditions' in art which they carried with them into their art therapy practice. (It is obviously easier to make such an analysis several decades later, especially with the work of Raymond Williams (1958), Ed Berman, Ivan Illich, and other critics of art and society to draw on. In attempting to popularise art, Hill and Petrie seemed, in fact, to try to impose a set of artistic cultural values on the recipients.)

Hill's public relations drive

Hill began his campaign to publicise art therapy by sending some patients' work, accompanied by an article, to *Studio Magazine*, where it was published in 1942 under the title 'Art as an aid to illness'. He had a letter published in *The Times*, describing the work at King Edward VII Sanatorium and asking for information about similar schemes to be sent to him. He received a mass of mail, all of which he answered and acknowledged in a further letter to *The Times*. He noted the positive response to his ideas. 'My scheme was welcomed as a most valuable contribution to what was termed a virtually new science!' (1945: 67). The correspondence contained many requests from occupational therapists for advice on how to teach patients in bed, and from army education officers seeking to introduce art in military hospitals, and from ex-patients, deploring the lack of pictures in hospitals. (It is difficult to imagine, now that we are used to seeing paintings, sculptures, and prints in hospitals, that it was once forbidden to hang pictures because they gathered dust.)

Hill also sought the co-operation of other health care workers in his schemes, being sensitive to the problems involved in introducing 'messy' activities like painting on to hospital wards. He was careful to keep the goodwill of the nursing staff, and maintained close contact with OTs

> to ensure that our proposal did not cut across their province of work. They were found to be helpful and cooperative but anxious that we should not call it 'diversional therapy' as they maintained that therapy was a term implying a 100 percent curative benefit and this form of therapy would only affect those who had artistic inclinations.
>
> (Hill 1945: 88)

Hill does not appear to have questioned either of the assumptions in the above statement: that therapy could ever be 100 per cent effective or that in order to benefit patients should be artistic to begin with. Waller and Gilroy discuss the 'myths' which have arisen in art therapy as a result of such assumptions going unchallenged in the past, considering that they have led to art therapists today having constantly to describe and justify

The role of individual artists and psychotherapists

their work in the face of misunderstandings from other professions (1986: 54–7).

Hill as organisational leader

Belver Griffiths and Nicholas Mullins (1972) have discussed the communication and organisational patterns that underlie major advances and changes in direction in science. They take up the question of leadership roles, making a distinction between 'intellectual' and 'organisational' leaders, suggesting that these are often different people, although occasionally one person could occupy both roles. The 'intellectual' leader lays the original conceptual framework for work through research and theoretical publication, and the 'organisational' leader arranges funds, facilities, and means for communicating findings and ideas.

Hill had little pretension to be an intellectual leader, admitting that he had come by art therapy 'by accident', and he produced no research or elaborated theory on how, and in what conditions, it was successful. He used his skills as an artist, his love of teaching, and his desire to make art accessible to all as a basis for the work. On the other hand, Naumburg in the USA and Champernowne in Britain had produced some theoretical arguments as to why image-making, or free expression, could be valuable within the psychotherapeutic process (see Chapter 1).

Throughout the 1940s and 1950s especially, Hill strenuously campaigned for 'art therapy' and was actively involved in organising the first working parties and in distributing questionnaires to hospitals. He was also preoccupied with organising the details of the scheme to take pictures into hospitals and to arrange art classes in co-operation with the British Red Cross, a plan which was finally put into operation in March 1944. He travelled the country, lecturing and advising hospitals on the scheme, and played a role in trying to have art therapy 'officially' recognised (Large 1986).

In the final chapter of *Art Versus Illness*, he admitted to an 'obsession' with art therapy, but felt it would be very difficult to establish officially. Acknowledging the abundance of sympathy and good wishes for the scheme, he nevertheless admitted that these were insufficient on their own:

> There is a kind of admiration which has a tender, thoughtful grace, but is far too often accompanied by a certain melancholy. It is a compliment which is generally accompanied by a slight shake of the head. A more spirited gesture is wanted, one which inspires with a prophetic optimism, a genuine exhortation to carry on with cheerful hope and

Adrian Hill

confidence in the future. Indeed, there is much to be said for 'honest animal spirits and riotous impulses'. Such energies get things done.

(Hill 1945: 96)

He castigated the British public for too much caution and distrust of innovations, especially where art was concerned, feeling that on the one hand the 'custodians of custom and authority' were opposed to radical change, but on the other there was an opposing class 'obsessed by novelty'.

His vision, then, was of a new democratic state in which the National Health Service would replace private medicine and the Welfare State ensure a secure future for all. Art would have a central role to play in such a state; the creative artist would be venerated and each art centre would adopt its own neighbouring hospital or sanatorium. (This somewhat utopian vision of the arts was also shared by the Elmhirsts of Dartington. See Young 1982 and discussion in the section on Withymead later on.)

Adrian Hill continued to work tirelessly for his concept of art therapy, and it was his influence, together with that of Adamson and Champernowne in particular, which led to the formation of the British Association of Art Therapists of which he was the first Vice-President and later President.

Chapter six

Edward Adamson and Rita Simon
Moving from commercial art to art therapy

In this chapter I shall discuss the work of these two important figures in British art therapy, both of whom began their professional lives as commercial artists and 'accidentally' found themselves working with patients, which led them to abandon commercial art in favour of another occupation, not yet defined, but later to be known as 'art therapy'.

Adamson's background

Adamson was trained as a commercial artist in the 1930s, and along with Adrian Hill became involved with the British Red Cross picture-lending scheme during the Second World War. He lectured on art both in sanatoriums and in mental hospitals. Adamson had no particular knowledge of or interest in psychology, initially at least, and had never been psychoanalysed. He was, as Cunningham Dax, the medical superintendent at Netherne remarked, particularly interested in the evolution of artistic products and the use of art activities in the treatment of psychotic illness. Why this was so is not clear. It appears that Adamson came 'accidentally' into art therapy. We may speculate that he was not satisfied with being a commercial artist, nor did he wish to go into school teaching or practise as an artist full time. It seems he was looking for a directly socially useful role as an artist, hence, like Adrian Hill, was drawn towards giving art appreciation lectures in hospitals.

In their paper on the origins of psychology, Ben-David and Collins note that an individual who is moving from one role to another, such as from one profession or academic field to another, may be placed in a position of 'role conflict', and might try to resolve the conflict by giving up the attitudes and behaviours appropriate to the old role and adopting those of the new. Or, the individual might try to fit the methods and techniques of the old role to the materials of the new one, with the deliberate purpose of creating a new role. They refer to this process as 'role-hybridisation' (1966: 459). As far as Adamson is concerned, it is possible that his initial role conflict was in using his art training for

52

Edward Adamson and Rita Simon

commercial purposes and that he tried to resolve this by associating with the world of psychiatric rehabilitation.

Adamson gives a brief description of his entry into the world of psychiatry in *Art for Mental Health*:

> The aftermath of the war was an inauspicious time for drawing and painting to be included in the treatment programmes of British psychiatric hospitals, which were already undergoing considerable reorganisation as a result of the inception of the National Health Service. It was just at this point, in 1946, that Millicent Buller, of the Red Cross Picture library, invited me, as an artist, to assist her scheme by touring various British hospitals to discuss with the patients pictures that had been lent to the hospitals. In the course of this tour I visited Netherne and Fairdene Hospitals, Coulsdon, Surrey, where I met Dr Cunningham Dax. He subsequently invited me to join the staff of his hospital, as a practising artist, to open an art studio for the patients. I believe that this was the first time that such an appointment had been made on a full time basis in a state hospital.
>
> (Adamson 1970: 149)

Adamson thus adopted the role of 'artist', although he was required to facilitate the work of patients rather than do his own work in the studio, and, as we shall see, he worked under a very stringent set of guidelines.

Cunningham Dax and the experiments in 'psychiatric art'

In Chapter 3 I mentioned that Dax and Reitman were instrumental in having Adamson employed as an artist to help them in their research. In *Experimental Studies in Psychiatric Art* (1953) Dax explains that his own interest in 'art therapy' began when he heard about the work with servicemen with severe neurotic difficulties mentioned in Chapter 3. In a letter dated January 1986, written from his home in Australia to art therapy student Stan Roman, Dax comments:

> This Unit where Foulkes and Main were had much to do with the development of group therapy in England... an army sergeant had organised free painting there and Sybil Yates, an analyst with Freudian training who had been to the Tavistock, Mrs Bach, a Jungian, and I went there. When I returned to Netherne the staff were enthusiastic and Dr Freudenberg, with many cultural interests, Dalberg, with a wide European experience, and Reitman who had been at the Maudsley before the war with Guttmann and Maclay, all supported the project. Fortunately we were able to build a studio and gallery. Reitman told us about Edward Adamson, who was then a commercial artist and I persuaded the Committee to employ him. I don't remember the exact

53

The role of individual artists and psychotherapists

timetable but he agreed to a number of principles which we laid down for him, especially that he was to stimulate and receive, not to teach, not to analyse, but observe and never to touch the patients' paintings.

Dax considered painting to be 'more of a therapeutic aid rather than an occupational diversion' and Adamson 'more than an occupational therapist but not an analyst'.

Adamson perceived himself as an 'artist', but in fact his role could be described as something like a research assistant in the experiments which the medical staff were engaged in. Roman, in his essay concerning art therapy in its relationship to clinical investigations, discusses the research into leucotomy in which Adamson played an essential role, making the comment that:

> Little reference has been made in the past as to the association of art therapy with clinical investigation. This is to some extent understandable, particularly in view of an intense physical treatment like leucotomy. For a new profession such as art therapy there may well have been an unconscious unwillingness to mention its clinical links and thus add to the suspicions and misunderstandings surrounding it.
> (Roman 1986: 48)

Adamson's brief

So Adamson had a clear brief from the medical staff at Netherne. He was not to attempt to 'interpret' pictures nor to show any interest in the patient's life history or psychological problems in case he may have influenced the work produced. Both Dax and his colleague Reitman were very wary of the approach of Jungian and Freudian analysts, believing that the analyst would join the patient in a dialogue about the symbolic content of the work which would lead to a certain kind of painting being produced (Dax 1953; Reitman 1950). Reitman in particular saw such a process as circular, in that the therapist would interpret the picture according to Freudian or Jungian theory, which in turn would influence the next painting, which would again be interpreted in terms of the symbols produced. Thus, he felt, the pictures would have no diagnostic value and serve only the therapist's need.

Dax and Reitman wanted the painting to be carried out under 'standard conditions capable of being reproduced so that controlled experiments could be made'. The studio was erected specially for this purpose in 1948 and details of all aspects of the building were noted so that the same environment could be reproduced in comparative experiments or studies. Materials were standardised, a colour range of eleven posterpaints, two brushes, large and small, and a small enamelled tin with six divisions to be used as a palette and standard-size paper were provided for each

Edward Adamson and Rita Simon

patient. Dax (1953) concluded that paintings could be of diagnostic importance and that information gained from painting had on occasion helped to avert a possible suicide or other crisis. He felt that, in some cases, painting had shortened treatment. He acknowledged that it could also provide a tool for use in psychotherapy.

Adamson was not, then, regarded as a 'therapist' by his medical colleagues but rather as an 'artist' and 'observer'. His role in the hospital appears to have been rather difficult to maintain, in that he was to take no active part either in communication with patients, other than minimum technical advice about materials, or in encouraging them in their creative efforts. He had simply to 'be there and observe' and somehow to maintain a supportive attitude. Yet his stance was not unlike the approach recommended by Dewey (1934), Tomlinson (1934, when Senior Inspector of Art in the London County Council), and other advocates of the 'child-centred' approach to art teaching. Although Adamson was working with adults who happened to be in hospital, he provided an environment with materials and himself as a concerned other who did not, and was not allowed to, intervene, but somehow facilitated the creative process. Despite the fact that Adamson's 'passive role' is stressed time and again by the artist himself and by Dax, the latter observed that when Adamson was absent, attendance at the studio declined and those who painted 'did poor work of little psychiatric value' (Dax 1953).

Perceptions of Adamson's role by his patients

It is a reflection of the effects of chronic institutionalisation on mentally ill patients that so many people who worked in Adamson's studio were still in Netherne to give their reflections to Rona Rumney, a postgraduate art therapy student who did her placement there in 1980. She met several patients who commented on Adamson's 'charisma':

> There is no doubt that Adamson generated a particular atmosphere in the studio and it is difficult to analyse from this distance in time how this was done. One patient said: 'The atmosphere was mostly serene and deep. Everyone who came there found themselves expressing a new world of ideas that were suppressed in them. Their success was very great. He left us totally free to express ourselves.'
>
> (Rumney 1980)

But according to another patient he was dogmatic and would not tolerate talking or noise. 'Even staff were not allowed in.' He managed somehow to inspire creativity without making patients feel that they had to be creative artists. The general impression was that he did nothing while in the room, although one patient said that he was 'encouraging and said nice things' about their work. Another described him as 'a very quiet man who

The role of individual artists and psychotherapists

made people interested and created a very good atmosphere... he had a very great gift: he would just sit down next to someone and ask them if they would like to paint'. Another echoed this: 'Adamson used to be looking out of the window for hours and one wondered what he was doing. He generated a therapeutic atmosphere' (Rumney 1980).

This seems to be an occupation far removed from that of the commercial art world, with its strict deadlines and demands for work to be produced to a specific formula, although he was still working to a strict brief set by his medical colleagues.

Later on, in the 1950s, Adamson was allowed more freedom in his approach and opened the studio on four afternoons a week. During the mornings, he worked with thirty long-stay, mostly schizophrenic female patients in a ward in the main hospital. He told Rona Rumney that these were very sick people who liked to copy. He had to be with them continuously but once they got started they produced 'excellent work'. Here, apparently, the atmosphere was much freer and noisier than in the studio. Although the patients were chosen for research purposes, they painted for their own pleasure. There was some anxiety from the medical staff that 'too uninhibited a transference situation might affect the content of the painting' (Dax).

The conditions that were set by the doctors and Adamson's desire to carry them out enabled art therapy to be distinguished from occupational therapy. Patients were able to paint without recourse to selling their work or being concerned about aesthetic standards.

Rumney suggests that Adamson's passivity might have been a result of his unwillingness to deal with the psychological content himself, combined with his willingness to hand over the paintings to the doctors for analysis. In this respect he differs considerably from Naumburg and Champernowne (whose work will be discussed in the next section) who felt that the art therapist should be able to help the patient explore his or her own paintings. (As Naumburg puts it, 'The art therapist does not interpret the symbolic art expression of his patients but encourages the patient to discover for himself the meaning of his art productions' (Naumburg 1966).)

Some contradictions in Adamson's role

Rumney points to a central contradiction in Adamson's role. According to Dax (1953: 23) patients knew that their paintings would not be returned as they were regarded as 'case notes', so they would not be seen by relatives or friends or put on walls for decoration. She asks:

If they were to be treated as case notes, why were the paintings exhibited publicly in the gallery? What chance did they [the patients] have of relating to their own work after they were named, dated and filed away if their doctor did not choose to use them in therapeutic sessions? It is impossible to know how most of the patients felt about the total lack of control over their work.'

(Rumney 1980: 14)

As we shall see later on, Champernowne was very critical of this approach to patient art work, especially to the notion of exhibiting work. Yet she and Adamson and Hill were all members of the same working party to promote an 'art therapy' which obviously meant very different things to each of them.

Adamson's organisational role: exhibitions

Adamson himself gave the issue of exhibitions some consideration. He asked, why hold exhibitions at all, but suggested that the reasons were mainly didactic in that they would give mental health workers some idea of what it felt like to be mentally ill (1970: 149). He established the gallery at Netherne for this purpose in 1956.

In fact, most of his public relations work for art therapy was carried out through organising exhibitions of his patients' work. For instance, in July 1949, an exhibition was held at 1 Grosvenor Crescent, London SW 1, and reviewed in the *British Medical Journal* of 23 July 1949. The (anonymous) review mentions that Dax had said that the term 'art therapy' should not be used for 'there were nearly as many therapies' in psychiatric nomenclature as there were phobias; and it brought only disrepute on their experimental methods of attacking psychiatric illness if they were labelled as curative without statistical evidence to support their claims. He did, however, feel that painting provided emotional release and that patients who were able to reflect their state of mind in their drawings felt better for it. Dax added that he thought patients often did their most interesting work when their minds were disturbed.

It was in 1949 that Adamson joined Hill on the National Association for Mental Health working party on art therapy, thus beginning to engage in promotional activities which were to lead to the subsequent formation of the British Association of Art Therapists of which Adamson was the first Chair in 1963.

Rita Simon

Like Adamson, Rita Simon worked as a commercial artist, at the publishers, Harrap. She was not interested in using her art training in teaching nor did she find commercial art satisfying. She too became involved in art therapy 'by chance' through a friend who was a psychiatric nurse and

The role of individual artists and psychotherapists

who suggested she might like to do some voluntary work for a group of ex-psychiatric out-patients. This was in Dr Joshua Bierer's social club in Kingsway Hall. Rita Simon says of her work at that time:

> I was a sort of helper, a socialising person, but Joshua Bierer came back from the army one day and immediately asked me if I would teach some patients to paint. I said, No, I didn't think I could do this. I remember saying that you couldn't just teach anybody to paint. You had to have an innate talent. So he said, would you like to try? You will have to do it in your own home because we have no premises. So on Sunday mornings for two years people trooped up to my front door; I knew nothing about them or mental illness or what to expect.
>
> (Simon in interview)

In 1944, Joshua Bierer asked Rita Simon if she would contribute a piece on the work she had been doing to a booklet he had produced on therapeutic social clubs, and attend weekly staff meetings at the Social Psychiatry Centre which he had started in Hampstead. She recalled her experiences in the Centre:

> It was a multi-disciplinary setting. Bierer was an Adlerian, but there were Freudians, Jungians and eclectics and straightforward Harley Street psychiatrists as well. It was very informal and free and supportative.

Eventually, through an occupational therapist friend, Beryl Harris, Rita Simon met Adrian Hill, who in turn introduced her to Nancy Overend at the National Association for Mental Health. Rita commented on the fact that Hill and Overend wanted to go beyond the initial idea of the Red Cross picture-lending scheme which was to give talks on art, and to introduce painting. Rita was gradually drawn into working with TB patients in the wards of the Royal Free and Paddington Hospitals. At the time, 1944, she felt:

> At a certain point I had to choose between being a commercial artist and getting into this much more interesting area. So I gave up my job at Harraps and took on one day a week teaching at Medway School of Art, Rochester.

For the rest of the time, Rita took on part-time work with TB patients, and other physically ill patients, including those with accident trauma and brain damage, as well as psychiatric patients in hospitals.

Apparently the climate of opinion towards art in hospitals was very favourable after the war. Rita Simon felt that Adrian Hill's work had been significant in producing such a climate, together with the approach to group psychotherapy for traumatised servicemen and the search within the health service for improved rehabilitation schemes for psychiatric patients following the war. As a member of staff at the Social Psychiatry Centre, she had continued to work with groups in an informal setting, entering into her own analysis as a way of better understanding her own and the patients' psychology. In this way she was different from both Adrian Hill and Edward Adamson, who expressed themselves not interested in this aspect of art therapy.

Rita Simon attended the first art therapy working party at the NAMH in 1949, but in 1952 left for Ireland with her husband and baby, returning only for the founding meeting of BAAT in 1963 and then in the early 1980s permanently to London. She continued to work and to write on art therapy while in Ireland, especially in the field of art therapy with children and the elderly, and on changes of style during art therapy. Her articles appeared in a wide variety of art therapy and medically-related journals (1970, 1974, 1981, 1985).

Chapter seven

The Withymead Centre

The role of Gilbert and Irene Champernowne in promoting the theory and practice of art therapy

At the same time as Adrian Hill was attempting to set up art classes in sanatoriums and general hospitals, and Rita Simon had begun to work in Joshua Bierer's social psychiatry clubs (1942 onwards), an experimental centre for psychotherapy through the arts was established in Devon, under the direction of Dr Irene Champernowne and her husband Gilbert.

The Champernowne's had been bombed out of their London flat and sought refuge in Devon, near to Leonard and Dorothy Elmhirst, trustees of Dartington Hall. At the time at which Withymead was established, there had been a gradual decline of private patronage of the arts due to severe restrictions imposed upon the accumulation of wealth. Private collectors still bought works of art from dealers in the open market but, according to Herbert Read, 'They no longer command the artist like the monastery or the guild, the court or the castle' (1952: 18). This did not apply to the Elmhirsts, however, who were described by Young as wealthy enough to defy the trend (1982: 195). The Elmhirsts were responsible for saving Withymead from financial disaster in 1950, and over the following ten years donated £70,000 (Young 1982: 212)

It was in 1941 that the Champernownes bought Withymead, and in 1942 the first patients arrived.

Background to Withymead

The only book about Withymead is by a one-time resident and close friend and colleague of Irene Champernowne, Dr Anthony Stevens, a psychiatrist and Jungian analyst (1986). This is a descriptive account of the history of the Centre from its formation to its demise in the late 1960s, and of the role of Gilbert and Irene Champernowne. Shortly before the publication of his book I was able to interview Stevens about his personal experience of living and working in the Centre. Other published material about Withymead is by Champernowne herself (1963, 1963). A later paper, which clearly presented her views on the relationship between art and therapy, appeared in *Inscape* (1971).

The Withymead Centre

Fortunately, many art therapists who spent some time at Withymead are still living and were prepared to be interviewed in connection with this book. They include therapists who were officers and council members of BAAT at the time of its formation and later.

I have also drawn on my personal acquaintance with Irene Champernowne, working closely with her for two years, and on a weekend visit to her home in Stanton Broadway to make a study of her archives on Withymead and art therapy in general. At that time I met and discussed the work of the Centre and of the individuals who had practised there with Molly Kemp and Euanie Tippett, both of whom had remained at Withymead until its closure.

The Withymead Centre has had a considerable influence on the development of art therapy in Britain, in that it provided some of the first informal training schemes in the subject in the 1950s and 1960s. It was a source of personal learning and therapy for several founder members of the British Association of Art Therapists (many of whom later became prominent in teaching and research); and its founder, Irene Champernowne, actively campaigned for art therapy until her death, aged 75, in 1976. 'Withymead-style' summer schools still continue under the auspices of the Gilbert and Irene Champernowne Trust.

The fact that Withymead was the first community on record where psychotherapy was combined with art therapy, together with the points made above, ensures its place in the history of the profession.

Background of the Champernownes

Gilbert Champernowne came from an old Devonshire family who had lived at Dartington Hall for several centuries. The Elmhirsts had bought the estate from them in 1925. Stevens describes Gilbert's unhappy childhood which had severely affected him psychologically, and physically too, as he had lost a leg in an accident. These misfortunes, Stevens suggests, had contributed to his humanity and commitment as administrative director of Withymead (1986: 10–11).

Young offers the following description of the Champernownes and their relationship to the Elmhirsts:

Irene's husband Gilbert was the brother of the man who sold the property to Leonard. He would have inherited Dartington eventually if it had not been sold. Born in 1884, he was the ninth child of Arthur Champernowne, Squire of Dartington Hall. He remembered what the Hall was like in the 1880s and his father pretending to be a roaring lion when he chased his children down the back corridor of the Hall's Elizabethan wing. This background made for a special bond between him and Leonard. But the dominant one of the two, for Dorothy

61

The role of individual artists and psychotherapists

[Elmhirst] in particular, was not Gilbert but Irene. He was tall, thin and frail. She was as large in personality as in person, with tremendous energy and presence, a psychotherapist who had been analysed by Jung himself, in Zurich, and for twenty years from 1942 practised in Exeter.

(Young 1982: 210–11)

Irene Champernowne was born in London, the eldest daughter of a missionary who had served in China. She had wanted to be a doctor but was advised by her school that she was not suited to a university education. Undeterred, however, Irene enrolled at Birkbeck College, studying botany, zoology, and chemistry, to prepare herself to enter medical school later on. She financed her studies herself by teaching biology and mathematics. Eventually, after a personally stressful and exhausting period of time, she gained a second class honours degree.

Stevens recalled that, while in her early 20s, Irene Champernowne became severely depressed and, in an attempt to recover, went to stay on a farm in Kent, an experience which deeply affected her and inspired her later on at Withymead. She was able there to maintain her love of country life. After the successful stay on the farm had eased her depression, Irene embarked on personal analysis at the Tavistock Clinic with Leonard Brown, a Freudian. She did not consider this to be very productive, and, despite discovering a more promising situation in the Adlerian school in London, could not find what she was looking for in England so in 1930 decided to go to Vienna to study at Adler's clinic.

In order to finance her psychotherapy studies, Irene obtained a lecturing post in biology at the Gipsy Hill Teachers' Training College for half the year. The rest of the time she studied in Vienna. She was impressed by the way that Adler used his audience as a therapeutic group and this gave her the impetus to examine the value of working therapeutically through a community, an approach which she used later when she established the Withymead Centre on the lines of a therapeutic community with much emphasis on the whole staff meeting as a decision-making forum. Her analyst at that time was Dr Leonard Seif, and Adlerian from Munich, who advised her to read Jung's works.

For two years Irene moved back and forth from London to Vienna and Munich, eventually becoming a senior lecturer at Gipsy Hill. In 1935 she enrolled for a BSc psychology course at University College, London.

At that time the activities of the Nazi party in Germany were growing more noticeable and alarming, and in 1936 Irene stopped going to Munich. During her last visit, Irene wrote to Jung. She had read *Modern Man in Search of a Soul* and she felt that he provided just what she needed 'to fill the gaps left by Freud and Adler'. Jung invited her to Ascona, where he was attending a meeting. Her description of her first meeting with Jung, which I recall from discussions with her in 1970–2, revealed the enormous

62

The Withymead Centre

admiration, perhaps even passion, that she had for his teaching and personality. Jung suggested that Irene should obtain her BSc and then go to Zurich to analyse with him, and, at the same time, prepare a PhD thesis on an aspect of his 'word association' test.

On return to London, Irene began to analyse with Godwin Baynes, a Jungian analyst. She felt that she learned about art therapy for the first time from Baynes and his *Mythology of the Soul*, a comprehensive demonstration of the combination of analytical psychology with art, became a kind of bible for her. His work also influenced her at Withymead, where she saw a clear distinction between the role of art therapist and that of psychotherapist: the art therapist would help the patient to *produce* the pictures but it was the psychotherapist who would enter into the deeper *meaning* of the work with the patient. Irene was inclined to refer to the art therapist as a 'midwife' in the process.

In 1937, having obtained her BSc, she went to Zurich and had regular analysis with Jung, and at the same time collected material for her PhD thesis. She also analysed with Toni Wolff, a pupil of Jung's and learned that it was possible to work with two therapists provided that they were working in a similar way and that they were in close contact with each other. This ran counter to the accepted psychoanalytic view, held by Freudian analysts in particular, that such practice caused 'transference' phenomena to be split between the different therapists, thus leaving the patient unable to resolve his or her early childhood difficulties. Again, Irene was to use this somewhat unorthodox experience at Withymead.

In 1938, she married Gilbert Champernowne who had been working with the Discharged Prisoners Aid Society, had been in analysis with Baynes, and was then an occupational therapist at the Mill Hill Military Hospital, doing pottery and woodwork with the patients. When the bombing raids on London intensified they started looking for accommodation in Devon.

As a result of a chance meeting with her old headmistress, Irene learned of a Georgian house at Countess Wear near Exeter. They bought the house in 1941 and in May 1942 it became a base for refugees from Exeter which had been heavily bombed.

Physical attributes of Withymead

Irene Champernowne always held the view that the environment was important to the practice of psychotherapy, and Withymead was, from its photographs and by the accounts of all who went there, a very beautiful site standing in about six acres. There were two Georgian houses and an adjoining cottage and several outbuildings, which were converted into studios for painting, music, pottery, etc. Ex-residents of Withymead

The role of individual artists and psychotherapists

invariably speak of the peace and tranquillity of the surroundings and the attention paid to decor.

There was, at the same time, a sense of 'other worldliness', as described by the American art therapist, Eleanor Ulman, after a visit to Withymead in July 1962:

> Given the intimate loveliness of Devon's rolling green hills, flowering hedgerows and thatched cottages, the residents of Withymead have made their home of a piece with the country around it. The gardens where they grow vegetables for their table and flowers for their pleasure, rooms furnished plainly but well, the beauty added to by the vital products of studio, pottery and garden – all reflect the wise expenditure of little money, much artistry and loving care.
>
> (Ulman 1963: 96)

This carefully planned, peaceful environment, attested to by residents and visitors to the Centre, could however prove inhibiting at times. Two art therapists, one-time residents at Withymead, made similar comments, illustrated by the following extract from an interview:

> Much as we respected Irene, there had developed a rather cosy atmosphere and something about the real world needed to come into the situation. I think we missed something on reflection, though, which was the wisdom of an overview that she had. You could also say a moral view, or an ethical one... she had a kind of wisdom of which our use was a bit irresponsible. At the same time we felt it needed opening up.

Treatment philosophy and structure

The attention to creating harmonious surroundings was not unusual at that time in approaches to emotional disturbance in both adults and children, and in special education (see Wills, D., Neil, A. S., *et al.*).

The patient group itself also appears to have influenced the style of treatment, as Stevens suggests.

> Withymead's success, however, depended not only on Gilbert and Irene Champernowne and the talented staff they gathered round them to form what Irene referred to, somewhat mystically, as the 'therapeutic ring' but also on the kinds of people they attracted as patients. These came from all walks of life, but they were predominantly drawn from the culturally more advantaged sections of society. Thus of the 240 adults who were admitted between January 1942 and October 1954, 151 were connected with the professions or with the arts, while only 47 belonged to a miscellaneous group of occupations such as secretaries, clerks, domestic workers etc. The remaining 42 were women

The Withymead Centre

who were full-time housewives, married to the most part to professional men.

(Stevens 1986: 57)

Stevens echoes a commonly held assumption of the time, and one which is also still held today in some analytic circles, that:

It is well known that people of good cultural background, ready verbal facility, and above average intelligence are those who are best suited to analytic treatment and most helped by it. But it is only fair to bear this limitation in mind when comparing Withymead with state run institutions, which must accommodate patients of much more diverse social origins.

(Stevens 1986: 58)

Such patients were to be found in the hospitals served by Adrian Hill, Edward Adamson, and in the social psychiatry clubs formed by Joshua Bierer in which Rita Simon began her art therapy career.

One patient, who became a member of staff later, remembered:

There was a folksy, cottagy thing about it, which was very nice, especially if you'd been in the city. Some of the time, anyway. But when I first went there they had people who were very much middle-class, but gradually, due to economics, thy needed other people to be referred there. People were referred from local authorities who were glad to have Withymead there. They referred very difficult cases there, and the place wasn't actually designed for very difficult cases. They struggled very well and hard, but....

(The issue of suitability for psychotherapy has been investigated by many authors (see especially Yalom 1983) who suggest that it is the therapist's technique that may need adapting to specific circumstances, rather than certain patients being excluded from psychotherapy. The art therapist quoted above is referring to the later years of Withymead, when finances were very low and attempts were made to increase referrals, resulting in the admission of borderline psychotic patients who found the open structure of the centre hard to cope with.)

As a treatment centre, then, Withymead was established to be as different as possible from the 'conventional' mental hospital of the time, where the emphasis was on isolating the mentally ill from the rest of society in a custodial framework. (Stanton and Schwartz (1954), Barton (1959), and Goffman (1968) have all written extensively on the problems of 'institutional neurosis' among long-stay patients, resulting in apathy, lack of initiative, loss of contact with others, all of which contributed to worsening the patient's original illness.) Irene Champernowne deplored

The role of individual artists and psychotherapists

such conditions and was determined that Withymead should contain none of the features of such hospitals.

The role of the arts at Withymead

The desire to introduce art into the therapeutic programme at Withymead came directly from Irene Champernowne's personal experience as an analysand, and from her work with Jung, who encouraged his patients to paint and model and who found making art valuable himself. Her association with H. G. Baynes was a strong motivating force as well. Gilbert Champernowne had also had some personal involvement in arts and crafts, and had been inspired by Adrian Hill's work, resulting in his teaching woodwork and pottery in a north London hospital.

Irene wrote in 1963 that she found words to be an extremely difficult medium through which to convey deep experiences of life:

> It was clear that the mind was filled with visual, aural and bodily images which were suitable containers for emotions and ideas that were otherwise inexpressible. Images give a means of communication between one human being and another, and also a means to a more conscious understanding to the individual himself.
>
> (Champernowne 1963)

Despite her previous personal involvement in image-making, however, Irene remained firmly in the role of psychotherapist, and one member of staff at Withymead during the 1960s felt that 'art therapy had to take second place to psychotherapy, in a nutshell. The psychotherapist was the person who held the power. The other could hold it too, but on condition'.

Eleanor Ulman (1963) presented a transcript of a conversation with the Withymead staff group. She pointed out that it was unusual to find a number of different people (professionals) working together in a team, and also a number of different arts which interrelated. She was concerned to know whether these arts overlapped or were interchangeable and Irene had replied that people were encouraged to be spontaneous but there came a point where they needed the discipline of a technique, to give security to the colours or chaotic forms. It was the role of the 'teachers' as she referred to the artists, to be sensitive to the patients' expressions and to pick up cues from them and their work to see when they might be ready to move into another medium or develop further technical skills. Irene had warned:

> One has to be careful if a person goes into the painting room and wants to keep everything in a straight line and a border with a pencil, won't use colour or a brush... one has to be warned that the person may need to stay in that rather conscious framework and the other only be let in

The Withymead Centre

with the greatest gentleness, or he might either 'split' or *fall* into the unconscious... you can't let the unconscious in deliberately except by absolutely skilled means.

Here Irene was drawing attention to the need to take into consideration the power of the medium, for the art form was considered to be the container of strong emotions, which could include anger and violence, for example. Irene considered it essential that the art therapists (or teachers) should be highly skilled in their own art form in order to understand the expressive and communicative possibilities of the medium. This notion still lies at the base of art therapy training and practice today (1989).

Withymead as a therapeutic community

Maxwell Jones, writing in *Therapeutic Communities: Reflections and Progress*, comments that the Second World War acted as a stimulus to himself and his colleagues in deviating from the 'strict orthodoxy' of the Maudsley Hospital in London towards a mode of treatment in which patients and staff co-operated and staff became 'facilitators' rather than 'curers'.

> The war years heightened the dissatisfaction that many of us felt with traditional psychiatry and gave birth to a new ideological approach. Because the climate was ripe for changes in many directions, parallel developments were occurring elsewhere, notably among the ex-Tavistock Clinic army psychiatrists at Northfield Military Hospital, where they were inspired by Kurt Lewin's concept of life space.
>
> (Jones 1979: 1–9)

According to Stevens (1986) the first therapeutic community was established by Tom Main in 1946, at the Cassel Hospital in Surrey. He says that Withymead was in many ways 'a model therapeutic community' but that it had important differences. Yet, further on in his book, he rather contradicts this statement by declaring that Withymead was 'the first therapeutic community to be established in Britain'. It seems that he felt the differences to be of a conceptual nature, in that Withymead analysts were all schooled in Jungian analytical traditions, whereas other communities, he felt, displayed 'a conceptual vagueness and uncertainty in conducting their affairs'. He suggests that these 'other' communities lacked the 'archetypal exploratory dimension which permeated all activities at Withymead and gave a ready understanding of psychic needs characterising different stages of the human life cycle of individuals and the group' (Stevens 1986: 84–5).

The role of individual artists and psychotherapists

Stevens's ambivalence about the therapeutic community movement in terms of its 'group' orientation is revealed throughout the book and the following statement is typical of his reservation:

> That communication and sharing should be elevated to such a high status is typically to be expected of a peer-orientated society which has lost respect for traditional values and has experienced the progressive relativisation of all canons and ethics. When authority is no longer ordained by the gods, one citizen's opinion becomes as good as the next, nothing can be known for certain, and the media emerge as the only means by which a culture can sustain itself.
>
> (Stevens 1986: 86–7)

If we accept that communication and sharing of tasks, close patient–staff contact and decision making being carried out through the staff meeting were fundamentals in Withymead's structure, then it appears as if Stevens is attacking the Centre itself. I do not think this was his intention. Rather, he was attacking the democratic, humanistic, and perhaps even Marxist base of the whole therapeutic community movement, seeing Withymead as different because it focused on 'the individual' rather than 'the group'. (Irene Champernowne herself had many misgivings about the power of the group, especially during the late 1960s and early 1970s when the 'encounter group' movement emanating from the USA became very popular in Britain.)

Issues of control and power

There is no doubt, according to both staff and patients, that Irene was firmly in control. As one interviewee said:

> It's this thing about being in control... she was in control for years and years and when somebody gets to be like that, it gets mixed up... she had some blind spots... her thinking was so shaped by Withymead, being a psychotherapist and having art therapists on the spot, so to speak. It's a totally different relationship to how people are in the world outside.

Stevens believed that the success of Withymead lay in the fact that the staff and patients accepted the 'complete authority' of Gilbert and Irene as charismatic leaders; that there were no therapeutic group and community meetings (save the staff meeting); that there was no 'radical political intent'; and that Withymead was a 'genuine community' and not a 'synthetic' one (1986: 99–100). He does not elaborate on these last two descriptions, but his statements call attention to the problem of 'idealisation' of the therapeutic community and its leader (Hobson 1971: Lemlij *et al.* 1981) and the dangers inherent in such a situation.

The Withymead Centre

Baron discusses the issues of 'idealisation' and 'charismatic leadership' in her account of the demise of the Paddington Day Hospital during the late 1970s. In examining the role of the medical director, Baron draws on Weber's definition of 'charisma' (Roth and Wittick 1975). She says:

> Given that in the area of professional autonomy he was entitled to define the area of his responsibility, his definition remained unchallenged. This is an example of how charismatic authority is not externally constrained. The bearer of charisma is 'delimited from within, not by the external order' (Weber). Charisma usually operates within specific social, political or ethnic groups and tends not to extend beyond the group.
>
> (Baron 1987: 76)

Baron goes on to say that in the NHS the group of mentally ill patients have a relationship to other specific groups of staff – social workers or the administrative staff, for example, who generally run the material side of the hospital. At Paddington there was 'a clash in the day hospital between the charismatic authority of the medical director and the bureaucratic authority of the administrative or managerial level' (1987: 76). (Such a clash may well have contributed to the demise of Withymead in the late 1960s, when, in the face of ambivalence and misgiving on the part of the staff and in particular of Irene Champernowne, Withymead came under the NHS and hence subject to 'outside' management.)

Male and female roles at Withymead

Further evidence of Irene Champernowne's authority can be found in an interview with a female art therapist who worked at Withymead in the 1950s onwards. She made the point that Irene preferred to have women run the painting studio while men were in the pottery:

> Irene thought it was best to have a woman in the painting room. She thought it was particularly the job for a midwife, as it were, in the painting room. I don't quite know why. I think Mr D would rather have liked to be in the painting room. He was a much better painter than I was. Much. But Irene didn't think it best for him to be there when he joined the staff.

Interviewer: 'Was it possible for you to go into the pottery room, or would that have been difficult?'

> It might have been difficult to find me another niche... I don't think Irene wanted to move me. She never suggested it. She didn't say that clay was all right for either a man or a woman but she did say that she thought a woman was better in painting. Clay being such an earthy

The role of individual artists and psychotherapists

material, one would have thought that if there were any sexual discrimination it would have been more suitable to have a woman there! For the throwing, and that side, probably a man is better, for the heavy, more technical work.

It seemed that this interviewee would have liked the opportunity to work in the pottery. However, such was Irene's authority that she did not even question her decision.

That Irene had such strong feelings about what was appropriate work for men and what for women, as far as duties in Withymead were concerned, is confirmed by Mr G who went there in the early 1950s as an art student and stayed on to work as an art therapist until the late 1960s:

> Irene had this thing about the men. They were supposed to be doing work outside the art. You know, we were all supposed to have been doing proper painting, and then, of course, to be sensitive therapists. And the women she saw as being the midwives. The men were downstairs in the stables, which was the pottery, and doing a lot of modelling... there was the building squad which did all the repairs, and that was the men.

In his chapter on 'Man, woman and creativity', Stevens explores Irene's attitudes to the roles of men and women in society. He cites an incident when Robert Hobson was talking about his therapeutic community and the issue of freedom being balanced with authority was being discussed. Hobson asked Champernowne:

> 'Do you believe that someone has to have the last word in a community?' and she replied, 'Yes, I do, and the last word should be from a man, but the man must be a very special kind of man, one who is deeply related to the community and capable of listening to its soul, which is feminine.'
>
> (Stevens 1986: 108)

I have referred earlier to art therapy gaining a strong matriarchal role model in Irene Champernowne. She herself did not consider that she was a matriarch. Indeed, she believed that matriarchies had never existed and could never survive, and that men were 'better at authority' than women.

(It is beyond the scope of this book to delve further into the issues of masculinity and femininity as they apply to the role of art therapist. [See Walter (1983) for further discussion and Stevens (1986: 229–37) on the 'split' which occurred between the men and women at Withymead.] I have raised the issues here, in connection with Withymead, to highlight the openings for future research to examine the influence of Withymead on male and female authority within the art therapy movement itself.)

The Withymead Centre

Irene Champernowne as an intellectual leader

As remarked earlier, Adrian Hill emerged as an 'organisational leader' of the art therapy movement during the 1940s and 1950s. Concerning the 'intellectual leader', Griffiths and Mullins (1972) suggest this is someone who lays the original conceptual framework for work by making public statements on theory and research which normally result in an acknowledged theoretical break, and who approves and validates others' work. The intellectual leader also functions as the central communicator within the group, although this role may be dispersed among members of the group. It is unlikely that Irene Champernowne herself would have identified her role in this way as she saw herself primarily as a practitioner. However in combining the theoretical frameworks of Jungian and Adlerian psychology with the developments in art education outlined earlier on in this thesis, and in combining them within the framework of a 'therapeutic community', she made an active contribution to the theoretical bas of the movement. In so far as Withymead acted as an informal training base for future leading art therapists, she can also be considered to have inspired and validated others' work. By her lectures and her writing and her formulation of short training courses at Withymead, she acted as a communicator within and without the movement.

She never referred to herself as an art therapist, however, even though by today's criteria she would be so regarded. She seemed satisfied with her role as psychotherapist, but it was extremely important to her to promote and encourage the development of both art therapy and art therapists.

Summary of Withymead's contribution to art therapy

Withymead, then, offered an opportunity for selected patients to experience Jungian analysis combined with art therapy in safe, comfortable, and empathetic surroundings, contained by an enthusiastic team of staff, for the experience of the Withymead art therapists appears overall to have been a positive one, especially if we compare it to that of art therapists in psychiatric hospitals. The artists who worked at Withymead were searching for a meaningful use of their art skills, not to be found in teaching or commercial art, nor in conventional adult education classes. The fact that staff also had access to psychotherapy seems to have been attractive to those who were wishing to develop and change, and perhaps to find a new direction in life. They could participate in the therapeutic team, although the 'last word' lay with Irene, or Gilbert. Total dedication of the staff to the ideal of the community was essential.

The staff and patients were prepared to accept the authority of the Champernownes, Irene in particular emerging as a 'charismatic leader'

The role of individual artists and psychotherapists

with all the problems inherent in that position. Staff had to be very motivated, as they had to be prepared to work and study for long hours for little pay in return for the privilege of being part of the Withymead 'family'. It is probable that Withymead became an 'idealised community', its closure in the late 1960s resulting in attempts to continue the movement elsewhere by Irene Champernowne and those closest to her. This then was the situation of Withymead from 1942 to the late 1950s and the context from which Irene Champernowne made her contributions to the first working parties on art therapy in the NAMH.

Chapter eight

The influence of psychoanalysts on the intellectual development of art therapy

As we have seen in previous chapters, art therapy had seemed to emerge as a segment both of art teaching and also of psychoanalysis. The emphasis in the model practised by Hill was on the process of painting, drawing, etc., as an enjoyable, fulfilling, and creative pastime, whereas the focus in Champernowne's model was on the communication of unconscious conflicts through image-making within a prescribed relationship.

I have suggested that Irene Champernowne could be considered as an intellectual leader in the field of art therapy, in terms of her synthesis of models from analytical psychology with a developmental model of art, within the context of a therapeutic community. Irene Champernowne never referred to herself as an art therapist, but always as a Jungian psychotherapist. She did, however, spend much of her life promoting the discipline and her own practice was similar to what is defined as art therapy today, except that she asked the patients to bring their work into the session, rather than make it there and then.

Other prominent figures in the art therapy movement also came from non-art backgrounds, and while engaging in practice which could today be defined as art therapy, retained their original role as psychotherapists (or, in the case of Ralph Pickford, psychologist and psychotherapist). In this chapter I shall discuss the work of Marion Milner and Ralph Pickford, both of whom became deeply interested in the process of image-making as an aspect of psychotherapy, partly as a result of their own Freudian analyses. Pickford was a founder member of BAAT and of the Scottish Society for the Study of Art and Psychopathology, and Milner succeeded Hill as Honorary President of BAAT.

This chapter also gives an opportunity to draw attention, albeit briefly, to the work of Donald Winnicott, as one of the psychoanalysts who gave inspiration to many generations of art therapists, particularly those working with children. Winnicott never referred to his work as 'art therapy' but, in his regard for and use of drawings, could be said to have acted as a role model for future art therapists.

The role of individual artists and psychotherapists

Donald Winnicott

Winnicott was born in Devon in 1896 and completed medical studies in Cambridge. He began to train in Freudian psychoanalysis in 1923, in the same year that he started to work as a consultant paediatrician in Paddington Green children's hospital and Queen Elizabeth hospital in East London. He was somewhat isolated in this position, being the only analyst who was also a paediatrician.

Winnicott felt that classical Freudian theory at that time was limited as far as the treatment of children was concerned. His work as a paediatrician had revealed that disturbed children showed difficulties in their emotional development as infants and as babies. He was much interested by the work of Melanie Klein in Berlin and Anna Freud in Vienna, both of whom had undertaken psychoanalytic treatment of children using new techniques, particularly play, for communication. When Klein came to England, Winnicott studied her methods at first hand and began to develop his own theories.

Davis and Wallbridge, in their book *Boundary and Space* (1981), give an excellent description of the way that Winnicott's therapeutic methods evolved. Of particular interest to art therapists is the concept of the 'transitional object' (for example, a piece of blanket or a woolly jumper that is of central importance for an infant and the loss of which causes extreme distress). In a chapter entitled 'A search for meaning: loss and transition in art therapy with children', Caroline Case explores this phenomenon.

> Winnicott sees the role of the creative impulse being a prerequisite for human development. This starts in a small way, through the use of objects between mother and child. As we develop into adults, the ability to use objects to communicate with the world, to make space and belongings personal, becomes the basic mechanism by which we attempt to maintain degrees of health over ill-health on personal, environmental and cultural levels. A transitional object is a first object that a baby attaches importance to. Winnicott suggests that the mother's breast is first perceived to be part of the infant. The object seems to come into the space between the mother and baby.... The ability to play comes into being. He is able to manipulate transitional objects to meet his needs. A range of creative responses develops, including drawing and painting.
>
> (Case 1987: 68–9)

The use of a transitional object as forming a bridge between the child and the outside world has been found to some extent to be culturally and socially determined. Nevertheless, Winnicott observed that 'the babies who came to his clinic were inseparably attached not only to parents but

Psychoanalysts and art therapy

to blankets, rags and other soft objects' (Case 1987: 71). Winnicott developed his paper on 'Transitional objects and transitional phenomena' (1951) into the book *Playing and Reality* (1971a). In a chapter in this entitled 'Creativity and its origins', he links the ability to be creative with psychological health (a concept which has been taken up not only by art therapists but by the Artists in Hospitals movement in Britain).

> The creative impulse is therefore something that can be looked at as a thing in itself, something that of course is necessary if an artist is to produce a work of art, but also as something that is present when anyone – baby, child, adolescent, adult, old man or woman – looks in a healthy way at anything or does anything deliberately, such as making a mess with faeces or prolonging the act of crying to enjoy a musical sound....
>
> It is not of course that anyone will ever be able to explain the creative impulse, and it is unlikely that anyone would ever want to do so; but the link can be made, and usefully made, between creative living and living itself, and the reasons can be studied why it is that creative living can be lost and why the individual's feeling that life is real or meaningful can disappear.

(Winnicott 1971a: 69)

In describing an interview with an adolescent, Winnicott refers to the 'squiggle game', in which he uses spontaneous drawings, or 'squiggles', to start a process of communication. This game is described and illustrated through case examples in 'Therapeutic consultations in child psychiatry' (1971b), published at the same time as E. M. Lyddiatt, an art therapist, published *Spontaneous Painting and Modelling*. The fundamental approach is similar, in that image-making (in two or three dimensions) is encouraged by the therapist. The image acts as an intermediary between patient and therapist, may be retained as a valued object in itself, or transformed and eventually discarded.

Winnicott's books, especially those mentioned above, find a prominent place in current art therapy bibliographies and it is clear from more recent art therapy literature at least that his influence has been pervasive, despite the fact that he did not write on art therapy *per se*.

Marion Milner

Her published works have, according to many art therapists interviewed, had a profound influence on them. Two in particular, *On Not Being Able to Paint* (1950) and *The Hands of the Living God* (1969), appear on the recommended reading lists of the three training centres in art therapy. The combination of object-relations theory with image-making in the analytic process, which she developed from her contacts with Melanie Klein, has

75

The role of individual artists and psychotherapists

in more recent times served as an important model for art therapists. (See Dalley *et al.* (1987) and Gilroy and Dalley (1989) for several references to her work and influence.)

Marion Milner was born in 1900. At the age of 18 she began to train to work with young children, then went on to take a degree in psychology and physiology at London University. After successful completion of her degree, she entered the field of industrial psychology, and studied for two years in the USA on a Rockefeller scholarship. She wrote *A Life of One's Own* (1934), based on her diaries, and *An Experiment in Leisure* (1937), based partly on memories from holidays:

> Images that had been increasingly intruding into my thoughts with a particular quality of still glow, a quality that was quite different from that of ordinary memories. So much so that I felt the need to try and find out what it might mean.
>
> (Milner 1987: 4)

From 1934 to 1939 she was doing research work in girls' day schools in England, and published her third book, *The Human Problem in Schools*, in 1938.

While working with the girls, Milner became increasingly impressed by Freud's ideas on child development, something she had not found in Jung's work. She regularly read Susan Isaac's contributions to the magazine *The Nursery World*, and through this encountered Melanie Klein. It was, however, after attending a public lecture by Winnicott in 1938 that she decided to begin a Freudian analysis with Sylvia Payne, and in 1939 to apply for training to the British Psycho-Analytical Society. Milner says about that time:

> I do not remember at all what was said in the lecture, but I did get the feeling that, contrary to the impression that some Freudians had given me, the main ideas that I was pre-occupied with could be accommodated creatively within the Freudian metapsychology. Also, although from time to time, I had made small excursions into Jung's writings, other than *Psychological Types*, I had given it up because I found that, while there were many illuminating remarks, the whole structure of his approach seemed to elude me.
>
> (Milner 1969: xxvii)

She goes on to say that, when in analysis, she had found it possible to do 'doodle' drawings which turned out to have 'meaning for me far beyond anything that my deliberative mind was aware of while doing them. It was the sheer surprise of this that led me in 1939 to begin writing a book about them' (1969: xxviii).

Milner subsequently wrote *On Not Being Able to Paint* because she thought that by exploring an activity in which she had failed to learn what

Psychoanalysts and art therapy

she wanted to, she might find out something of what she had felt to be left out of the school system. She recalled her early attempts to learn how to paint, making connections between aspects of visual perspective and outline and questions of personal boundaries, separation, and distance.

In 1940 Milner was accepted for training with the British Psychoanalytical Society, and in 1943 she took on a patient called 'Susan' on whom the book *The Hands of the Living God* (1969) was based. This was an account of a long individual, Freudian-orientated analysis in which Susan, after spontaneously beginning to 'doodle' in the sessions, then produced and took to the analysis over four thousand drawings. It appears that Milner was not aware of the work of Hill *et al.* during the 1940s, or, if she was, she does not refer to it. Although she does not mention Champernowne's work at the Withymead, they seemed to work on similar lines, that is, encouraging patients to bring art work into their analysis and having been personally involved with painting at important times in their lives. It is possible that they did not encounter each other, and this might be to do with the 'distances' between the various analytic schools, i.e. Jungian, Freudian, Object Relations, and also to the fact that Champernowne did not publish any books or major articles until the late 1960s. Marion Milner was not involved in the art therapy working parties of the late 1940s and has been influential mainly through her works which deal with the use of art in psychoanalysis.

Ralph Pickford

Ralph Pickford could also be regarded as an 'intellectual leader' in the field of art therapy, through his substantial publications and foundation, with Joyce Laing, of the Scottish Society for Art and Psychopathology in the early 1960s. Pickford was Professor of Psychology at the University of Glasgow and had become interested in the psychology of art in the late 1930s, mainly from the point of view of the psychological analysis of historical factors and social psychological factors affecting art. He was intrigued by a picture which one of his students presented as part of his practical work for the examiners in the psychology department at Glasgow, and, when the exam was over, Pickford and the student talked about the picture at length, as it expressed many aspects of the student's life and his problems. Pickford wrote an article about this experience which he sent to the *British Journal of Medical Psychology*. The editor, Dr Rickman, asked if Pickford didn't think that 'the picture has some implications of a therapeutic kind'? Pickford said that it had not occurred to him, but it started him thinking about the therapeutic implications of art. From that time on he became more involved with therapy and, after meeting Dr Margaret Lowenfeld, child psychologist, went to work at the Notre Dame Child Guidance Clinic in Glasgow. In his interview, Pickford admitted:

77

The role of individual artists and psychotherapists

I had no idea how to do art therapy with children. I had read it up in books and thought I could do something... the first experiences with a boys' group were rather disastrous and I was then much more wary about how I treated the children... difficult to say how but I didn't do anything which would lead to unnecessary excitement... what happened in the Notre Dame Clinic led me to become gradually more interested in art therapy but I didn't regard myself as an art therapist at all for at least twenty years. It hadn't occurred to me that there was a concept of that kind... in fact it wasn't until other people spoke to me and asked for my articles as examples of art therapy in practice that I began to think that there was something that perhaps I had overlooked and I was in a sense an art therapist.

In the late 1940s, Pickford became discontented with his approach to patients, and entered psychoanalysis with a Dr Rushworth in Edinburgh. He commented:

She was very astute and understanding and insightful. She was eclectic in the sense that she wanted to combine Jungian and Freudian approaches, which always seemed to me to be extremely difficult. We got on very well together and she concentrated on the Freudian approach, because she knew that appealed most to me, and she gave me the necessary insight that I wanted in order to go on with the sort of work I was interested in.... While I was a patient with her, I also produced lots of pictures which she was very interested to see. Her handling of these was quite instructive and characteristic. I produced these pictures at home and took them along. Very often I couldn't say anything about them... but I just left them with her and she said she would look after them for me and finally gave them back to me.

Pickford noted that a colleague of Dr Rushworth's was a Miss Romanes, a psychotherapist who was also an artist. He observed:

They didn't really consider themselves art therapists, they were just psychotherapists who were using art materials as a bridge in the process of psychotherapy.... It is very interesting that psychotherapists should use pictures in this way and assume that they are a sort of communication with the therapist, and there is often a great disadvantage in trying to turn these things into a verbal form.

Following his own analysis, Pickford began to work individually with patients, encouraging them to draw and paint. During the two days that I spent with Professor Pickford and his wife, Ruth, I saw many of the paintings and sculptures that his patients had made during analysis, and which they had subsequently left with him.

Psychoanalysts and art therapy

In 1967, Pickford published *Studies in Psychiatric Art*, based on thirty years' work an showing his increasing interest in the use of art in psychoanalysis. He lectured on the first art therapy course at Hertfordshire College of Art, and wrote extensively for *Inscape* and other journals on the subject. Pickford had, then, a dual identity: his first and major one, as professor of psychology, and the other as a psychotherapist. He also referred to himself, on occasions, as an 'art therapist', but tentatively, due to his lack of an art background. He was a founder member of BAAT, a founder of the Scottish Society for the Study of the Psychopathology of Expression, and remained a registered member of the BAAT until his recent death.

Chapter nine

Reflections on being a pioneer art therapist

Nowadays, schoolchildren can have art therapy as a career in mind and follow a recommended path culminating in postgraduate training. In the 1940s to late 1960s, though, there was no such structure and many pioneers have said that they got into art therapy 'by accident'. In the following section, I have drawn attention to the background and involvement in art therapy of a cross-section of founders, using comments from their interviews, from their own writing and from the impressions of others who knew them. There were thirty-two members of BAAT when it was formed in 1963 and I have selected the following because of their long-term commitment to art therapy, and based my comments on the interviews in which I asked the question 'How did you get into art therapy?' This account is not intended to be exhaustive as research into occupational choice in the case of art therapists is currently being conducted by Andrea Gilroy (see *Inscape* spring 1989). I was interested in the 'chance encounter' element mentioned by so many interviewees and by the fact that they were all searching for a meaningful role which did not seem readily available with an existing range of career options.

Jan Glass

Glass was the first membership secretary of BAAT. She was a graduate from Chelsea School of Art, and like Hill and Adamson worked for the Red Cross picture-lending scheme. While working on the scheme, she met a psychiatrist who was interested in introducing paintings into his hospital in Surrey. Jan Glass described the way that she became involved in art therapy:

> I was looking for something to do, and had thought of teaching children.... I'd only just come from three glorious years and had a vision of myself setting up a studio and drawing and painting. Totally unrealistic!

Pioneering art therapy

She felt that she got involved in art therapy 'accidentally' through the chance meeting with Dr R who was very interested in art, and who paid all her expenses to lecture on art in hospitals around the country.

Jan did not have a teaching qualification, nor would she have needed one to teach in the 1950s and 1960s, for qualified teacher status was available to persons holding the National Diploma in Design or the BA in art. So there was nothing unusual in her expecting to acquire a teaching post post-art college without further training. It appeared from her interview that she had never identified herself wholeheartedly as a teacher, and was attracted to working in hospitals because of the possibility of working with individuals and small groups, rather as in art college. She felt that making art was in itself therapeutic:

> The use of paintings and clay modelling by patients as an aid to diagnosis has long been recognised as valuable in psychotherapy, but as far as I know, very little has been said about art as a therapeutic activity in itself... work produced by individual analysis I would not in any case describe as art therapy.
>
> (Glass 1963: 57)

Although taking a very active and central role in the early days of the BAAT, Jan considered herself first and foremost an artist. (She now runs a pottery class from her own studio and does not see herself as an art therapist any more.)

Michael Pope

Michael Pope trained as a teacher in the 1950s and then took an NDD in ceramics. He worked for several years as a special education teacher in schools both for delicate and for deaf children, before moving into the role of teacher/art therapist in schools for 'ESN' and 'maladjusted' children in London.

His experience of being an art teacher with 'slow learning children' is described in an article in *Special Education*.

> It is generally agreed that the art teacher or the class teacher who is teaching art has a special role. He makes an atmosphere, he motivates but does not impose, he looks for creative insight rather than imitation or repetitive memory, he moves in the direction of the unknown where there is not a correct way of doing things – although there may be 'correct' technical procedures and a certain body of knowledge to support the creative search. He is a tightrope walker with errors of emphasis yawning on both sides.
>
> (Pope 1970)

81

The role of individual artists and psychotherapists

Pope was Honorary Treasurer of BAAT from 1965 till 1971 and in 1974 to 1976 was Honorary Secretary and a member of BAAT's Training and Education Committee. Although his official title was 'teacher', Michael Pope always identified himself as an art therapist, though with a strongly 'educational' bias, and he played a consistently active role in the internal organisation of BAAT, eventually taking the Diploma in Art Therapy course at Hertfordshire College of Art. He was made an Honorary Member of BAAT and continues to work as an art therapist within the Home Office.

John Timlin

Timlin was training as an art teacher when he met Edward Adamson on a visit to Netherne Hospital. He was very impressed by the visit, and remembered it four years later when put in charge of forty 'rebellious primary schoolboys'. Timlin comments that their standards of work and behaviour were so appalling that they ended up in the special class, but there were no problems when it came to art. One of the boys painted unusual pictures which reminded him of Adamson's collection, so he got in touch for advice. Later he took a sabbatical year to take the diploma in the field of 'maladjustment' at the Institute of Education, London University, under Dr Edna Oakshott. Adamson was invited to lecture, and again impressed Timlin. Timlin firmly supports the notion of 'art as healing' of emotional and behavioural difficulties and advocated the use of 'spontaneous art' in education (1983: 64–8).

Timlin's background in art education and his views on the use of art in education – i.e. influenced by the 'child-centred approach' – were similar to those of Jan Glass. Timlin continued to work in education as a lecturer in teacher-training colleges. He was for a time active in BAAT and remains active in promoting Adamson's work (e.g. he is now Honorary Chair of the Adamson Collection charity). To change from the position of a lecturer in higher education to that of art therapist would have meant a loss not only of status but of money. Like Champernowne, Timlin was an advocate of art therapy but never totally identified with the occupation himself.

Michael Edwards

(Michael Edwards's considerable role in the professional development of art therapy will be dealt with at length in later sections, particularly in the section concerning training.)

Edwards's introduction to art therapy also appears to have been 'accidental'. Just after the Second World War, he completed the National

Pioneering art therapy

Diploma in Design at St Albans School of Art. The principal was Mary Hoad who had worked with Herbert Read and, according to Edwards, was 'psychologically minded'. Hoad suggested that Edwards should meet Mary Webb, who was working with patients at Kingsbury Hospital. Edwards remembers being overwhelmed by the pictures in the art room. He recalled that when he first met Mary Webb in 1953, she did not call herself an art therapist although she seemed to have inspired the patients to make very powerful images. She told Edwards about Withymead and he subsequently visited and stayed for two months while still an art student. He was advised by Champernowne to finish his training and acquire an art teacher's certificate, which he did before returning to Withymead where he stayed for several years.

He noticed how his style of work changed while at Withymead:

> I was amazed at how my style of painting changed... just poured out of me... at college I would sit around trying to scrape up an idea... I was desperately trying to think of things to do. There it was totally, totally different. At Withymead everything was reversed. At art college I couldn't draw from memory... but in these dream paintings, I could draw a human figure with no difficulty at all. That was a revelation.

Edwards established the first option in art therapy as part of the postgraduate art teacher's diploma course at the School of Art Education in Birmingham, leaving in the late 1970s for a professorship in art therapy at Concordia University, Montreal. He has remained an active contributor to art therapy through publications and participation in the Champernowne Trust summer schools, as well as through clinical work and supervision of art therapists.

Mary Webb

A letter from Napsbury Hospital Management Committee to myself dated 14 June 1971 states that Mary Webb was employed as an art therapist at Napsbury Hospital from 8 May 1947 to 26 February 1960. She was an artist who had spent some time at Withymead and was influenced by the work of Jung. Although Webb did not refer to herself as an 'art therapist' according to Edwards, it is interesting that the hospital itself should have bestowed that title as early as 1947. This may, in fact, make her the first 'art therapist' to have been employed in the NHS. Although she participated in the early art therapy working parties at the NAMH, Webb did not take an active part in later organised professional activities, seeming to be a retiring person who is best known for her influence through her art therapy practice.

The role of individual artists and psychotherapists

Joyce Laing

Joyce Laing graduated in art in Scotland and went on to teacher-training college in the 1950s. However she felt that teaching was not for her:

> I wanted to paint and I wanted to have freedom, not to clock in from 9 to 4 each day. So I decided to 'go it alone'. I had not heard of art therapy at this time, nor had it occurred to me, but two things coincided in my life at that time: one was that a friend developed tuberculosis and was in a sanatorium in Aberdeen, the other was I discovered the books of Adrian Hill (on art therapy).

As a result of these two events, Joyce Laing felt that there should be an artist visiting the two sanatoriums near Aberdeen, so she applied to the Position Superintendent and was subsequently interviewed by the various members of their board. She was appointed as a 'cultural visitor'.

> The remit was to interest patients in the arts and it was left almost as vague as that.... I was lucky enough to work with a young registrar and I confided in him about the interest I had and how it seemed there was a relationship between the paintings and the illness.

The registrar was interested enough to go through the paintings with her, and Joyce Laing noted that there seemed to be some correlation between the content and the patient's condition.

Laing comments that art therapy and occupational therapy were always seen as separate and that a friendly relationship was established with OTs in the hospital. She defined herself as an art therapist and continues to do so and was very active in BAAT, in forming the Scottish Society for Art and Psychopathology and in writing and making films on art therapy. She established a satisfactory status for herself by quickly making close working relationships with the medical profession and jointly producing articles and films with psychiatrists.

John Henzell

Henzell was another artist who came into art therapy 'by accident'. He completed his art education in Australia where he first encountered art therapy in a chance meeting with a painter who had been helped by Adrian Hill at the King Edward VII sanatorium. On return to Australia, the painter started to work like Hill and offered some of his sessions to Henzell, who had just left art school and was searching for work. Henzell said that he had taught in a school for three months but didn't enjoy this, finding the experience frustrating. He was intrigued by his first experience of work in hospitals and started to work with alcoholic groups, mostly returned servicemen. In 1959 he came to Britain, met Hill and through him many

Pioneering art therapy

other art therapists, eventually finding a job at a Surrey hospital, working under Jan Glass. He became actively involved in negotiations for career and salary structures, and training for art therapy and was an early chair of BAAT

Hansi Bohm

Hansi Bohm started her art training in Austria, having been a pupil of Cizek's Vienna art school. She trained as a commercial artist in the early 1930s. When she came to London, she learned photography and illustrated book covers. She later trained as an occupational therapist, with a view to entering art therapy which she had learned about from Marie Petrie. Bohm was employed as an occupational therapist by an Essex hospital, where she had two small rooms for pottery and painting. Bohm visited Adamson in the early 1950s, at the time when he was engaged with Cunningham Dax and Reitman's research projects. She was not impressed, finding it 'over-formal, run like a school room'.

Hansi Bohm said of her own work:

I got my ideas from Marie Petrie and had my own thoughts. I didn't realise at the time how fortunate I was, to make my own department... they gave me a marvellous building which was a disused laundry. This was in 1954. The room was used for very psychotic people mostly, who needed to be on their own and not too much disturbed.... I was in constant contact with the medical staff and the consultants were particularly interested and co-operative.

As a qualified OT, Hansi Bohm had a place in the medical hierarchy, but she identified herself as an art therapist, feeling that in that way she was more valued and able to act on her own initiative, certainly having more sway with the consultants.

Elizabeth Wills

Elizabeth Wills trained as an occupational therapist. She was working in a chest hospital in Birmingham when she read Hill's *Art Versus Illness* and wanted to try art therapy herself. She had previously attended the Segal school in London but had not found this a satisfactory experience as there was 'no scope for imaginative painting'. Elizabeth recalled that

When I first heard of art therapy, I thought it was just what I wanted, it would combine my two interests, the artistic one and the side that was interested in people... but I found that the artistic side was very much less in evidence than I would have liked. We were hampered by having such a large number of patients to cover in a relatively short

85

The role of individual artists and psychotherapists

time so we were less creative in the things that we did than we would have been if we'd have had more time for each individual.

Elizabeth's first meeting with Hill was on the occasion when she invited him to open the art therapy area of her hospital, but it was, she felt, 'a fiasco' because she experienced Hill as deeply prejudiced against occupational therapists at that time, and advised the person who was to be the art therapist (from the Segal school) that she should not work in an OT department.

Following her Jungian analysis in Birmingham, Elizabeth went to the Withymead Centre where she remained until it closed. She continued to work as an art therapist privately, with students on the residential child care course at Ruskin College, Oxford, and for the Champernowne Trust, until her recent death.

Diana Halliday

Diana Halliday was Vice-Chair of BAAT between 1973 and 1974 and an active council member and promoter of art therapy through seminars, workshops, and exhibitions from 1960 to the present. She was born in London of East European *émigré* parents and she remarked that her father was much influenced by the anarchist Kropotkin. She was influenced by her parents' atheism. After passing her baccalaureat at the French Lycée in London, she was torn between academic studies and art school. A meeting with a Freudian analyst from the British Psychoanalytic Society influenced her decision to go to art school. She contemplated studying medicine, but was put off this by the need to pass maths, which she could not do.

At the Central Art School, Diana spent five years studying textiles, painting, and graphics, then went to Paris. In 1940 she married and went to Canada, then to New York, where they stayed for sixteen years. Diana had already encountered therapeutic art education in Canada, when she taught patients with terminal cancer:

> That's when I first realised that art could be something more than art education and that it could cure people. They had very serious depressions. Unconsciously integrating inner feelings with the outer, it could happen that they got a new sense of the beauty of the natural world and could take some of that inside. In six months they were less depressed.

During the war years, Diana took a specialist art teacher training course and her first job was in a school for delicate children in Clapham. She had, at that time, still not heard of 'art therapy'.

86

Pioneering art therapy

While in the USA, Diana had undergone Freudian analysis which she did not find helpful, and later followed it up with a Jungian analysis. She met Naumburg in the USA in the late 1950s, referring to her as the 'great grandmother of art therapy in the USA', and again in 1960 at a conference in Madrid. She also met Adamson, whom she referred to as the 'first art therapist she had met', at the suggestion of her Jungian analyst. He went to the lycée where Diana was working part time and lectured to the children, then Diana took them to visit Netherne. She also worked part time in a child guidance clinic in Sussex, as a child psychotherapist. Diana eventually left the lycée, becoming frustrated with the demands of the art syllabus:

> I was a renegade. I was trying to pay lip service to the needs of the curriculum but choosing to give far more free projects. My job was to teach O and A level and S level art. None of the kids suffered from the way I was teaching. I also had a policy of work which did away with competitiveness. The absence of competitiveness in teaching is absolutely essential.

Diana was offered, and took, a full-time post as a child psychotherapist on the strength of her two analyses: 'It was understood that I was an art therapist, but there was no such post. I worked with children individually. I felt a bit of a fraud as I didn't have a five-year training.' Although Diana's 'official' title was 'child psychotherapist' she always identified herself as an 'art therapist', feeling that role to encompass her talents and her occupational needs.

E. M. Lyddiatt

Lyddiatt is best known for her book *Spontaneous Painting and Modelling* (1970) in which she explains the purpose of this activity through detailed case studies of patients whom she worked with in a range of psychiatric hospitals and clinics. Lyddiatt trained at Birmingham School of Art and from 1934 to 1950 taught art in a school, craft in a hospital, and lectured in art and craft in teacher-training colleges. She became interested in Jung's work in 1935, and undertook a Jungian analysis. She became involved in art therapy in 1950 'Because it appeared likely that spontaneous painting and modelling might help those who were ill. Thus the hospital background became an important factor that could not be ignored' (1970: 4–5). She advocated close co-operation between artist, doctor, and other medical staff, and found her ideal state as one in which she could work alongside a psychiatrist with whom she was in tune.

Lyddiatt started departments for art and art therapy in Fulbourne Hospital, Cambridge, Runwell, Essex, Leavesden in Hertfordshire, St

The role of individual artists and psychotherapists

Marylebone Hospital for Psychiatry and Child Guidance, and Halliwick Hospital, London, and at the private Bowden House Clinic, Harrow.

As a person, Lyddiatt was somewhat shy and self-effacing, despite her energy and commitment in building up several large art therapy departments in the early 1950s and later. Martina Thompson, who knew her well, says:

> Lyddiatt's house was somehow expressive of her approach to art therapy. She recognised and treasured the value – which to her was synonymous with the therapeutic value – in her patients' paintings and models. She did not impose herself as a therapist but allowed the work to happen – and the work that went on under her care was remarkable. She was not inclined to follow the profession to a more sophisticated level, to a more worldly, official and self-conscious stance.
>
> (Thompson 1989: 15)

Lyddiatt remained a member of BAAT until her death in 1981, but never participated in any working parties or 'political' activities of the profession. She always identified herself as an art therapist.

The search for a role

I have already referred to the issue of 'role-hybridisation' discussed by Ben-David and Collins (1966: 559), and to their suggestion that an individual who is moving from one profession or academic field to another may experience role conflict and that this may be resolved by giving up the attitudes and behaviour appropriate to the old role and adopting those of the new. In such cases, identification with the old reference group must be withdrawn. It is possible, though, that the individual may be unwilling to give up his or her identification with the old group as it may carry higher status, intellectual as well as social, than the new one. In such cases the individual may attempt to resolve the conflict by fitting the methods and techniques of the old role into the materials of the new, with the deliberate purpose of creating a new role.

Adrian Hill, having coined the term 'art therapy', remained in the role of 'artist' and is best known for his series of 'How to Paint' books, and for the radio and television appearances in which he popularised drawing and painting. Adamson was employed at Netherne as an artist, but later on adopted the title of 'art therapist'. Rita Simon, too, became an 'art therapist' by virtue of working with psychiatric patients, even though at first she had no pretensions to psychological training.

Artists who went to work in hospitals did not have a clearly defined role in the structure of the hierarchy and we have seen that this may have been an attraction in the first place. As far as the hospital management (medical superintendent or counterpart) was concerned, the occupational

88

Pioneering art therapy

group which these artists could most easily be identified with was occupational therapy, as this was primarily concerned with rehabilitation.

One can see that this would be a logical connection to make as far as Adrian Hill's work was concerned, as it had an overtly rehabilitational and diversional aim and was intended to occupy purposefully those recovering from illness, as well as to provide a release from boredom and tension. However, it had little connection with the work that was going on at Withymead, which had a central aim of promoting insight and change in personality and behaviour. Hill appears to have been contented to be included in the occupational therapy service, but the majority of artists strongly objected to being so defined.

Champernowne, too, as we shall see later, felt that art therapy was a very different occupation from occupational therapy.

It is interesting to consider why this situation occurred: I suggest that the role of 'artist' was a more attractive one than 'occupational therapist' both for the psychiatric profession in terms of the 'otherness' of artistic achievement (Reitman *et al.*) and for the artists themselves as, despite having little inclination to dedicate themselves totally to art, they strongly wished to continue to maintain their identity and to pursue their art 'part time', while using their art skills in a socially useful way. Another attraction was that, as artists, they were difficult to place within the hierarchy of the hospital, whereas as occupational therapists they would have a low status and be identified with instructors and craft workers. In the art world, this was not desirable. But artists could hardly be allowed to be directly concerned with patients' treatment for they were neither medically nor psychologically trained. So a resolution needed to be found which would enable artists to maintain their higher status identity than occupational therapists as they saw it, yet be able to participate more fully in treatment.

This section, then, has given us background material about important individual contributors to art therapy, and leads us into the next phase of development: namely the development of organised, as opposed to individual, activity in the service of promoting art therapy.

Part III

Beginning of organised activity: the first working parties in art therapy

Introduction

In Part II, I discussed the role of several individuals in introducing and promoting art therapy in Britain. In this part, I shall trace the development of co-operative and organised activity in the form of conferences, working parties, and exhibitions designed to bring art therapy to the attention of the general public and other health care workers (such as doctors, psychiatrists, hospital administrators). These events served as an opportunity for the participants to try to understand how the term 'art therapy' was being used in hospitals and to debate such issues as who should practise it and if and how they should be trained. Between 1949 and 1963 there were many attempts to 'regularise' the procedure and limit its practice to 'suitable' people. However, without a clear agreement on what was actually meant by 'art therapy' and an investigation into the role of both art and therapist in the therapeutic process, it was not possible to devise a system of training, though, as we shall see, many ideas were put forward.

Chapter ten

Art therapy in the witness box

The title of this chapter is taken from Adrian Hill's book *Painting Out Illness*, from the section in which he describes his participation in an international conference – the first Commonwealth and Empire Tuberculosis Conference to be sponsored by the National Association for the Prevention of Tuberculosis (NAPT) in Westminster in July 1947. Hill was invited to present a five-minute paper, to be augmented by an exhibition of patients' work. He took every opportunity to publicise the work during the conference, presenting his paper on the last day. 'Thus art therapy made its first official public bow, and in the months that followed many enquiries arrived from Medical Superintendents and others interested' (1951: 28).

In 1948, Hill was invited to show a collection of patients' paintings at the Professional Nurses' Conference, organised by the *Nursing Mirror*. He gave a talk on 'Art Therapy in Hospitals' and met HRH Princess Louise, who was opening the exhibition.

In 1949, Hill prepared yet another exhibition of over 500 paintings and drawings from thirty sanatoriums. On this occasion the exhibition was hung by the Art Exhibition Bureau, and was opened by P. H. Jowett, one-time director of the Royal College of Art.

Hill considered that the widespread interest and official recognition that art therapy had begun to enjoy was due mainly to these three exhibitions. Between 1948 and 1949, the NAPT sponsored a series of tours which took Hill to Scottish hospitals where he tried to press his cause to convince the medical superintendents to employ half-time art teachers to practise art therapy, but most were able to afford a teacher for only one afternoon a week. Hill commented:

> While I have not access to the actual number of those at present employed, NAPT stated in June 1949 that their panel of artists had risen to twelve and these had paid no less than 400 visits to sanatoria in the past three and a half years. This in itself offers a significant clue as to the extent of the propaganda now pursued and which has in many cases

94

Art therapy in the witness box

resulted in establishing regular visits to sanatoria over an increasingly wide area.

(Hill 1951: 33–4)

In 1948 Hill visited Holland, as a guest of the Dutch Art Therapists Committee to contribute a selection of paintings by British patients to the first exhibition of hospital patients in Holland. He also received letters from Australia and Canada where Hill-style art therapy appeared to be flourishing in sanatoriums. He continued to broadcast on BBC radio, both home and overseas, and in 1949 became the chair of the first Art Therapy Committee set up by the SW Metropolitan Regional Hospital Board.

The first art therapy conference

The first conference entirely devoted to art (and music) therapy, at which Hill was a speaker, was sponsored by the British Council for Rehabilitation at 32 Shaftesbury Avenue, W1 on 23 March 1949, with Dame Georgiana Buller DBE in the chair. It was reported in *Rehabilitation Journal*, October 1949, No. 3. The first speaker was Dr Cunningham Dax. In a paper on music therapy, Dax made a comparison with art therapy. 'The difficulty arises that whereas painting is comparatively easily capable of analysis by the psychotherapist, music is very difficult, at least in our present state of knowledge' (p.11). This suggests that Dax saw the production of paintings by patients as having diagnostic potential and had a method of analysing the paintings that Adamson was helping to produce, but he does not indicate what this method was. Dax referred indirectly to Adamson's role, but not to him by name:

There are, I think, two particular points of importance. If the artistic products are to be used for emotional expression and psychological investigation, it is useless for the same person to give the educational talks and also to expect to encourage free and independent production for emotional release. Secondly, that to obtain these therapeutic effects, the artist in charge must assume a passive role.

Here again we have reference to the so-called 'passive' role of the artist in encouraging the production of art objects for analysis (see Chapter 6).

Dax's talk was followed by Irene Champernowne's, on 'Painting and Modelling as an Inner Process', in which she stressed the power of the 'inner symbol' for recreating life and the necessity to value and respect patients' art works as 'self-healing, self-regulating mechanisms at work within the individual' (p.13).

There were two art therapists present from Withymead, Jo Guy and Nora Godfrey. Jo Guy gave a demonstration and described her work in the pottery at Withymead. Nora Godfrey gave a painting demonstration,

95

Beginning of organised activity

mentioning that she was an art teacher 'specially trained for this type of therapeutic work'.

We see in the presentations by Irene Champernowne and the two art therapists quite a difference in style: Irene's puts forward the theoretical basis for using the arts in therapy and the two art therapists gave practical demonstrations of the media.

Other contributors included Dr W. J. T. Kimber, whose talk entitled 'The Patient with the Paint Brush' emphasised the value of painting in treatment, but questioned how accurate it was possible to be in assessing the extent to which any patient's recovery could be attributed to the 'paint brush' rather than to other therapeutic interventions; Elsie Davies from the City Sanatorium, Birmingham, described Arthur Segal's methods, which came across as a form of art teaching in which the individual's needs and wishes were taken very seriously.

Adrian Hill made the concluding remarks at the conference and unequivocally claimed parentage of art therapy. 'In 1942, when I first launched this then novel form of diversional therapy at the King Edward VII Sanatorium, I little thought that two influential bodies would so quickly spring to my aid' (p. 21). (He was referring to the British Red Cross and the NAPT.)

Hill suggested that the British Red Cross Picture Lending Library might never have come into existence but for the fact that Millicent Buller saw his original letter in *The Times* and had the vision to invite him to explain his schemes and put them into operation.

It is quite clear that Hill had no hesitation whatsoever in regarding himself as the 'father' of art therapy, despite the fact that at the Withymead Centre a different version of 'art therapy' had also been practised since 1942, and Naumburg in the USA had used the term 'free expression' in the 1930s to refer to work very similar to that undertaken by Champernowne in Britain. Hill had no interest in psychology *per se*, and his use of the term 'diversionary' to describe his form of 'art therapy' seemed accurate, and led to art therapy being related to occupational therapy in its rehabilitative and diversionary role, a link which has remained until the present day. (Art therapy is described as a 'linked' profession to occupational therapy by the Department of Health.)

Two very different strands of 'art therapy' emerge from the papers and demonstrations at this conference:

(a) where the emphasis is on making paintings or models as ends in themselves, as recreational or rehabilitative functions;
(b) where the emphasis is on the production of 'inner images' which express unconscious feelings and may subsequently be used for diagnostic or therapeutic-analytic purposes.

Art therapy in the witness box

The role of the art therapist was similar in both situations: to assist the patient to produce the art work; to remain firmly an artist or art teacher and not to intervene in the therapeutic process. In the first strand, the therapy would seem to take place incidentally through the pleasure of picture making; in the second it would happen as a result of the intervention of the psychotherapist or psychiatrist in interpreting the patients' unconscious symbolism.

The first art therapy working parties

In February 1949, Hill was invited to become chairman of an art therapy committee set up by the South West Metropolitan Regional Hospital Board. He was proud of this fact:

> I hope I may be forgiven if I confess to a certain feeling of sober elation, for such a position does convey a generous measure of official recognition in one region at least, and one in which some of my more ambitious schemes may in time be officially accepted and put into practice. To be able to discuss future problems with such medical experts as Sir Geoffrey Todd and Drs Cunningham Dax and Louis Minsky in a spirit of friendly cooperation is for me a real reward for the ups and downs, hopes and fears, successes and failures when striving in the past capacity of what might be called 'private enterprise'.
>
> (Hill 1951: 40)

In order to ascertain to what extent art therapy was being practised in this region, and whether or not its introduction would be welcomed in other general hospitals, a detailed questionnaire ws prepared in April 1949 and duly circulated throughout the region.

In December 1949, the National Association of Mental Health sponsored a working party on art therapy to consider the responses to the questionnaires. Members of the committee at that time included John Trevelyan (who later became the film censor but was then director of research into hospital administration), Gilbert and Irene Champernowne, Rudolf Laban, dancer and choreographer, Dr Culver Barker, a psychiatrist, Mrs Coote, a music therapist, Misses Metman, Tarrant, and Rivett, psychotherapist and occupational therapists respectively. Adrian Hill was the only visual artist present and took the chair. The results showed that there were three ways in which art therapy had been understood in the hospitals which had been circulated:

1. In sanatoriums and long-stay hospitals the emphasis was on occupying patients, filling time with creative work.

Beginning of organised activity

2. In mental hospitals, art therapy was used to indicate states of mind and the progress of the patient, and was considered to have some 'therapeutic value' (as well as diagnostic importance).
3. In general hospitals (and also long-stay hospitals) the provision of pictures on the walls of the ward and the organisation of the means of changing them took priority.

We see that art therapy as practised at Withymead did not feature: that is, no hospital reported using art as an aspect of psychotherapeutic practice.

Following his discussion of the survey results in *Painting Out Illness*, Hill offers a definition of art therapy which was later used by officers of BAAT in their campaigns for improved salaries and conditions:

> Art therapy is a highly specialised form of 'teaching' involving enterprise, intuition, tact and patience. The power to stimulate confidence and sustain interest, a sympathetic approach to every type of patient, young and old, and obviously a real sense of humour – all these are necessary.
>
> (Hill 1951: 43)

Hill went on to stress the importance of the teacher's personality in the process of bringing to light hidden mental conflicts

> which through the right contact with the patient and under the ameliorating creative impulse are naturally translated in terms of picture-making and thereby exorcised of their dread. Especially is this realised in mental hospitals where many of these subliminal outpourings of the patient's imagination have a potential diagnostic value in indicating the source of the malady and perhaps some change of treatment. Thus while the main benefit to the ordinary patient lies in the therapeutic aspect, the problem patient, like the problem child, sometimes reveals an unsuspected self when 'talking' with a pencil or brush.
>
> (Hill 1951: 43)

He appears to suggest here that making paintings is cathartic for the patient as well as being useful diagnostic material for the doctor, which in turn could influence the patient's treatment.

Hill goes on to quote Marie Petrie, in supporting her view of the 'artist' who is 'receiving' such paintings as needing to possess

> some of the qualities demanded of nurses and doctors, the intuitive understanding of what a particular patient needs, the sympathetic and patient help at the right moment, the knowledge of what can and what cannot be demanded of a sick person.
>
> (Hill 1951: 43)

Art therapy in the witness box

There is evidence here, then, that by the time he wrote *Painting Out Illness* between 1949 and 1950, Hill had come to appreciate that art therapy had a meaning over and above that of alleviating boredom and providing a pleasant hobby, and that persons who intended to practise it needed certain personal qualities in addition to art-teaching skills. Such development in his attitude may have been partly a result of frequent meetings with Champernowne (he visited Withymead in 1945 and had encountered her at conferences and meetings about art therapy) and partly a strategy to increase the status of art therapy above that of a 'hobby' or an activity that could be carried out by an occupational therapy aide.

Anthony Stevens felt that the basic difference between Hill's and Champernowne's approaches was that Hill's stressed the 'diversionary' role of art therapy, whereas Champernowne's stressed the 'healing power of the symbols which patients produced'. He considered that

> The work of Adrian Hill and others in sanatoria and hospitals was admirable as far as it went, for it demonstrated clearly that creative activity was itself beneficial, but it would not do for Withymead because it neglected the transcendent function: it did not set out to activate the compensatory, homeostatic potential of the unconscious.
>
> (Stevens 1986: 124)

Looking at these approaches in terms of Bucher and Strauss's model of professions (1961), it seems as if at this point Hill's version of art therapy was a segment of occupational therapy (as it was then), whereas Champernowne's was a segment of Jungian psychotherapy. Adamson's could be said to fall somewhere between the two, and perhaps was a segment of 'child-centred' art education (as described in Chapter 2).

Chapter eleven

A struggle for ownership

From the minutes of these early meetings it seems as if a 'struggle for ownership' of art therapy was beginning in the arguments which developed between the occupational therapists and Irene Champernowne. It was always her aim to see art therapy established as separate from OT. At the December 1949 meeting at the NAMH, she suggested that OT was concerned with the 'outside world', designed to prevent the patient from 'unhealthy brooding', as suggested by Iveson (1938) among others, whereas art therapy was 'an inner psychological process which could be brought to birth by somebody who understood psychological symbolism, as a healing method'. The minutes state that the occupational therapists present denied this and claimed that OT could encompass the whole field of rehabilitation, including art therapy.

According to Bucher and Strauss's process model of professions, such attempts to separate out a particular area of expertise are common in the early days of specialities (1961: 326) and art therapy was no exception in very quickly making arguments which would declare its separateness from OT (and, later on, from art education). It appears form the minutes of their meetings that the committee were concerned on a more general level at what they perceived as a 'very obvious trend towards systemisation and uniformity in all departments of life'. They saw the establishment of the NHS as contributing towards this trend and as an intrusion into therapeutic work. Mrs Champernowne in particular was anxious about moves towards 'groups rather than psychotherapy' (meaning influences from, for example, Joshua Bierer's social psychiatry movement as opposed to individual psychotherapy) and in the medical field 'a growing predilection for treatment of emotional disorders by shock therapy rather than psychotherapy'. They appeared to see art therapy as going some way to correct these trends. However, from these minutes it does not appear that the committee attempted to consider in any depth the definitions of 'art therapy' which appeared in the questionnaire responses. Rather, they moved quickly to debating the qualities needed for practising it.

A struggle for ownership

All agreed that the personality of the art therapist was important. Dr Barker was in favour of an art therapist having an analysis as he felt that the analysand was 'someone who has experienced his own unadapted inner energy – an energy by which the artist groans and suffers to express himself'. This came out of personal experience and therefore could not be taught 'in the ordinary sense'. John Trevelyan considered that 'the real educationalist' would be in complete sympathy with the patient and that it would be possible for him to be both educator and healer. He suggested that a centre for training should be established, rather like Withymead, where various professions could be represented and work together. The problem then arose as to who would train the art therapists.

John Trevelyan felt it would be wrong to enlarge Withymead because the therapeutic value of the centre was bound up with its small, homely atmosphere and family pattern – but unlike in the family, 'psychological insight was present'. Miss Tarrant, OT, said she had tried to set up something similar to Withymead in a centre in Tottenham Court Road, in central London. She claimed that the 'government had asked OT to embrace art therapy and she thought it should come under the heading of OT'.

The idea of forming another centre in Devon was put forward and the committee started to plan how many people it could cater for and what would be the initial expenditure needed.

Conference of art therapists

In December 1950, Trevelyan chaired a conference of art therapists in hospitals and clinics, at which he invited suggestions about the standards which should be observed by those practising as and training future art therapists. These were subsequently discussed at another working party chaired by Adrian Hill in February 1951 at the NAMH. Those present included Irene Champernowne, Dr Culver Barker, Millicent Buller from the Red Cross, Elsie Davies from Birmingham Sanatorium, Mary Webb, art therapist, Dr J. Hadfield, a psychiatrist, Mrs S. Bach, a psychotherapist, Miss Sowerby, Mr McKinnon, Mrs Williams, occupational therapists. It was suggested that the secretary of the Courtauld Institute for History of Art be co-opted at a later meeting.

The committee discussed the issue of training for art therapy. Some members felt that art training was not necessarily a good foundation for art therapy 'since art students frequently lacked the necessary personality and experience of human relationships'. Others thought it essential to have 'deep insight and knowledge of psychology', while others wanted a good knowledge of art history and an art teacher's diploma. They arrived at the following list of possible criteria (noted in the report of the conference):

Beginning of organised activity

1. understanding or have psychological training necessary for the welfare of the patients;
2. a knowledge of hospital etiquette;
3. that useful knowledge might be given by a candidate joining a class of patients for a short time;
4. that he should work in conjunction with psychiatrists, psychologists, etc.

It is worth noting that having an art background is not mentioned. This may be because it was taken for granted, or because of ambivalence about this requirement due to the statement about art students lacking suitable qualities for the work. An art-teaching qualification was not included, but later on (1965–75) this was seen as essential by the British Association of Art Therapists. (These debates will be considered again later on, in the chapters on training.)

At the close of the meeting, Irene Champernowne recommended that a panel of art therapists be formed to assist hospitals wishing to employ art therapists. It was suggested that Irene Champernowne, Adrian Hill, Edward Adamson, Elsie Davies, Mary Webb, and a Mrs Rubenshaw be members.

Rita Simon attended the conference of art therapists in 1950 and remembers that Adrian Hill was approaching the newly formed Health Service to persuade the Minister of Health to take on the expense of paying the art therapists, in place of the hospitals, who had to find the money from private funds. Nancy Overend, of the NAMH, convened the first art therapists' panel and Rita Simon remembers:

> We talked for a long time about bringing together a corporate body of ideas as to what we were doing and how far there should be analytical training for art therapists in the future. I by that time was quite deeply into analysis and felt very strongly that you couldn't really get over your own prejudices and projections unless you did have an analysis... anyway, the upshot of that meeting was a great disappointment to me because they decided that there was no common body of opinion on which one could base an organisation. Everyone was working individually.... I didn't see why we couldn't become part of an organisation, or a society, in which people had a common interest but could meet with their different points of view. However, it didn't come about and nobody pushed it.
>
> (Simon in interview)

Conflicts were, then, apparently too deep to be worked with at this time.

A struggle for ownership

Moves to define art therapy as a profession separate from occupational therapy

Although the NAMH had offered hospitality to the working party meetings, the Association, represented by a Dr Torrie, was expressing disquiet because the art therapy panel were increasingly tending to emphasise the differences between art therapy and occupational and play therapy (which at that time was concerned with the welfare of children in hospitals). The discussions on training and suitability to practise were leading in a direction which suggested that the art therapy panel saw art therapy as more than a series of techniques which could be practised by other professionals and thought that a new occupational group should be formed to practise it. (We shall see later that the DHSS had similar reservations about separating art therapy from OT, and these still exist today (1989).)

The promotion of art therapy through exhibitions

Adamson and Cunningham Dax had organised an exhibition of Netherne patients' art work at 1 Grosvenor Crescent, SW1, on 11–16 July 1949. This exhibition was reviewed in the *British Medical Journal*, 23 July 1949, p. 4. In discussing the pictures, Dax had suggested that the term 'art therapy' should not be used, as 'it brought only disrepute on experimental methods of attacking psychiatric illness if they were labelled curative without statistical evidence to support their claims'.

The art therapy panel were not deterred from their purpose of promoting art therapy by the reservations of the NAMH. In order to reach and inform the general public, as well as other professions, of the potential for art therapy as a treatment method, the panel organised an exhibition of patients' work, entitled 'Schizophrenic Art', which took place at the Institute of Contemporary Art in 1955 and was opened by Kenneth Robinson (later to become Minister for Health).

It is curious why the title was chosen, since the exhibition contained paintings made by people with a wide variety of emotional difficulties and not only those suffering from schizophrenia. The pictures in the exhibition were mostly water-colours, collected by Professor G. M. Carstairs (later to become the first President of BAAT) from several mental hospitals. He had grouped the pictures to illustrate what he felt to be four aspects of the art work of mental patients: the first group showed changes in the form and content of art works during the onset of acute schizophrenic illness; the second included examples of the imagery of psychotic patients; the third suggested rigidity and stylisation in the work of schizophrenics; the fourth illustrated a combination of verbal material and pictorial imagery. Herbert Read wrote an introduction, in which he suggested that 'a schizoid

103

Beginning of organised activity

personality is not necessarily pathological' and that it was probably true to say that most artists were schizoid, their art being a way of balancing their minds between the world of fantasy and world of reality. This view of artists put them only a step away from psychiatric patients, and presumably the idea was that if patients could paint (like artists) they might achieve the same balance, or be 'rebalanced' towards reality. In his book *Studies in Psychiatric Art*, in a comment about the exhibition, Pickford says that the sponsors hoped that the public would not see much difference between the work there and that of 'modern artists'. It was intended to show the affinities of schizophrenic art with experiences which normal people have shared, and not to assert only its abnormality' (1966: 179).

It was reviewed in *Art News*, which declared that:

Schizophrenic art was popularized by the Surrealists who, cued by Prinzhorn's great book on the most inspired of all amateur artists, sought out the maddest images with the most kicks... in England, since the early 'forties, however, public exhibitions of psychotic art have stressed the therapeutic rather than the spectacular aspects of the subject.

(1955, 54: 58)

The reviewer went on to say that there had been a series of exhibitions of art work of tuberculosis patients and epileptics as well as psychotics. The review ends with the following comments about art therapy:

increasingly, in other institutions (as well as Maudsley, Springfield and Netherne) art therapy has a future. It is no longer regarded as a hobby merely but as a means of communication. The dangers of this approach, that the patients will be influenced by the doctors to produce the kind of drawings the doctors expect, is guarded against by making the art therapist an artist whose function is restricted to getting the patients to work independently.

Adamson (1970) observed that the exhibition afforded a 'social commentary' on art in mental illness in 1955. The exhibition received much publicity through the press and, as in the past, many critics were stimulated to compare the works with those of the Expressionist, Dada, and Surrealist movements in art, a comparison which was later strongly criticised by Plokker in his book *Artistic Expression in Mental Illness* (1964: 71–3).

One reviewer considered the exhibition 'an unwarranted eavesdropping on the sufferings of the insane' and unsuitable for the general public to visit.

A struggle for ownership

Identification with the art world

We see that the art therapy panel had identified themselves closely with the 'art world' in having the exhibition at the Institute of Contemporary Art in London, and later at the McLellan Galleries in Scotland, instead of, say, at the Royal Society of Medicine, and in framing the pictures and presenting them in every way as works of art. Irene Champernowne was ambivalent about the value of such exhibitions, despite their obvious public relations attraction in promoting art therapy, for she was concerned that the audiences would be carried away by the power of the images and forget about the creators. She expressed her thoughts about this matter some years later in 'Art and therapy: an uneasy partnership' (1971).

However, the mounting of exhibitions of patients' work remained a major means of promoting art therapy throughout the 1950s. Most of these were held in the hospitals where art therapists worked, with only a few being held in large public galleries.

Nowadays this situation is entirely changed, as the Principles of Professional Practice of BAAT actively discourage art therapists from displaying patients' art work for other than purely didactic aims.

We have seen, then, the emergence of the first organised and collaborative activities of art therapists towards building a profession in terms of career and salary structure and training, and in seeking autonomy from occupational therapy. Much of this activity devolved upon Adrian Hill and his colleagues and took the form of conferences and exhibitions and informal meetings, some under the auspices of the NAMH. In the next chapter I shall trace the development of the British Association of Art Therapists from the beginning of the 1960s.

Chapter twelve

Moves towards organised activity:
The idea of forming a professional association

During the 1940s and 1950s, the idea had gradually been spread that art could be used in the treatment of emotional and physical disorders, so that, by the end of the 1950s, many artists and art teachers had begun to work in general and psychiatric hospitals, and in sanatoriums under the National Health Service. A movement had also developed in the private health sector, at the Withymead Centre, where art – including visual, dance, and dramatic art – was used as an adjunct to psychotherapy. There had been some attempts to form an association in the early 1950s but these had not succeeded, so individuals had continued to work on their own, with occasional meetings, usually on the occasion of exhibitions of art therapy. There was increasing dissatisfaction on the part of these artists and art teachers about the difficulties they encountered in working, not least in having poor physical conditions and rates of pay which could vary from those of 'cleaners' to those of 'adult education tutors'. The idea of an association had become increasingly attractive, together with the possibility of art therapists being recognised as a new occupational (or 'professional') group.

Bucher and Strauss's concept of 'profession', as 'loose amalgamations of segments pursuing different objectives in different manners and more or less delicately held together under a common name at a particular period of history' (1961: 326) is useful as a model for examining the development of art therapy, but was probably not what art therapists had in mind when they used the term. It seems that they saw a profession more as a 'desirable symbol', as offering recognition of their practice (by the public and the State) through good conditions, salaries, and career structure, and as an opportunity to work with relative freedom and with the same status as art college lecturers.

Bucher and Strauss suggest that:

It is characteristic of the growth of specialties that early in their development they carve out for themselves and proclaim unique missions. They issue a statement of the contribution that the speciality, and

Forming a professional association

it alone, can make in a total scheme of values and, frequently, with it
an argument to show why it is peculiarly fitted for this task.

(Bucher and Strauss 1961: 326)

The 'mission' of the early art therapy working parties, as we have seen
from the minutes and from the recollections of their members, was to
make public the idea that art could be healing, whether this was by means
of painting under the guidance of a sympathetic art teacher or artist (Hill,
Adamson) or painting during or in conjunction with an analytic session
with the aim of reaching unconscious material (Champernowne). All
could share in the overall belief (and I use the term 'belief' because there
ws no body of research which could prove this, despite countless testi-
monies from recipients of the process), but there were disagreements
about ways of promoting art therapy and of achieving 'recognition' as a
'profession'.

It seems that, throughout the 1950s, art therapy may have been developing from segments of other professions (occupational therapy, art
education, psychotherapy). These segments were represented by the
individuals already discussed and there were, not surprisingly, conflicts
over practice. But in the interests of achieving autonomy from other
groups, and to promote their work, and themselves, in ways other than
mounting art therapy exhibitions, they wished to come together under the
common umbrella of a 'professional association'.

In 1962, Alexander Weatherson (who became Chair of the British
Association of Art Therapists in 1967) wrote an article in *New Society*
entitled 'Seeing Insanity Through Art'. He was then art therapist at
Springfield Hospital and wanted to draw attention to the very broad
definition of art therapy that existed at the time:

> On the surface, the sphere of activities covered certainly appears rather
> variable; an art therapist, it seems, may be anything from an old
> gentleman visiting the hospital once a week to encourage a little group
> of flower painters to greater efforts, to a formidable lady holding a
> diploma in psychology (German) investing cathartic procedures with
> some of the characteristics of a purge. The exact functions of an
> individual department often seem to depend upon what the hospital
> deems itself to require and the extent of the knowledge of the subject
> by the medical staff in question.

(Weatherson 1962: 18)

Weatherson went on to suggest that there were two basic groups of art
therapists: those who asserted its diversional and occupational aspects
(Hill, Breakwell) and those who wished to stress its access to the continually changing mental condition of the patient, with cathartic, analytic,
and diagnostic possibilities (Champernowne, Simon, for example). The

Beginning of organised activity

former tended to gravitate towards general hospitals and had more or less the same background as OTs, the latter had a background in Jungian or Freudian thinking and were aware of modern psychological and psychoanalytical developments.

Weatherson pointed out that this had led to both problems and possibilities in that the emphasis of analysts who used paintings had been on getting the patients to bring their pictures into the session, rather than make them there and then, and attention had been on the nature and content of the imagery produced, rather than on the process of making a painting or model. Yet the latter was often as revealing of the patient's state of mind as the former:

> This fact obviously creates difficulties vis à vis the relations of the therapist and the psychiatrist... naturally many psychiatrists are reluctant to accept the findings of an individual beyond the medical professions... as a result one of the most valuable sources of information offered to the psychotherapist by the patient himself is rejected.
>
> (Weatherson 1962: 18)

From the tone of his article, it is clear that Weatherson's own preference was for the latter of the two groupings mentioned above, and that he was hinting at the possibility of the art therapist being in a better position to understand what was happening to the patient than either the OT or the psychotherapist, in that the art therapist was present while the painting was made and could, given a background in psychology or psychoanalysis, engage in the exploration of both process *and* content.

Weatherson seems here to claim a unique *mission* for art therapists (Bucher and Strauss 1961: 326), namely that they could, with the right background, be involved in both the *making* of the art work (process) and also in *discussion* of and perhaps *interpretation* of the content, instead of handing that task over to a psychotherapist or doctor. Weatherson demonstrated his claim for the scope of the art therapist's role with illustrated case studies from patients he had worked with. An elaborated version of his work was presented at the exhibition to mark the foundation of BAAT at the ICA in 1964. (Although Weatherson was a founder member and chair of BAAT for a short time, he had left BAAT by 1968 and lectured in art at Leeds Polytechnic.)

By this time, the early 1960s, then, the concept of an 'art therapist' as well as of 'art therapy' had emerged. The foundations were being laid for a new discipline, and occupational group, as opposed to a set of techniques and functions which could be carried out by any health care worker. Weatherson's article spelled out some of the issues which he felt needed to be addressed by an association if art therapy was to develop and art therapists to form a new occupational group: namely, who art therapists

108

Forming a professional association

actually were, in terms of background, qualifications, and attitude; and what art therapy consisted of in practice.

Formation of the British Association of Art Therapists (BAAT)

By the early 1960s, it appears, sufficiently large numbers of the general public, members of the medical profession, hospital administrators, artists, and art teachers had expressed interest and involvement in art therapy that it was felt timely by those individuals who had been trying to promote the work to form an association which would co-ordinate the work of individuals and put it on a more 'formal' basis.

There are no recorded minutes of the meetings that preceded the formation of BAAT (other than those of the early 1950s working parties), but some of the founder members had strong recollections:

> The first meetings were in 1961 and 1962. There was an exhibition at the ICA where a number of art therapists had been asked to contribute. JG contacted me and we and five or six others all contributed work to the exhibition which was called 'Communication Through Art' about psychotic art, psychiatric art, art therapy, etc. That group of people then became the nucleus of a further group that set up BAAT. In the first place this was jointly with NAMH. It was a very small outfit: all founder members took turns at being officers and I became treasurer, secretary, chairman and was very closely involved with BAAT until the early 1970s when I moved away from it.

> How it started... Edward and his group (two or three people around him who supported him and their own view of things), Irene, who represented Withymead and psychotherapy, Adrian Hill, John and Jan Glass came into that first meeting and John asked me if I'd like to be on council. I used to drive up to council meetings from Devon, and became secretary while still down in Devon.

> I came back to London as I was invited to become a founder member of BAAT... that first meeting, I was uncomfortable about it, in some ways. I felt it was fractious... I was met in the corridor by Adrian (Hill) and Frank (Breakwell) and they were troubled. They felt it was moving in a way they didn't like. But I couldn't understand. I felt I was being plunged into politics and this was a shock. I didn't like this. There were so few of us that it was all right that we worked from different points of view, and now there seemed to be pressures that one was going to be better than the other, one the right way, one the wrong.... I remember Michael Edwards standing up and talking about Withymead, and talking about it well, and trying to pour oil on troubled waters – because there were troubled waters right from that first meeting.

Beginning of organised activity

Other founder members also sensed that there was dissent right from the start and profound differences in what was meant by art therapy:

> I met X very early on. He greeted me in a starched white doctor's coat, very clinical... the emphasis on the interpretive and the diagnostic... schizophrenic paintings in which he would point out the schizophrenic expressions. How could one tell from a painting that this was either the onset or a full-blown schizophrenic experience. I have NEVER approached it like this, never did or wanted to. I was against it.

The same art therapist says of meetings with other art therapists around the time of the formation of BAAT:

> There was a very nice man who worked with Adrian, same sort of background.... I saw a lot of them at one stage. He was absolutely lovely. I liked him very much as a person, but he had distinct ideas about techniques and he did beautiful, delicate watercolours, quite unrelated to expressing anything in a p.. ological sense...., I've no doubt he did a great job because of his personality.

(The person referred to was Frank Breakwell, who also worked at the King Edward VII Sanatorium in a similar way to Hill. He became Chair of BAAT for one year in 1970 after John Henzell resigned.)

In spite of the differences of opinion within the small group, an association was formed in 1963 out of the informal meetings described above, and its formation was marked with another exhibition at the Institute of Contemporary Arts, from 5 May 1964. The exhibition was previewed in an extensive article in the *Sunday Times* of 3 May 1964 illustrated with pictures from Netherne Hospital (Adamson), Springfield (Weatherson), Warlingham Park (Jan Glass, and St Bernards (John Henzell).

It was opened by Professor Carstairs, who drew an analogy between the artist and the mental patient:

> They are both in a sense under privileged 'out' groups. That is why painters, as a whole, share a sympathy with the psychiatrically sick who paint. There is no clear dividing line. The greater the acceptance of gifted eccentricity in society, the larger will be the understanding of mental patients.
>
> (Catalogue note: May 1964)

Here we see that Carstairs is linking art and eccentricity and perhaps unintentionally suggesting that art therapists, by virtue of being artists, were destined to be an 'out' group. Yet the struggle which was ahead was, perhaps, about becoming an 'in group' in terms of recognition by the NHS.

Forming a professional association

Membership criteria are established

Shortly after the formation of BAAT but before the inaugural meeting of 1966, a council and officers had been elected by the membership of thirty-two people. Adamson was the Chair, John Henzell the Honorary Secretary, Jan Glass Membership Secretary, Michael Pope, Treasurer. One of the most pressing issues, as the council saw it, was to determine membership of BAAT, which would in turn determine membership of the emergent profession. A sub-committee was established which proposed that those applying for full membership should satisfy the council in following respects:

a) mode of employment:
   that they were employed as or working as art therapists or remedial art teachers (the latter term was used when referring to art therapists who were also teachers and working in special schools);
b) training and qualifications:
   an art teaching qualification was felt by the committee to be desirable. Certain other qualifications were accepted – for example, an art degree plus working experience and/or analysis;
c) experience:
   in art therapy or art teaching, or in a related field such as psychology or psychoanalysis;
d) number of hours working:
   this was applied to ensure that the person applying for full membership was working primarily as an art therapist. The rule was not to be rigidly applied, but if an applicant was considered to be primarily engaged in another professional role (e.g. psychiatrist or teacher) they were offered Associate Membership;
e) provision of a statement:
   to give the applicant's views on the aims of art therapy, in order that the committee could get an idea of their attitude and approach. (This practice continued until about 1984 when it was finally discontinued. There had always been disquiet among applicants for membership about making such a statement and the use to which it would be put. There had been a somewhat vague intention to retain the statements for possible future research, but perhaps the more telling reason was that the BAAT Council at that time had views on what they felt was 'true' art therapy practice and the applicants with statements which accorded with these views were looked upon more favourably: that is, admitted to membership.)

The emphasis that the committee placed on the art teaching qualification stemmed from two main sources:
   most founder members had experienced the 'child-centred' (or

111

Beginning of organised activity

person-centred, see Chapter 3) approach to art education themselves, while at school or art college, and had also taught art, most probably using that approach (e.g. Diana Halliday, Michael Pope);

and for reasons of 'prestige':

they wanted to include in the association people who were likely to be sympathetic to art therapy as a result of being artists BUT who had been 'vetted' by another professional group (teachers). Art teachers were thus chosen as a comparability group.

There was anxiety in the committee about the kind of activity that was taking place in hospitals, etc. under the name of art therapy and about the personalities of the people who were practising it. Adamson recalled some of this in an interview:

Seftel: I know that in the really early days you and Adrian Hill and Irene Champernowne were trying to form a professional organisation?
Adamson: Yes. We did this with the assistance of the NAMH. But it was many years later than I formed BAAT.
Seftel: About 20 years? Why was there such a hiatus between your forming this idea and its eventual realisation?
Adamson: Actually, it was because other people were starting to work and I was trying to stop the lunatic fringe from getting in and taking it over. There were so many people saying 'I can do that' but they were not artists. Unfortunately the non-artists have crept in now... it wasn't the medical side as much as it was the people from the outside thinking that they could come in and do this. Just anyone, more or less; those who were impelled by their own problems.

(Seftel 1987: 50)

Referring back to Carstairs's comment about artists, we see that the artists saw themselves very much as the 'insiders' as far as art therapy was concerned, or at least those whom Adamson represented. Adamson's reference to the 'lunatic fringe' seems to be based on fears that artists who were themselves disturbed may be drawn to art therapy for their own needs. Yet it seems that Adamson was not so concerned about these artists as about 'people from the outside' who were also non-medical. It is not clear what is meant and is not followed up, but it is an issue which recurred persistently when considering not only membership but also training criteria. Adamson may have had in mind 'fringe therapists' (such as members of the many 'growth movements' stemming from the USA in the 1960s – Quaesitor, Esalen, EST, and so on). Being seen as associated with such groups might well have made acceptance by the medical profession unlikely. (Such issues of 'respectability' were cited by John Evans in connection with the formation of the Certificate in Remedial Art at St Albans School of Art in 1969 – see Chapter 23.)

112

Chapter thirteen

The inaugural meeting of BAAT
Aims and objects established

The preliminary meetings of BAAT prior to its inauguration had been concerned with membership criteria and drafting aims and objects for the constitution. These were presented to the Inaugural General Meeting, held at the NAMH headquarters in London on 8 January 1966.

The title of the association was the British Association of Art Therapists (Remedial Art Education), and art therapy was defined as: 'the use of any creative means of self expression for the purpose of maintaining and improving mental and physical health'. We have seen in the previous chapter that art teachers had been chosen as a comparability group, hence the subtitle 'Remedial Art Teaching'.

The objects were as follows:

a) to promote mental and physical health in every way but especially by the use of art and other creative activities as forms of therapy;
b) to protect and promote the interests of its members and to provide and maintain such services for the benefit of members as may be approved by the Council from time to time;
c) to promote the exchange of ideas concerning health in general and art therapy in particular, and to place the views of members before the various authorities and other bodies with interests in this field and before the general public;
d) to enable its members to co-operate as a body with other organisations in pursuit of the objects of the Association;
e) to encourage suitable persons to enter the profession, to devise and establish courses of training for such persons and to see that proper standards of professional competence are maintained by members and associates.

These were very complex objects for such a small group and gave BAAT the following functions:

1. a learned society (c) and (e);
2. a union (b);

113

Beginning of organised activity

3. a pressure group (a, c, d);
4. a professional association (c) and (e).

The objects were statements of intent, and, by voting for all of them, the members were putting a very heavy load on the council and officers, and, of course, on themselves.

The most contentious of all the objects was (e) concerning membership. The members agreed to five grades of membership: *Fellow* (who had to have been practising art therapy for seven consecutive years and have a thesis on some branch of art therapy approved by a panel of the Council); *Honorary Member* (a person of distinction who had rendered some distinguished service in furthering one or all of the objects of the Association); *Associate Member* (anyone actively concerned in furthering the objects of the Association, who could receive information but not vote); *Student Member* (a student in full-time training for 'teaching service' in art therapy, who had the same status as an Associate); and lastly and most problematic, *Full Member*, which I shall consider below.

Full membership The founder members of BAAT, who had been responsible for drafting the aims, objects, and membership criteria and for beginning the process of admitting members to the new association, were in a position of some power when laying out the constitution. The process of admitting members had begun immediately after BAAT was formed in 1963 and the first officers invited applications from intending members. As I have said, early membership forms included a section for applicants to write a personal statement on their approach to art therapy. I have suggested that this was partly to gain 'archive' material, but more importantly to distinguish between those with no qualifications, or working in OT departments, and those with a higher status, in terms of qualifications or position, and views which accorded with those of the council and officers. Pursuit of the 'honorific symbol' (Becker 1971) implied being able to demonstrate that the occupational group were high enough in status to be good runners.

Those forms submitted between 1964 and 1972 show that there was a definite preference for people with degrees or diplomas in art or design and art teaching qualifications over people who had other qualifications but who were working under Ministry of Health conditions of service. To illustrate briefly here:

Applicant A admitted in 1964 worked for 18 hours per week in geriatric and psychiatric hospitals and had a National Diploma in Design in Sculpture, a postgraduate qualification from the Slade and an Art Teacher's Certificate.

114

Aims and objectives of BAAT

Applicant B was working full-time as a teacher but had had a personal analysis and wrote a piece on the use of art therapy with handicapped children. This person had a graduate art qualification and an ATC, and was offered full membership.

Applicant C who had similar qualifications to those above but who worked part-time in an OT department was offered associate membership at first, but on appealing became a full member.

These examples highlight the importance of these early decisions on the kinds of qualifications and attitudes that the first council and officers of BAAT felt desirable for the new discipline.

The criteria for full membership which were eventually approved at the inaugural meeting were as follows

Any person who is or has been engaged in the practice of art therapy in the British Isles who can prove his or her professional competence to the satisfaction of the Council of the Association. (This would include any Qualified Art Teacher who can satisfy the Council that he is engaged in the practice of art therapy.) Admission to Membership shall be in the absolute discretion of the Council and no applicant shall become a Full Member until notified in writing by the Council. The Council may in its absolute discretion refuse membership to any person without assigning any reason.

An appeals procedure was available for those who felt unfairly treated.

One founder member was disappointed by what she felt was 'exclusiveness' in the new association, preferring to see BAAT as a loose association of interested people:

Much as I longed for a group of friends, I withdrew from the Association.... The Art and Psychopathology Group [formed in Scotland by Professor Pickford and Joyce Laing, having no union or professional association functions] seemed to be much more open. I feel they have an open or scientific spirit where people are interested in sharing whatever they feel is important.

Although this member had been in accord with the objects of the constitution which were to do with promoting the notion of art as healing, she felt uneasy about the methods of achieving the aims right from the start.

Another founder member recalled:

When I first went to Council meetings, we used to hold them in Edward's flat, and there was a group, Edward's friends. I can't remember them all – they were all mates and tended to hold the thing... they held the power. And it seemed, was it going to be their way, or was it going to be London University training at this stage... as it seemed that was the main first option. But there were always problems with that.

115

Beginning of organised activity

Then things changed. H became Chair, I was Secretary, M was treasurer.

It seems the conflicts were present even in the small group which formed the first BAAT council, to such an extent that they drove some members away. It is not clear from interviewees' recollections whether these were conflicts over strategies for promoting art therapy and art therapists or struggles for leadership. It was probably a mixture of both.

Forming the identity of BAAT

It appears then that the political orientations of the leading members (then Adamson, Hill, Henzell, Cable, Breakwell) were an important consideration in shaping BAAT in the early days. There were several main issues as well as membership criteria which had to be considered:

1. The nature of art therapy itself: was it 'art' which was inherently healing or was it really 'psychotherapy through art' (Hill or Champernowne)?
2. The nature of BAAT: should the association focus on 'ideas' and members meet as a kind of 'learned society' rather like the Society for Art and Psychopathology which any interested person could join?
3. Should it be a political pressure group, carving out a clear definition of art therapy and seeking a career, salary, and training structure?
4. Should it be a group of friends who were feeling themselves isolated by the unusual work, as artists involved with psychiatric patients?

Having taken on the objects under the constitution, it seemed that the small group of officers and council were in an impossible position in trying to fulfil all the objects equally. So priorities had to be established and the issue of who would decide these became paramount.

The first annual general meeting of BAAT

This was held on 26 June 1966 in the Gallery of Netherne Hospital. Besley Naylor, a founder member, had kept a report and minutes of the meeting which he kindly sent to me. The report states:

There among the strange pictures and models which their first Chairman Edward Adamson had collected over twenty years, the first meeting of the BAAT got underway. Even for one of the youngest professions in the world it had seemed long overdue, and members had come from as far away as Dublin and Aberdeen and from establishments as different as psychiatric hospitals, orthopaedic hospitals and special schools.

Aims and objectives of BAAT

Progress reports were submitted to the members about different aspects of the council's work. There were plans to become an incorporated society affiliated to the National Association for Mental Health, to be 'recognised' by the International Society for Art and Psychopathology. But the item which dominated the meeting was that concerning moves towards obtaining improvements in salary and conditions of service for art therapists, and a plan to start a training leading to a degree-status qualification.

Before the AGM, members had been circulated about their qualifications, training, experience, and salaries. A total of thirty-six full members and eight associates had replied, almost 100 per cent response. Of twenty-five art therapists working in hospitals, six had arranged to be paid by local education authorities and ten were being paid on an *ad hoc* Whitley Council rate. Five were paid below this rate and four above it. The report notes that:

> Mr Henzell himself, having at one time jibbed at accepting a post because of the low salary, was told that this might be overcome by employing him, on paper at least, as a refuse collector.

The Council informed members that a questionnaire was to be sent to all psychiatric hospitals and other medical institutions in Britain to see if present and future demand for art therapy could be ascertained. The last such questionnaire had been sent out in 1949 by Hill (see Chapter 10).

The council was left with the brief to improve communications among members, to increase awareness of the achievements and potential of art therapy, especially among the medical profession, and to raise finances for these purposes. They were also asked to continue with the work in hand, already discussed. A very large agenda for such a small group.

In this chapter we have seen how a group of people designated, either by themselves or others, as art therapists, came together to form an association. The early meetings of the association (BAAT) were devoted to drawing up a constitution with aims and objects, and membership criteria. The objects were broad and covered learned society and union activities. Membership criteria were established which were designed to exclude those who did not fit in with the proclaimed mission. Segments had already begun to develop within the small group of art therapists (BAAT), different forms of art therapy were being practised, and, from founder members' recollections, conflicts of interest were present from the start (see Bucher and Strauss 1961: 325 for discussion of conflicts of interest and the consequences for change). Different weighting was given by the council of BAAT, who had set the criteria for membership, to different kinds of work. Bucher and Strauss discuss this issue in reference to medicine, where, within a core speciality like internal medicine, there are

Beginning of organised activity

many different kinds of practice, ranging from the 'family doctor' to highly specialised consultation, a service to other doctors. They comment:

> These differences in the weights assigned to elements of practice do not begin to take into account the further diversity introduced when professionals assign different weights to such activities as research, teaching and public service.
>
> (Bucher and Strauss 1961: 327)

The different weightings given by BAAT were to ensure that only persons of status equal to that of art teachers, preferably postgraduate art teachers, who had allegiance to an 'educational' model of therapy as opposed to a 'medical' or 'occupational therapy' model, were admitted to full membership. Others were offered associate (non-voting) membership.

In the next chapter, we shall see how the council and members set about fulfilling their objects and in particular examine the change of status of BAAT in becoming a Central Association of the National Union of Teachers in 1967. This in turn had an effect on membership criteria and on the strategies which were employed in fulfilling the objects.

Chapter fourteen

Some of the main issues influencing BAAT's decision to become a Central Association of the NUT

Parallel to and to some extent affecting the debates about membership criteria, and crucial to the future structure of BAAT, were the negotiations which resulted in BAAT acquiring the status of a Central Association of the National Union of Teachers. These negotiations were conducted by Graham Cable (a potter and art teacher by background), on behalf of the council, and the outcome was to have profound effects on the future of both BAAT and art therapy training until the mid–1970s and beyond.

Background to the negotiations: the position regarding employment

During the first years of BAAT the Council had collected a body of information on conditions of service and rates of pay of would-be members, revealing a confusing and complex picture, which the council considered needed rationalising. According to surveys conducted by BAAT, the position regarding employment of art therapists in 1964–7 was as follows.

1 Employment under hospital management committees

The minimum requirement set by the MoH for working as an 'art therapist' was a qualification gained two years after A level art (although not specified, this was the Intermediate Certificate in Art and Design which was phased out in 1964). Although a hospital might wish to employ an 'art therapist', job titles varied and ranged from art therapist to staff nurse, OT helper, art director, craft instructor, hospital porter, play therapist. These were usually vacant establishments used when the hospital wanted an art therapist, as of course there was no official establishment. HMCs had to get the permission of MoH (later DHSS) to employ an art therapist.

119

Beginning of organised activity

2 Employment under educational services

Some art therapists were employed by a local education authority and seconded to hospitals as part-time adult education tutors. The contracts were subject to a maximum of fifteen hours per week for forty weeks per year. Minimum attendance and enrolment requirements were the same as for adult education classes, i.e. around twelve to fifteen people. Qualifications were not specified but usually a National Diploma in Design (NDD) was necessary. (This was a two-year course following the Intermediate Certificate, and examinations were set by the Ministry of Education.) Payment was at approximately double the hourly rate of MoH sessions, but there were no paid holidays or sick pay.

3 Employment in special schools

Art therapists who were also art teachers were sometimes employed in special schools by local education authorities and paid in accordance with Burnham agreements, often with responsibility allowances. Employment was as 'teacher' and, although the art therapist might have been allowed to spend part of their timetable seeing individual children in the role of 'art therapist', this could change if the headteacher changed and their successor did not want the teacher to use their time in this way.

4 Employment by private or other arrangement

Hospitals that had 'free monies' could employ art therapists by private arrangement. A small number had been paid at a rate agreed between the art therapist and the hospital before the inception of the NHS and these rates of pay had been pegged there. Some clinics converted 'psychotherapy' posts into art therapy posts, but this was very rare.

Employment from the point of view of the pioneers

In the years before BAAT's formation, the pioneers had not tended to concern themselves much with the poor conditions in which they had worked. Indeed, some felt them to be adequate, and that they were privileged to be employed. From the interviews and from my personal acquaintance with many of the founder members in the late 1960s I understand that some had private incomes, some were married to high-earning spouses, some had lucrative part-time work. Others got by on very poor salaries because they enjoyed the work (and may have thought it an artist's lot to be poor, as in the 'Romantic Tradition'), others simply did

BAAT and the NUT

not care about financial rewards because they believed passionately in their cause.

They were not unaware of the problems (for instance, having to work in a corridor, or a room designated as a 'store room', or go on to the wards with a trolley of paints, etc.), but it seems that their enthusiasm for working with patients, combined with their lack of expertise in institutional politics, and perhaps fear of losing their job, prevented them from doing much about the conditions. From interviews and from letters to newsletters and discussions with those who were art therapists in the 1950s and early 1960s, it seems as if they saw their main task as 'getting on with the job, seeing patients and trying to convince other staff about the value of the work'. To take a few examples from correspondence and from newsletters of 1967, a founder member wrote:

> W. Hospital was the second largest psychiatric hospital in the British Isles – the therapeutic staff consisted of one occupational therapist, myself as an art therapist and two OT helpers. We were responsible for the entire hospital therapy service. There was no art department at that time. I had to carry around large cardboard boxes with my art materials, round a limited number of wards. When I took early retirement there was no qualified OT but a newly created Diversional Therapy department with a manager and over 20 staff and my art therapy department, that I had to fight tooth and nail for... the manager promised when I retired they would employ another art therapist... this was never done, even after seeing my MP and informing BAAT of the situation.
>
> (Letter to author 10 February 1986)

Another member had a more fortunate experience in an orthopaedic hospital where had had managed to

> establish a happy state of co-operation with the physiotherapists in which from the very start the newcomer, art therapy, was welcomed and accepted as one of the working team for the patients' welfare.

Yet another, working in a unit for alcoholics, complained that the consultant 'refused to hold discussions with the staff and herself in order to discuss problems and work out a proper function for the art therapy sessions'. This member felt that her case illustrated a larger problem:

> A mere human being, a professional in his own line, but not necessarily in the line that 'holds the reins of government' (in this case the medical profession) is not allowed to express an opinion on matters that involve some of the basic problems of humanity because his restless unhappy searching may embarrass, disturb or threaten the convenient 'structure of the establishment'.

Beginning of organised activity

A member with a National Diploma in Design, working in a large Birmingham psychiatric hospital in 1965, was paid 27/6 per three-hour session on MoH rates. He worked twelve hours each week in the hospital and also taught art at a college of further education. He had been working at the hospital since 1958. (Initially this member had been offered associate status, due to his working in the OT department but this was changed some months later to full membership.) He was advised by BAAT:

> I suggest you approach your hospital and ask them to employ you as an art therapist with your own department. There is a rate of pay for art therapists authorised by the Ministry of Health and although this Association strongly disapproves of it – it is only half of the minimum paid to Art Therapists and Specialist Teachers working for local education authorities – it is rather better than the rate you are being paid at present.
>
> The ideal solution is to have your own department within the hospital but to be employed by your local education authority or College of Further Education as an adult education instructor, until the seconding of Art Therapists by LEAs is standard practice.
>
> (Hon. Sec. of BAAT 11 August 1966)

A member who was an Associate of the Royal College of Art (ARCA), one of the highest art qualifications available, was employed by a Sussex hospital management committee in a small therapeutic community in 1965 for six hours per week at £2 0s 3d per three-hour session. This member had taught full time in grammar and private schools and in adult education for twenty-three years. She had her own department (there was no OT) and was offered full membership immediately.

Surveys conducted by BAAT and outlined in a submission to the NUT in 1970 noted that:

> the conditions of service under which many art therapists were employed in the 1960s were prejudicial to the proper performance of their duties and in turn they inhibit many developments that are desirable in the interests of their patients and pupils.

The problems were seen as too complex for a small organisation (which also had other functions than that of union to fulfil) to tackle alone and as needing the power and advice of a union.

The Ministry of Health's attitude to the employment of art therapists

In 1964 the MoH had a definition of an art therapist which was 'A person with two years post A level study of Art'. So, according to the MoH, art therapists were artists but had no therapy training or experience.

We have seen that one of BAAT's objects was to:

BAAT and the NUT

encourage suitable persons to enter the profession, to devise and establish courses of training and to see that proper standards of professional competence are maintained by members and associates.

(BAAT Constitution)

We have also noted in the previous chapter, and from some of the examples mentioned above, the strategies which the council employed to ensure 'suitable' persons became full members of BAAT.

BAAT did not agree with the MoH that someone holding in effect an Intermediate Certificate in Art (and exam set by the Ministry of Education) could properly practise under the title of 'therapist', but, on writing to the MoH to try to set in train some discussions, BAAT received the following response to its suggestion that art therapists be compared to teachers and be paid at the same rate:

Teachers give instruction in recognised courses, many of which lead to some qualification while art therapists necessarily work alongside other members of the hospital staff, all of whom are contributing in their various ways towards the patients' recovery.

(letter from MoH to Hon. Sec. of BAAT 1964)

This response is somewhat ambiguous, in that it seems to imply that contributing towards patients' recovery is less financially worthy than providing courses of instruction.

The other arguments that BAAT presented concerning poor pay did not impress the MoH, for they commented that other paramedical staff received almost as poor wages, and the exclusion of married men due to inadequate salaries on which to maintain families (which had been cited by BAAT's – predominantly male – officers as a problem) applied equally to nurses, OTs, and physiotherapists as to art therapists. The rapid turnover of staff might have posed a problem to the MoH, but there were plenty of volunteers to perform what the MoH (represented by various civil servants) defined as 'art therapy'.

On various occasions during 1964–7 in letters and phone calls, the MoH had declared that occupational therapists could provide art therapy – using 'craft work' as a definition of art therapy. As we have seen from previous chapters, BAAT had not been able to provide a clear definition of art therapy, so it was not surprising that the MoH was influenced by the most publicised (and probably most economic model) – that of diversional art activities as practised by Hill and others, and not the model of 'psychotherapy through art' as practised by Withymead staff, which, in stressing the need for one patient to one therapist, and for highly trained therapists at that, implied an expensive service.

Given this situation, BAAT considered further negotiations with the MoH would be unproductive, and this influenced the decision to seek

123

Beginning of organised activity

employment through the local education authorities, with the help of the National Union of Teachers.

The officers persuaded the membership of BAAT that the best way to achieve pay and conditions of service equivalent to those of art teachers was through becoming a Central Association of the NUT. The proposal was approved by the membership at the AGM of 1966.

The affiliation agreement

The affiliation document, establishing BAAT as a Central Association of the NUT, was signed on 1 January 1967 by the President of the NUT Oliver Whitfield, the General Secretary Sir Ronald Gould, Edward Adamson, Chair, and John Henzell, Secretary of BAAT.

The association to NUT was made on the basis that BAAT should preserve its autonomy in respect of the following:

a) formulation of its own policy on matters solely pertaining to the organisation of the art therapy service;
b) representation on the existing or any future national salary negotiating machinery concerned with the salaries of members engaged in the administration of LEA services;
c) representation on other national and international bodies dealing with the art therapy service;
d) changing of its own rules and standing orders subject to the provisions of the rules of the NUT.

After payment of the appropriate subscriptions to BAAT, all persons eligible for full membership of BAAT would be entitled to all benefits enjoyed by NUT members. The council of BAAT was to act as an advisory committee of the NUT on all questions concerning art therapy and a representative of the NUT would sit on BAAT council.

Regarding membership, the NUT did not insist that BAAT full members had to be qualified teachers, but, since this criterion had already been set by BAAT itself, there were few problems about this as exceptions were rare.

BAAT in the context of the 'professionalism versus unionism' debate

By deciding to become a Central Association of a (non-TUC-affiliated) union, which represented the interests of a group with which art therapists had begun to compare themselves (art teachers), BAAT had, I suggest, intended to focus on strategies for achieving all the objects in the constitution.

124

BAAT and the NUT

Discussions with members who were in BAAT at the time reveal that there were some anxieties lest 'politics' (in the form of 'trades union politics') take over during the battles for salaries. As I have mentioned before, some art therapists were not much concerned about salaries, but were keen on promoting the practice of art therapy and setting standards for training. The salary issue was usually linked with provision of better service to patients through provision of qualified, well-paid personnel.

One member interviewed was on the council at the time when BAAT joined the NUT:

> As I remember it, the main thrust of our argument was that people should be artists. That was the old school's view [Hill], that they should be artists. [We thought they should be] artists with some form of psychotherapy. I think what was confusing at the time was that as an organisation we were always looking to extend ourselves, and we extended it to all different sorts of people. Those who had expressed interest. It got to be a problem how to include all these people. Another thing that was complicated was how people were paid and often if you were working in the NHS your pay was negotiated through the education authority to get reasonable pay. So that was the best money available. That is why we became affiliated to the NUT. J and I used to go to meetings at the NUT. Not that they could do much.

There do not appear to have been any counter-proposals put forward at the BAAT AGM of 1966, or any suggestions for an alternative strategy for gaining salaries equivalent to the Burnham scales for teachers, other than joining NUT. The argument put to the membership by the officers and council (which included Adamson, Breakwell, Henzell, and Cable) suggested that the NUT would also help art therapists to fulfil the 'learned society' objects by spreading the word among the public, other professionals, and members of parliament. This was confirmed later, by Breakwell in a letter to members in the BAAT *Newsletter* of January 1971:

> Recently Michael Edwards and I saw the NUT's representative and discussed with him the most effective strategy to adopt. He suggested, and we agreed, that the best course was to establish a group in the House of Commons interested in our work and sympathetic to our case. As a preliminary step he kindly offered to approach and brief a Conservative MP and a Labour MP whom, he was convinced, would be both interested and sympathetic. Michael and I would see them later and give them a complete briefing with the full background. Simultaneously the NUT's representative would see members of the County Councils' Association and brief them, also.
>
> (BAAT *Newsletter* January 1971: 2–3)

Beginning of organised activity

In the same *Newsletter*, there are reports of BAAT's contribution to the International Society for Education through Art's annual conference in Coventry, by Michael Edwards, Dr Edmund Miller, a psychiatrist who was also an artist, and Anna Robinson, a council member of BAAT who was also headteacher of a Birmingham nursery school, and a report of an art therapy session held during the conference by Elizabeth Wills. A copy of the document of affiliation between BAAT and the Society for Education through Art was also included.

I make this point to show that BAAT was trying to fulfil all its objects, both trade union and learned society-professional functions, and there did not appear to be a split between them. Ozga and Lawn in *Teachers, Professionalism and Class* (1981) suggest that organised teacher activity is an area of study within education that has been neglected, and that part of the reason is that teacher union activity has been polarised in the literature into opposing areas: 'professional' and 'union'. 'The dominant assumption is that teachers have consistently struggled to achieve professional status and have identified themselves as professionals rather than union members' (1981: v–vi).

They offer a useful critical review of the literature on organised teachers, pointing out that:

> Histories of teacher unionism have created an image of consistent movement towards professionalism, an image which at once reflects and supports the 'natural history' approach to the professions. This concentration on progress towards professionalism has resulted in an underemphasis on contradictory or ambiguous actions on the part of teachers, not only among their historians, but among those authors writing about the unions' present status as part of the educational sub-government. Because they assume a history of consistent 'professionalism', the salary campaigns or sanction implementations in support of improved working conditions are considered to be eruptions of untypical militancy and to represent an alteration in union tactics which threatens the existence of educational government based on partnership.
>
> (Ozga and Lawn 1981: 34).

They further suggest that there were other consequences: that union strategies are assumed to be contradictory to the dominant professional ethic, individual members are supposed to experience tension between union demands and client-centred duties, the executive is assumed to be in conflict with its militant membership, and public support is lost along with departure from 'professional behaviour'.

Bearing in mind Ozga and Lawn's arguments, art therapists as a group appear to be unusual looked at in the context of the literature on professions which they have discussed, in that BAAT rejected this dichotomy

BAAT and the NUT

from its earliest days (although I have no evidence to suggest that this was a conscious rejection). It is not essential for qualified art therapists to join BAAT in order to practise, but if they do not (and this is *occasionally* explained as not wishing to join a union) then they do not appear on the BAAT Register of Qualified Art Therapists. There have so far been no attempts to form alternative associations specifically for art therapists, although a group consisting of a general practitioner, a Jungian psychotherapist, some drama and movement therapists, and interested lay people attempted to form an Institute for the Study of the Arts in Therapy (BISAT) in the late 1970s, which will be discussed later. BISAT folded after a few years through lack of support, in terms of both finances and members. Ozga and Lawn would prefer to see an approach (to professionalism) which would take into account the fact that it could have different meanings at different times for different groups and which 'could lead to progress in understanding organised teacher behaviour beyond the sterile dichotomy of professionalism versus unionism which dominates the literature at the moment' (1981: vii).

With these cautionary words in mind, I venture to suggest that art therapists, in their organised group in BAAT, did experience some conflicts between the 'image' of 'profession' – as being akin to medicine, law, i.e. academically respectable, high status, 'honorific symbol' – and 'union', i.e. conflicts about pay and working conditions more appropriate to 'blue-collar' workers. But the leadership of BAAT during the 1970s managed to prevent polarisation by dividing the organisation into subcommittees to take on various operations which could be loosely categorised into 'union' and 'learned society' functions, while it remained structurally part of a union.

(The association rejected the idea of applying for membership of the Council for Professions Supplementary to Medicine, which regulates occupational and physiotherapy, chiropody, radiography, dietetics, etc. in the late 1970s. If successful application had been made, it would have given state registered status to art therapists. The CPSM was felt by BAAT to be 'too prescriptive'. This issue will be discussed in more detail in Chapter 20.)

When BAAT became a Central Association of the NUT in 1967, it gave up any possibility of attracting grants or indeed any financial assistance other than its membership subscriptions – whereas music therapists, who had established a Society of Music Therapy as a charitable body, and had no association with 'union objects', were able to seek and obtain monies from trusts and other patrons (lately pop stars, such as the Beatles).

Given that the NUT represented teachers and adult education lecturers, with whom art therapists sought parity in terms of salaries and conditions (and status) in the 1960s, and that the union had offered help to BAAT in

Beginning of organised activity

promoting art therapy, it appears that Central Association status was popular among members generally. No proposals were made to council or to AGMs to change this status until in 1976 the council itself proposed that BAAT should cease its Central Association membership with the NUT but recommended that all full members working in the NHS should join another union, ASTMS (see Chapter 18.) The close link with the NUT, as representing teachers, did however contribute to the conflict between BAAT and St Albans School of Art, when it began to initiate art therapy training in 1969 (see Chapter 15).

I am suggesting that a mixture of idealism, in terms of the association of some of BAAT's leaders with trade union and left-wing politics, and pragmatism, in terms of gaining access to a pool of knowledge and support which might help BAAT achieve its objective to link art therapists' salaries with those of art teachers and, at the same time, to spread the word about art therapy's value, was at the root of the decision to join the NUT.

Very early on, then, BAAT was, in its association with the NUT, taking a clear stand as a trade union, protecting the interests of its members and trying to secure better salaries and working conditions for those it had 'approved' as full members. At the same time it performed the function of a 'learned society' by organising conferences and seminars, encouraging members to participate in national and international conferences, and by trying to develop standards for practice and criteria for training. Although sub-committees had been formed to carry out different tasks, the people involved were often the same, or at least membership of these sub-committees overlapped.

In the next chapter I shall explore some of the problems which BAAT faced during its campaign to have art therapists employed under local education authorities and seconded to hospitals.

Chapter fifteen

The campaign organised by BAAT and the NUT to gain comparable status with adult education lecturers

This chapter will describe the joint BAAT-NUT campaign for improved salaries and structural improvements in the employment of art therapists, in which the issue of comparability with other occupational groups needed to be addressed. At the same time, the question of content and level of art therapy training had to be considered, and these deliberations will be examined in detail in Part V.

Selecting and rejecting: the search for a comparability group

I have tried to show that by becoming a Central Association of the NUT, BAAT had for both pragmatic, historical (given art therapy's roots in art education; see Chapter 3), and idealistic reasons, chosen to ally with the teaching profession, and in particular with adult education lecturers. BAAT had on several occasions between 1964 and 1967 approached the MoH to see whether the Ministry would authorise a rate of pay to art therapists which was equivalent to the Burnham rates paid to adult education lecturers.

The MoH held the view that art therapy was a set of skills which could be practised by OTs:

> It has not been thought possible to draw a distinction between the work done by Art Therapists on the one hand and by Occupational Therapists on the other which justify fixing the remuneration of the former at a rate in excess of that fixed for the latter by the Whitley Council Agreement. The three year course for occupational therapists has been carefully designed to enable students to gain a knowledge and understanding of the physically and mentally ill during the first two years and a knowledge of the arts and crafts in the third year. The occupational therapist has therefore been trained to apply her instruction to hospital patients and performs a variety of activities whilst the Art Therapist undertakes only one.
>
> (Letter from the MoH, 14 December 1966)

129

Beginning of organised activity

The work of occupational therapists, however, covers a wide range of patients and activities whereas the scope of (the) art therapist is limited. For this reason their scales are lower than those of qualified occupational therapists.

(Letter from the Eastern Region Hospital Board, Scotland, after receiving advice from the Scottish Department, MoH, 9 July 1968)

There was clearly a difference of view between BAAT and the MoH concerning art therapy. This was outlined in a BAAT document prepared for the joint BAAT–NUT campaign for improved salaries and conditions of service for art therapists (20 June 1970) and can be summed up as BAAT (and its advisory body of consultant psychiatrists plus Sir Herbert Read and Sir Roland Penrose) seeing art therapy as 'a task similar in importance and scope to related disciplines such as teaching maladjusted children, Clinical or Educational Psychology or psychotherapy'. Whereas the MoH defined art therapy for the purposes of employment as

an activity of marginal importance in hospitals which in fact can be performed by an occupational therapist. Most of those they employ as art therapists are not members of this association and owing to their lack of qualifications for the type of work they do, could not be so. The conditions of employment relevant to the remedial art teacher or art therapist whose work is of a high professional standard are not traditionally encompassed by the medical, nursing and medical auxiliary structure of training and pay.

(BAAT 20 June 1970: 8–9)

These views represent different philosophical attitudes to art therapy, with BAAT aligning art therapy with 'education' in a broad sense as being to do with the development of a person's personality (see Herbert Read's *Education Through Art*, for example) and the MoH aligning it with art and craft activities as practised by some OTs or OT aides.

There were other problems for BAAT about alignment with occupational therapy, and these were to do with attitudes towards mental health care and treatment and the training of medical and paramedical staff. The influence of the 'anti-psychiatry' movement was strong and eminent people in that movement were often invited to BAAT functions (for example, David Cooper, Joe Berke). AGMs in the late 1960s featured films and discussions critical of 'traditional' psychiatric treatment, and *Inscape* was dominated by articles critical of such treatment – see especially Nos 1–5 between 1969 and 1972. (In a paper based on research into the relationship between psychiatrists and art therapists, presented for his Advanced Diploma in Art Therapy, 1989, Terry Molloy, who was Vice-Chair of BAAT between 1975 and 1980, confirms this view and suggests

130

Organisation and status

that, gradually, art therapists have ceased to challenge 'the medical model' and may have grown to accept it.)

Occupational therapy training in the 1960s took place mainly in private institutions and hospitals, in a system similar to that of nursing, which was seen by art therapists to be directed towards 'curing' illness and not questioning or entering into philosophical debate about the nature of mental illness itself (see Waller 1987: 198–9). Occupational therapy was considered by many art therapists to uphold the medical model of treatment and to be philosophically at odds with art therapy (even though in the 1940s there was much in common between art therapy as practised by Hill and arts and crafts activities provided by OTs).

A member who trained both as an art teacher and an occupational therapist recalled how she became involved in art therapy in a sanatorium in the early 1950s:

> I was appointed (as an occupational therapist to do art therapy) because I had done two years' craft work in my art training and because I had business experience. They wanted me to run workshops for patients who had TB and were living at home, not well enough to do full-time work – they could work perhaps five hours a day, mainly leather work or basketry. It was just that at first. So the commercial aspect of it was quite important, to try and get things that were saleable. It then spread out a bit more, and became anything that would interest or occupy the patients, ranging from perhaps a correspondence course to even a bit of clay modelling in bed, which is a bit tricky.... When I heard of art therapy I though it was just what I wanted. It would combine my two interests, the artistic one and the side that was interested in people...

This art therapist mentioned that some years after the War, craft work began to be spoken of in a rather derogatory way (by other professional staff). She felt:

> We were hampered by having such a large number of patients to cover in a relatively short time, so we were less creative in the things that we did than we would have been if we had had more time for each individual.

She went on to work at the Withymead Centre, where she was able to encourage patients to make art work without commercial constraints.

A widely used textbook for OT training (Macdonald 1961) sums up the aims of OT as follows:

> distraction from morbid preoccupation, deflection or diversion of drives, prevention of progressive intellectual or personality impairment, maintenance of the normal personal, social and work habits,

131

Beginning of organised activity

encouraging aspects of personality which militate against future break-down.

(Macdonald 1961: 110–16)

There is much emphasis on 'normalisation' of the patient through the provision of activities: for instance, diverting 'destructive energy' through tearing rags, wedging clay, tearing paper for papier mâché, etc.

From this standard textbook, we can see how rehabilitation at that time was orientated towards work – at a time when there were not three million unemployed. The kind of work available in hospital was of a fairly menial type, preparing patients for the (usual) reality of leaving hospital.

All activities suggested for various types of illness were carefully graded, as were the patients. The intentions were clearly well meant, but a very mechanistic attitude towards treatment is revealed. On the evidence of letters to BAAT, and from discussions with art therapists at council meetings and conferences, it appeared that many art therapists tended to be contemptuous of this and complained that patients were only allowed to go to art therapy as 'a treat' after 'doing time' in OT and its close relative, industrial therapy.

Yet, as I have suggested, Hill's model of art therapy fitted fairly well into the concept of OT of the 1950s and 1960s, in that he believed patients could be helped by diverting their minds from their problems and providing 'worthwhile' occupation. Some art therapists felt that, as long as art therapy was seen by medical colleagues to 'relax' patients and calm them down, it was encouraged, but if it started them questioning their treatment or evoked their angry feelings (which art therapists and psychotherapists would see as a positive sign in many cases, especially in depressed patients) then it was not.

In some OT departments art work had to be saleable, in order to recoup money for materials. This requirement clashed with the art therapist's aim of encouraging freedom of expression, regardless of aesthetic appeal, which often led to patients becoming confused. In short, each side saw the other as interfering with their aims. OTs, however, as the established profession, had some power in this situation, whereas art therapists did not. (There were, of course, many exceptions where working relationships were excellent, but the general experience of art therapists was as described above.)

On the evidence of meetings, interviews, and conferences of the early 1970s, there is little doubt that many art therapists felt they could do a better and more humane job of treating mentally ill patients than many of their medical or paramedical colleagues, largely because their philosophical attitude towards 'mental illness' was not influenced by the 'medical model'. An article by the Jungian analyst, James Hillman, in *Inscape* reflects views held by the leading members of BAAT at that time:

Organisation and status

Case histories have been accumulated in hospitals all over the world. They are a species of fiction that was developed in the last 40 years and there are massed tons of it. These histories or social-workers' write-ups speak in the fantasy language of problems without realising that they are fiction. Why do we not realise a case history is a story, and that we speak of life in the language of their fiction and create what Jung has called a 'healing fiction', an imaginal context for that life we are describing, whereby that life may imagine itself in another way. Why must the patient be the only one to paint himself a new existence? Cannot the therapist imaginatively write him a new history?

(Hillman 1970: 8)

In the same issue, John Henzell, then Chair of BAAT, wrote about a patient he was working with in a large psychiatric hospital. He concluded:

It is not necessary here to think in terms of effecting cures, of rehabilitating people to conform with some notion of a social norm. Through the experimentation with oneself and with others, a growing self-awareness makes it more possible to chose one's relationship to society.

(Henzell 1970: 16)

It was for some of these reasons, then, plus the fact that the paramedical professions were not graduate ones and were also poorly paid, that BAAT was anxious to dissociate itself from them in terms of qualifications, philosophy, and career structure, preferring art teaching or adult education lecturing as comparable occupations.

The employment position of BAAT members in the late 1960s

The 1968 survey mounted by BAAT to investigate the working conditions and pay of its members had revealed a chaotic state of affairs, with members having identical qualifications (often a degree and art teaching diploma) and doing the same work receiving grossly disparate rates of pay. This meant that art therapists could not easily transfer from one post or area of the country to another. Some therapists employed on NHS rates were either poorly qualified by BAAT's criteria or were surviving financially through having private means or were supported by a spouse, usually a husband, or had part-time posts in education which enabled them to tolerate the poor pay and insecure conditions involved in working as art therapists. Some had only their NHS salaries to exist on. The drop-out rate was high given not only the lack of financial incentives but also the low status. Even the pioneer members of BAAT, who were driven to the work by rewards other than financial, were not prepared to see the situation continue thus, as they saw that eventually their work would cease

Beginning of organised activity

to exist. Qualified people were unlikely to continue to be attracted to the work when they could obtain higher paid and better-status posts in education. (There were many founder members who moved into further or higher education in the 1960s, partly to initiate art therapy courses but also for improved conditions, one suspects.) Also, as we have seen, many founder members had part-time posts in education which allowed them to tolerate the poor pay and insecure conditions involved in working as art therapists.

BAAT–NUT attempt to persuade local education authorities to take over financial responsibility for art therapists

In 1968, BAAT and the NUT mounted a campaign to have the LEAs take over the employment of art therapists, whether they were working in LEA schools, hospitals, clinics, or Home Office establishments. The conditions of employment envisaged were comparable with those for teachers working in special schools and in FE, as embodied in the Burnham Reports and teachers' tenure agreements. The conditions of service were to be adapted according to the setting in which the art therapist worked, and would link in the courses of training being proposed at the Institute of Education of London University from 1965 on and at the School of Art Education in Birmingham.

Although employment through the LEA with secondment to a hospital was seen to be the most promising option of those identified in the 1968 survey, there were still many problems.

Briefly, these were:

a) employment was restricted to part time and was primarily designed for adult education instructors working in evening institutes and colleges of further education;

b) contracts were issued for only one year and could be terminated with a week's notice – not a satisfactory arrangement when treating patients long term;

c) there were limits on the art therapist's contact with other members of staff in that the contract was limited to 'class contact hours', allowing no provision for staff meetings, etc. ;

d) research and preparation time were not allowed for;

e) attendance requirements were often inappropriate: for example, the minimum 'class' size might be twelve, which would represent a fairly large group of disturbed patients. Individual work was not provided for in a 'class contact' contract;

f) there was no provision for art therapists to have time off with pay to undertake further training in this model, or in any other models of employment at the time.

Organisation and status

There were, however, examples of LEA conditions of service and salaries which were satisfactory. This depended largely on the principal of the relevant adult education institute being sympathetic to art therapy and 'allowing' flexibility in the interpretation of the contract.

One such was the Paddington Institute, which employed two part-time art therapists on secondment to the Paddington Centre for Psychotherapy. The art therapists enjoyed autonomous status, which resulted in equal working relationships with the clinical team and prevented them from being absorbed into occupational therapy. The need for attendance at staff meetings and case conferences was clearly understood by the principal and her staff. Regular visits from the art adviser provided managerial support for the therapists. (Later, however, problems arose when the principal retired and adult education suffered stringent cuts.)

Describing the difficulties

In 1968, BAAT Council prepared a document entitled *BAAT: Describing the difficulties facing a particular branch of this country's educational services and presenting proposals which the officers and council of BAAT believe will satisfactorily deal with the issues involved.* The aim was very clear.

> We propose that for the purposes of employment, all art therapists and remedial art teachers be put on a similar footing and that there is a parity between art therapists working in hospitals and prisons on the one hand, and teachers working in special and further education on the other.

The document goes on to claim comparability in work performed, qualifications, training, and experience. It further declared:

> Art therapists and remedial art teachers have their origins in the educational field and as such an LEA is the most appropriate employing body. Art teachers engaged in remedial work of this kind have, in almost all cases, been to colleges of art or had a teacher training. In addition to this, all courses of training at present proposed will take place in educational settings.

As well as laying out clearly the occupational identification with art teachers in special or further education, the document mounted a moral argument concerning the treatment of psychiatric patients. It stated that they had no pressure group to argue for their needs, and the consequences of NHS staffing problems had been serious and detrimental to patients' lives. It obliquely criticised the MoH for its definition of an art therapist and suggested that the situation could be remedied by the provision of qualified personnel, who would be trained at postgraduate level.

135

Beginning of organised activity

By suggesting that art therapists should have a 'postgraduate qualification', BAAT was offering a direct challenge to the MoH. BAAT's point was that, if the LEAs were to accept the responsibility for providing an art therapy service in hospitals on a 'more efficient and rational basis' they would be

> making possible the alleviation of much suffering and misery and using education in the most profound and human sense. It would be a most enlightened example of the much spoken of collaboration of the Health Service and the local authorities.

In this document, then, we can see the emergence of a strategy to be used by BAAT on many subsequent occasions, of quoting relevant passages of MoH (DHSS) and DES reports and circulars back at them in support of BAAT's own arguments. We shall see that this was particularly effective in the later campaign, from 1976 on.

BAAT's position was again declared unequivocally in a circular to members and for distribution in public places. This was entitled *Wage Negotiations and Status: 1968*:

> Within both the health and education sectors of public employment, workers are struggling for wage levels that will ensure that they can keep pace with an escalating cost of living... they will no longer be satisfied with some alleged 'status' or 'social standing'; they demand more concrete recognition of the inestimable value of their contribution than mere sympathy or the so-called rewards of altruism. Having a foot in each camp, art therapists are, of necessity, caught up in these struggles and must, if change is to be effected, stand in solidarity with trade unionists in both sections (health and education). *No illusions of professionalism* should be allowed to cloud their common interests. [This was prepared by the officers, John Henzell and Rupert Cracknell, with the NUT's help]

Here we can note the reference to the dichotomy discussed by Ozga and Lawn (p.126) between professionalism and unionism. This statement seems to have been addressed to the membership as a reminder that, in voting to be a Central Association of NUT, it had pledged its support for union activities and that these might include supporting other groups in their demands for improved pay and conditions. Although in the period following the signing of the affiliation agreement there were no outward signs of dissent, correspondence in the BAAT files around 1968, 1969, and 1970 show that there were beginning to be considerable stresses and strains in the association over the focus on determining career and salary structures as opposed to the 'learned society' objects. Council meetings of that period became long and fraught in the face of the prolonged campaign over salaries. It seemed that, for the Council at least, 'profes-

Organisation and status

sionalism' had become synonymous with acquiring a career and salary structure comparable with adult education lecturers or recognition of art therapists' own employment aspirations by the DES and DHSS.

By 1970, however, little progress had been made. The negotiations between BAAT and the NUT were being conducted by the Chair, (then Frank Breakwell), John Henzell, Rupert Cracknell, and Michael Edwards, who had just begun to run an option in art therapy for trainee teachers at the School of Art Education in Birmingham.

On 24 September 1970, Breakwell wrote to Bernard Mawby of the NUT, saying that it was becoming urgent for the LEAs to take over from the NHS the payment of art therapists' fees in hospitals and that he and Michael Edwards would like to meet Mawby. A meeting was arranged for October, and Breakwell reported the outcome in a letter to Joyce Laing of 19 October:

> The general strategy that Mawby suggested was that we set up a pressure group in the House of Commons. To this end he will get in touch with and give an outline of our case to Michael Roberts, MP for Cardiff (Con) and Barry Jones, MP for Flint (L).
>
> After this we will see the MPs and explain our case in further detail, and proceeding from this to a discussion of further strategy. This will include BAAT members contacting and putting our case to: MPs, individual constituency MPs, anyone who has influence with MPs, and any MPs who have been at the receiving end of art therapy, or whose family are connected with it in any way. Mawby quoted the case of teachers of handicapped children who had a powerful ready-made pressure group as several MPs or their close relations had handicapped children.

A need for urgency: the St Albans factor

In 1969, St Albans School of Art introduced a pilot course entitled 'Certificate in Remedial Art' which was open not only to art graduates and teachers but also to paramedical staff and nurses. Adamson was appointed art therapy consultant. The entry requirements for the course cut across BAAT's membership criteria, namely graduate status and art teaching qualifications and, in admitting people without an art or art teaching qualifications, posed a very serious problem in the negotiations to have art therapists paid by LEAs and compared to adult education lecturers rather than to OTs.

One of the reasons offered by the principal for starting such a pilot course at St Albans School of Art was that the college was in the centre of a large number of psychiatric and mental handicap hospitals, some of

137

Beginning of organised activity

which were employing art therapists on *ad hoc* scales. The principal had gained some support from these hospitals for the option of a training in course in art therapy, or remedial art as it was called then, but on condition that the course admitted paramedical and nursing staff as well as art graduates. There may well have been other reasons, though, to do with the position of the college within the general trend of art education at the time, stemming from the Coldstream Report.

The influence of the *Coldstream Report* on art college policy

It is useful to look at this development in the context of art and design education during the 1960s.

Art and design education was, with the exception of certain private and university institutions, the responsibility of local authorities and took place in art schools and colleges. The number of such colleges had declined annually from 180 in 1959 to 125 in 1969 and 111 in 1970 (Francis and Warren Piper 1973).

The *Coldstream Report* brought about important changes in the structure and content of art education, resulting in the National Diploma in Design and its two-year post-A level foundation element, the intermediate Certificate, being replaced by a new qualification, the Diploma in Art and Design (DipAD), which was to be taught in several different 'study areas' – e.g. fine art, textiles, ceramics, industrial design, etc. Throughout the 1960s, a validating body, under the chairmanship of Sir John Summerson, visited all the art colleges in Britain to determine which ones could offer the new DipAD, and in which study areas. Some were approved to offer fine art only, others fine art and graphics, and some gained approval in several areas. In spite of an impressive foundation course and popularity among students, St Albans School of Art did not receive permission to run it at all. Probably the main reason for this was to do with the prejudice that was developing against small art colleges which could not easily merge with larger institutions, thus offering the facilities of such. The college was required to develop its 'vocational' courses instead. The decisions of the Summerson Committee caused much bitterness in art schools throughout the country, as 'vocational' courses were, due to snobbery about 'pure' as opposed to 'applied' arts, regarded as lower in status than the new degree-level Diploma in Art and Design, which during the 1960s also qualified graduates to teach art in schools, although later an art teacher's certificate or diploma was needed as well. St Albans School of Art, which had previously offered a foundation course, an Intermediate Certificate and an NDD, was, in common with many other small art schools, left with its foundation course, a number of NDD-level art and design programmes and a problem of mounting additional vocational courses to keep the school open.

138

Organisation and status

These problems were noted by the ATTI (*Bulletin* March 1971):

A related and equally disquieting feature of the (Coldstream-Summerson) report is its assumption than non-Diploma art education, much of which caters for less educationally privileged young people, is justified only to the extent that it satisfies known skilled-manpower demand and that some courses for the Diploma should likewise be tailored to match, both in size and content, industrial 'needs' as they are at present conceived by industry and commerce.

(ATTI: 1971)

The issue of survival for non-DipAD approved colleges was, then, paramount, and an opportunity presented itself to St Albans in the form of remedial art, with its possibility of meeting health service manpower needs. Referring to Ben-David and Collins's discussion, in relation to psychology, of the growth of new ideas (1966: 452), I suggest that art therapy gave the college the means of establishing a new identity and its staff new occupational roles. (This issue will be considered in more detail in Part V, but it is essential to note it here as it had a profound effect on future negotiations for a career and salary structure for art therapists.)

Breakwell, in his letter to Joyce Laing of October 1970, alludes to the 'problems arising from the St Albans students and the difficulty of doing anything about it'. However, he saw that 'the problem' could be ameliorated in two possible ways:

a) by getting the Birmingham and London University postgraduate courses under way;
b) by persuading the LEAs to require higher qualifications than the St Albans course was reckoned to give, being, technically speaking, a certificated course at vocational level.

He thus presents exclusionary strategies, designed to prevent BAAT's mission from being diverted. Behind the anxiety over the St Albans' course was a fear that nurses and occupational therapists who were able to gain entry, though not in large numbers, would acquire a certificate in art therapy and return to the NHS to use it as part of their own professional work (as a series of techniques) thus preventing the emergence of a new occupational group of art therapists.

BAAT council was alarmed not only by the fact that this course had started with no regard to the negotiations already taking place with LEAs, but that their former chair, Adamson, was its art therapy consultant. This position did not seem to conflict with Adamson's usual way of working (at Netherne) because he was required to act as 'art therapist' to students on the course. As explained in Chapter 6, Adamson did not appear to be particularly interested in the psychological aspects of art, and he did not change his views while at St Albans. For their 'art therapy' experience,

139

Beginning of organised activity

students had a studio and worked individually, occasionally discussing their work with Adamson:

One interviewee who was a student during Adamson's time said:

We had an on-going group.... It was run in a totally non-directive way as in certain clinical settings. It was a Monday morning. We came and painted and at two o'clock you went for dinner, and the tutor would come in and say something like 'What are you going to do next?' That was it. There was no therapy between student and tutor. Not as I would have liked.

Another said:

Well, Edward Adamson was doing art therapy, which was one morning for three hours. The whole course sat in this big studio. I can remember quite clearly that we only did painting. For some reason he disapproved of clay being used, or any other materials. So we sat there and painted. I remember thinking the whole time that there was going to be some sort of revelation at the end of the year because we just sat and worked while he wandered around with his hands behind his back. I remember everybody thought that at the end of the year it was all going to be explained. It never was.

Despite the fact that the Principal was invited to and gave a talk at the BAAT EGM held at the Royal College of Art in 1971 on the rationale for the course, there was virtually no contact between St Albans and BAAT until 1975.

Maintaining the split

It is interesting to contemplate why neither side made any effort to pool experience and work together, nor to ascertain exactly what the other's position was. The systems model of group interaction proposed by Agazarian and Peters (1981) comes in useful here, in trying to understand what purpose was served by this evasive action by both sides, when, on the face of it, it should have been in both's interests, and in the interests of 'art therapy', to liaise. Such a situation is often seen in therapy or training groups, when the group-as-a-whole evades the central task of the group (to interact and understand both individual and group processes) by setting up two distinct sub-groups who will each engage in spinning fantasies about the other, or two members who will make projections about each other, never stopping to test them out. For both groups this avoids looking at the splits, or dissensions, within the sub-groups, which might threaten to destroy them.

Another reason is that having a new course which would enhance its vocational status was so vital to St Albans that the college had no interest

Organisation and status

in BAAT and its negotiations, but only in promoting the new art therapy course to as wide a group of applicants as possible. For St Albans, a long-established and well-recruiting art school, the inability to offer degree-level courses as a result of the Summerson inspection must have been a huge blow to staff morale. As a small college with no graduate or postgraduate work, facing growing cuts in funding for further education, the desire to be first in the field with a new vocational course, and one which could gain the support of the DHSS, may well have overridden any qualms about cutting across work already in hand by BAAT (which was dismissed as 'a group of teachers' thus misunderstanding the reasons for the alliance). (It was not only St Albans' staff who perceived BAAT in this way: one art therapist interviewed, who joined BAAT in 1972, said

> I was giving talks on art therapy and I gave a couple at the ICA. At one of them DH came up to me and I said, tell me about BAAT. I had heard at the Maudsley that there was an art therapy association but didn't really connect myself to it as I got the feeling that it was very union, or had to do with art teachers.... Unions were somewhere in the mists of time.)

Within BAAT (as seen from correspondence and records of council meetings) there was far from total agreement with the policy to align with art education and the NUT, and to devote energy and finance to 'politics' rather than 'learned society' functions. The council's view of 'professionalism' was, as already stated, to achieve a career and salary structure equivalent to that of adult education lecturers, but there was a growing body of members who construed 'professionalism' differently and thought it could be achieved through seminars, conferences, exhibitions, etc. Having the 'threat' of St Albans and their graduates united BAAT members, whose chair was ill and finding it hard to maintain the stress of the political negotiations.

The 'philosophical' position of art therapy was also an issue. As already mentioned, many members of BAAT held strong anti-psychiatry views, seeing art therapy as an alternative to traditional, drug-orientated psychiatric treatment. St Albans was appearing to encourage the view that art therapy was a 'paramedical' service – in the eyes of many BAAT members this was equivalent to approving of the despised 'medical model' of psychiatry. So the assumptions were formed and remained for several years, that BAAT was 'a group of teachers' and St Albans 'a collusion with the medical model of psychiatry'.

Whatever the reasons, the development of the new certificate course at the same time as Frank Breakwell's illness and subsequent death posed many difficulties for BAAT.

141

Beginning of organised activity

The campaign intensifies

Frank Breakwell became ill shortly after his last meeting at the NUT and the MPs who were contacted by Bernard Mawby do not appear to have taken any action. In the minutes of council of 16 October 1971, when Michael Edwards had become chair, there was a minute referring to the NUT:

> Graham Cable and Diane Waller had visited Alex Chappell (at NUT) but not much had been gained by this visit. Mr. Chappell had suggested we get in touch with a Mr. Maxwell of the Salaries Department with a prepared case for NUT to consider. Graham said he and Diane would be looking into this.

In January (minutes of 15 January 1972), though, it seems that Cable had withdrawn from the negotiations and his place had been taken by Mary Newton. She was a graduate in fine art from Reading University and had established the art studio at the Albany Community Centre in Deptford before taking up a part-time art therapy post at the Paddington Day Centre, where she was later joined by myself as the other part-time therapist. Since the Paddington Institute had an enlightened approach to employing art therapists, both of us had a clear model of the way that art therapists could function within adult education, and were eager to take up negotiations with the NUT.

Mary Newton and myself had visited Frank Maxwell, and he had agreed to what seemed like a shift in policy, in that he was prepared to look into the possibility of negotiating with the Whitley Council (which handled health service pay and conditions) to see if a rate for art therapists comparable to the Burnham rate for teachers in special schools could be agreed. In hindsight, it seems strange that such an unlikely proposition could have been put forward, given the structure of the Whitley Council and the lack of NUT representation on it. But it was seized upon by BAAT council who were becoming demoralised at their lack of progress and had little experience of the way that the NHS professions were managed.

Maxwell helped BAAT to draw up a questionnaire to be sent to BAAT members in order to obtain more detailed information about their qualifications, pay and conditions of service. A minute notes: 'Mr Maxwell was most concerned at the appalling state of affairs and agreed that we urgently needed to regularise pay and conditions' (15 January 1972).

Given the suggestion by Maxwell to commence negotiations with the Whitley Council, it was becoming urgent for BAAT to have a clearer policy on requirements for full membership and qualified art therapist status. This would have to take into account St Albans graduates who were a fact of life. There were two sets of graduates trying to obtain jobs in the NHS and elsewhere: one set approved by BAAT, the others not. This was

142

Organisation and status

seen by BAAT council, according to the minutes of 1971–2, as potentially very damaging to any aspirations for 'professional status', and certainly to the campaign for improved salaries and conditions.

Affiliation and training

The council set up a sub-committee, called the 'Affiliation and Training Sub-Committee', chaired by Michael Edwards. At its first meeting the committee examined the 'Professional Associations' section in the handbook on British qualifications and found that BAAT did not seem to fit exactly into any of the three categories of association listed, but that it was nearest to the 'Occupational Associations' category. The committee had also drawn up suggestions for full membership criteria as follows: intending full members should possess:

a) a first degree or equivalent with art as a major study, plus one of the following options –
 i) a period of, say, two years in an art therapy post;
 ii) ATD at Birmingham or similar college offering art therapy as an option;
 iii) St Albans Certificate in Remedial Art.

The certificate in Remedial Art would be accepted only if an applicant had an art degree initially. Those with nursing or OT qualifications, for example, would not. This inclusion of the Certificate was contentious, because it was seen to weaken BAAT's case and the sub-committee's suggestions remained 'on the table' and not ratified.

Bucher and Strauss's (1961: 330) discussion of 'colleagueship' is interesting to consider here. They cite Gross, who writes about the colleague group 'being in the same boat' and being fostered by such things as control of entry to the occupation, development of a unique mission, shared attitudes towards clients and society, and the formation of informal and formal associations (Gross 1958: 223–35).

Such a conception of colleagueship stresses occupational unity and, once entry to the occupation is controlled, it is assumed that members can be colleagues, rallying around common symbols. (Bucher and Strauss point out, however, that those very aspects of occupational life which Gross writes about as unifying the profession can also break it into segments, for when a person's group develops a unique mission, he may no longer share a mission with others in the same profession.) That art graduate holders of the Certificate should even be considered suggests that there was a wish on behalf of some BAAT members at least to include some of the St Albans graduates (i.e. the artists) as colleagues, even at the risk of breaking down BAAT's own case.

Beginning of organised activity

Progress in fulfilling objects

In his AGM report of 1970–1, Frank Breakwell had presented BAAT membership with an assessment of how far the aims and objects had been fulfilled. He reported that there were ninety-six full members and thirty associates and that the number of art therapists working in mental hospitals remained roughly stationary, while the number of art therapists (or specialist art teachers) in the educational field had increased strongly: 'This latter development is one which is to be welcomed most warmly.'

He also mentioned that the affiliation between the Society for Art Education and BAAT had been strengthened, and that BAAT members had played 'a fairly considerable part' in an international congress organised by the International Society for Education through Art (INSEA) in Coventry. BAAT had affiliated with the Association for Workers with Maladjusted Children, through contacts made by Elizabeth Wills. He noted that his request in the newsletter for views on the possibility of affiliating with or integrating with therapists in non-visual media had not been well responded to, adding that 'most Council members would be in favour of a close integration if the opportunity arises'. We see here a tentative move towards 'therapy' although the educational links were strongest and most welcomed.

As far as publications and events were concerned, the journal *Inscape* was appearing twice a year, several talks and a showing of a film by Dr John Birtchnell about a patient treated through art therapy had been arranged by BAAT; and an exhibition and talks at Eton School (on the invitation of the head of the art department who was interested in art therapy) had taken place.

A large section of Breakwell's report was devoted to the training issue and listing the current trainings acceptable to BAAT (Diploma in Art Education and ATD, which had art therapy options, and the Diploma in the Psychology of Childhood, all at the University of Birmingham School of Art Education). Breakwell noted that 'Other courses would however have to be considered carefully and with considerable wariness by BAAT.' The Certificate of Remedial Art was described as being 'of a much lower standard than the qualified teacher status required of full members of BAAT'. (This reflects the ambivalence in BAAT towards the Certificate despite the Affiliation and Training Sub-Committee's tentative suggestion to include it.)

Progress of the salaries campaign was notified, together with the rationale for continuing to press for art therapists to be employed by LEAs. This ended with a warning:

> The danger of these other courses is that they will provide graduates with too low a standard of qualifications and these graduates will not be qualified teacher status. They will have to accept MoH rates and

Organisation and status

consequently will be undercutting the LEA rates. This might well nullify our efforts to come under the aegis of the LEAs.

It is worth noting here that in July 1971, salaries for *ad hoc* grades including art therapists were notified to secretaries of regional hospital boards, hospital management committees, and boards of governors by the DHSS as follows:

Officers with some recognised qualification engaged in music therapy, art therapy, etc.;
sessional rate under supervision from £2.32 to £2.53 per 3 hours;
sessional rate single-handed from £2.70 to £2.97 per 3 hours;
for a 36-hour week £843–£1191 and £954–£1407 respectively.

This was better than the rate for handicraft teachers who got £2.00 and £2.18 per three hours but less than that for technical instructors who got £1104 to £1398 respectively. It was approximately half the rate paid to adult education tutors, although they could not be employed full time. The salaries of art therapists under the DHSS were 10 per cent less than those of occupational therapists (from DHSS Circular K/063/01B 6 July 1971).

The most crucial issues needing to be addressed, then, were those of full membership criteria and the development of training to produce art therapists who could claim parity with teachers, in order to back up the campaign for a career structure which was to include negotiations with the DHSS in the form of the Whitley Council. This implied taking into account the Certificate in Remedial Art at St Albans and a decision being made by BAAT as to whether or not to include the Certificate as a qualifying course in the case of persons having graduate art qualifications before entering the course.

Chapter sixteen

Some problems and contradictions within the campaign for employment under the LEAs

When considering the objects of the constitution and the ways in which BAAT was setting about achieving them during the late 1960s and early 1970s, it appears that there were some contradictions between the object of being incorporated into the state system of health and education services yet at the same time having the (unstated) object of retaining that aspect of art therapy which appeared to challenge 'traditional' attitudes in medicine and psychiatry. These contradictions produced conflicts within BAAT and the art therapy movement as a whole. Such contradictions were also faced by community artists and Owen Kelly in *Community, Art and the State: Storming the Citadels* makes the following observations, which seem relevant to the issue under discussion:

> What I am saying is that, regardless of the motivations and abilities of individuals working within them, at an institutional level the health service and the educational system are agencies of the centralised state and can be seen to behave as such. Thus doctors, whatever their personal beliefs, are obliged, by interlocking systems of legal rules and social expectations, to license illness.... teachers are obliged to license access to job opportunities and career structures through the licensing of certificates and diplomas.
>
> (Kelly 1984: 73)

Kelly places the development of many 'caring' services, each centrally determined and staffed by professional workers in the category of 'Radical Monopolies'. He cites as an example advice centres, where 'advice workers' had a quasi-official standing which served to 'exclude a number of other possible approaches to the same problem'. Kelly contends that there was no longer any point in tenants' associations forming their own advice networks of getting together to solve problems. Instead, they were given centrally produced pamphlets which contained predetermined solutions to their problems.

Many art therapists who were pioneers and active in the 1960s and 1970s in the organisational and political tasks of BAAT saw art therapy

146

Problems and contradictions

as a 'radical' element in the treatment of psychiatric or emotional disturbances, in that it encouraged patients to make choices, to feel they had the power to change, to take some responsibility for their own 'cure'. It was felt that to encourage patients to make full use of whatever artistic creativity they possessed would enable them to improve their potential for expression and communication, and to have some control over their own lives. This was in contrast to treatments which required taking anti-depressants and tranquillisers in large quantities or undergoing physical treatments like ECT. In other words, art therapists would not wish to be in the position of the 'advice workers' in offering predetermined solutions to life problems.

Yet, at the same time, they sough recognition by the State. The following quotes, to be found in articles, lectures, catalogue notes and interviews with art therapists and psychiatrists, are typical sentiments expressed by those working in the 1960s and 1970s:

> To many people whose contact with the world may be deeply threatening, no one before may have bothered to find out what their sense of private 'nonsense' is about. Just to mirror back feelings gives a sense of validation and appropriately timed interpretations may link previously unconnected feelings as insight.... We act as a bridge not only between a client's inner and outer world, while he may not yet be able to do so for himself, but also between himself and his outer social world... a connecting link but not a betraying one.
>
> (P. Gulliver *Inscape* 1 (15))

> So too the skill of the art therapist lies in offering oneself in an undogmatic way so as to catch the imagination of the patient without confusing it.... While one's opinions influence oneself and one's work, they should not overrule what the patient can say for himself.... We should be like our materials – involving, exciting and easy to use.
>
> (C. Walker, Exhibition Catalogue *The Inner Eye*, Oxford 1978)

> I realise now that the atmosphere I tried to create was something like that of my kitchen at home – a warm place, with an informal atmosphere in which people could feel free to come and go as they pleased.... During my time at the hospital, I saw that each person found his own way of expressing himself and his own way of working, each making use of the resources of my own personality and experience.
>
> (L. Doran *As We See It*, 1977)

> I find myself involved with the personality of the pupil through teaching him or her the technique of the job and I suppose it is in this way we make contact with one another.
>
> (J. Herbert *Art in Hospitals* Catalogue, 1972)

Beginning of organised activity

Aesthetic value judgements were not imposed on the work and the only valid interpretation was the client's own. Each person in turn talked about his work and if he said that he painted an eagle though it might look like a bath duck to an outside observer – during the session it remained an eagle.

(M. Rytovaara *Inscape* 1 (12))

I would remove the work when they were finished so that the prison staff did not get hold of it because they would have been tormented with non-sensical remarks about their work, and so confidentiality grew up between me and the prisoners. That was fine, but, obviously, alongside this grew up the paranoia from the staff – what was going on in that room with this artist and these fellows?

(Interview with art therapist describing work in early 1970s)

With some, I felt my function was to teach them to draw and paint, but with others, I seemed to be confidante, someone who was sufficiently removed from the ordinary hospital system to be in an odd, special position. So I seemed to receive stories from people and I was good at listening, probably because I was interested in what people were saying.

(Interview describing work in the mid-1960s)

An interpretation made within the context of the relationship, when the patient has the chance to acknowledge it, may, if well timed, be very important to the development of the therapy. Interpretations made outside this relationship may be inspired guesses or wildly inaccurate projections of the therapist's own inner state. In either case they are probably of little use to the person who painted the picture.

(D. Waller *Myths and Reality*, 1976)

It goes without saying that art therapy should have nothing to do with orthodox, mental hospital, medical model psychiatry.

(Dr J. Birtchnell 'Alternative concepts in art therapy',
Inscape 1 (15))

The art therapy department in a psychiatric hospital is often an asylum within an asylum. That is to say, it is a refuge from the depersonalising manoeuvres of a large institution and its agents.

(R. Holtom, Exhibition Catalogue *The Inner Eye*, 1978)

Does lack of structure mean that you are not making decisions for the patient but allowing him to be responsible for himself and for making his own decisions? You are giving him back control, the control of his life, which in so many other areas of the hospital is not considered, so extreme is the emphasis on organisation and collective activities.

(B. Warsi *What is Creativity?*, 1977)

Problems and contradictions

These quotes are included to illustrate the point that among art therapists at this time there was a strong sense of being engaged in an activity which challenged the *status quo* of medicine, and especially that of psychiatry. Influenced no doubt by events and attitudes of the 1960s, they invested art therapy with the potential to make changes in society as a whole. In this respect they had much in common with Hill, Petrie, *et al.*, having the vision of a new society, regenerated through art.

However, art therapists had come to expect to be paid well for their work. Otherwise, it was feared, wealthy amateurs ('do-gooders') in the tradition of British charities would move in and offer a kind of 'art appreciation class' designed to take culture to the 'deprived' (see Jones 1987: 34–5 for elaboration). (These fears had arisen as a result of several applications for BAAT membership which had come from persons with no qualifications in art or other disciplines, who wanted to 'help' with art and craft activities, and saw art therapy as a 'voluntary service'. On the one hand, these people were seen as being 'altruistic' and, on the other, as a problem, because they propagated the view of art therapy as being a 'hobby' or harmless pastime.)

Attempts to have art therapists state funded, as opposed to privately funded (as in the USA for instance) sprang partly from a desire to make this radical form of therapy available to all who needed it regardless of their financial circumstances. This was also the case with community artists, who wished to be engaged with local communities in the same way. Kelly points to a problem which these artists faced, and continue to face, over the issue of state funding:

> However vaguely community artists had defined their actions they had mostly nursed the desire to help achieve a movement within society towards equality of opportunity, social justice and communal self-determination. These aspirations were, in political terms, left-wing, and sprang from ideas about the nature of organisation and power within society which were also left-wing. Now that community arts was established as a legitimate area of state concern, there was no longer any reason why this should be so, and indeed, given the aura of neutrality with which the state's activities are cloaked, every reason why this should not be so.... What it actually does, of course, is to signal the demise of community arts as a radical, partisan activism and herald its arrival as one of the caring professions.
>
> (Kelly 1984: 36).

While not articulating these contradictions, it seems that there was an awareness of the issues among BAAT officers as there was much emphasis (in minutes of Council meetings, discussions, etc.) on the avoidance of the 'hierarchical' structure of the NHS. Being employed by a LEA as a specialist art teacher was seen as one way of being able to

Beginning of organised activity

work but avoiding participating in the hierarchy; in other words, maintaining some autonomy by not fitting in with any structure. Although there was a certain naivety in holding on to this perception, it enabled art therapists to continue to press their claim for total state funding through the LEAs, and to identity with 'progressive' art education models, without being overwhelmed by the contradictions in their position.

Chapter seventeen

First moves towards the Health Service

On 20 December 1973, BAAT received a letter from E. L. McMillan, stating that, in March 1973, the Secretary of State for Health, concerned at the problems facing the remedial professions and the lack of solutions to them, had set up an informal working party to make recommendations about the future role of and training for these professions. Some of the problems were to do with poor recruitment and wastage of staff, and with the organisation of the professions (including remedial gymnasts, physiotherapists, OTs, orthoptists and dietitians). McMillan enclosed a copy of the working party's report which considered the relationship between therapists and a number of other professions, including psychiatrists.

Paragraph 33 of the report referred to art therapists as a 'linked profession' with OT. A response was sent from BAAT, indicating its aim of establishing art therapy as a separate service from OT, since the function and training of an art therapist was very different and more closely linked with that of an art teacher in a special school.

A reply was received from McMillan, mentioning that 'more substantive guidance was needed' and that the DHSS was proposing to issue a health services circular on the operation and development of the remedial professions and linked therapies (Letter to BAAT, 13 March 1974).

Rejection of 'linked' status

This was the start of art therapy being referred to by the DHSS as a 'linked therapy' (to OT); it did not receive any support from art therapists, and made the campaign with the NUT all the more pressing.

At a meeting on 8 June 1974, Frank Maxwell reported on progress. There seemed to be three possibilities open to BAAT to continue the campaign:

1. presentation of a case to the DHSS for assimilation to the Whitley Council or

Beginning of organised activity

2. to the DES for payment on further education scales or
3. to the Halsbury Committee which was investigating nurses' pay, having been commissioned by Barbara Castle, then Labour social services secretary, following persistent action by nurses over pay.

The first possibility was considered most unpromising by BAAT. Art therapists employed by the DHSS were paid on the Professional and Technical 'A' *ad hoc* rates, which were 10 per cent lower than OTs' salaries and had only two categories, single-handed and under supervision. In any case, art therapists did not wish to become part of the NHS hierarchy, as they saw it.

The third possibility was more or less ruled out, because art therapists did not see themselves as linked to nurses, nor did they wish to be involved in nurses' pay disputes.

The second one, in which BAAT and the NUT would present their case direct to the DES, had more appeal in that art therapists might be eligible for secondment to the NHS under the adult education umbrella as part of the education in hospitals provision.

The Paddington Centre for Psychotherapy art therapists' case was a good one on which to try to base a future structure, despite the problems and insecurities of sessional employment.

By this time, June 1974, the BAAT–NUT questionnaires had come back from members, an 85 per cent return. The position was:

81 returns: 27 men, 54 women;
55 worked in hospitals;
16 in schools;
10 in other employment;
47 were referred to as art therapists; 20 as teachers; 6 as occupational therapists or OT aides; 8 had other titles – e.g. instructor, creative therapist, group worker, etc.

This information, together with a booklet giving a short history of art therapy and stating the arguments prepared by BAAT and the NUT previously, was sent to the NUT for forwarding to the appropriate section of the DES.

Rationale and proposals for having art therapy established and financed under local education authorities

In 1970, as stated in Chapter 15, BAAT and the NUT had prepared a detailed case for having art therapists employed by local education authorities, due, in part, to the attitude of the then MoH towards art therapy, i.e. seeing it as part of OT. Extracts from letters to BAAT from the MoH contained statements such as:

152

Moving towards the NHS

The work of occupational therapists, however, covers a wide range of patients and activities whereas the scope of the art therapist is limited. For this reason their scales are lower than those of qualified occupational therapists.

(9 July 1968)

It has not been thought possible to draw a distinction between the work done by art therapists on the one hand and occupational therapists on the other which justify fixing the remuneration of the former at a rate in excess of that fixed for the latter by the Whitley Council Agreement. [This letter also claimed that the third year of the occupational therapy training was designed to enable students to gain a knowledge of arts and crafts.]

(14 December 1966)

There was clearly a difference of opinion between the MoH and BAAT/NUT on the nature of art therapy and on the function of art therapists in relation to OTs. BAAT argued against the MoH view, accusing it of being 'curiously narrow in its definition of both education and therapy', citing a previous MoH letter of 14 August 1964.

The MoH had already refused to countenance paying Burnham rates for art therapists, pointing out that

whereby the local authority is providing a service for the hospital, those art therapists are not employed by the hospital, and the Remuneration and Conditions of Service Regulations 1951 do not cover them.

(Eastern Region Hospital Board, 5 July 1968)

So it was argued by BAAT that LEAs should take over responsibility for the employment or secondment of all art therapists, whether they worked in LEA schools, hospitals, clinics, or Home Office establishments, and the conditions of employment should be analogous to those for teachers in special schools and further education. In brief, the aim was to have art therapists employed full time within the NHS or other treatment settings, on Burnham salaries and accountable to the senior medical officer, usually the consultant psychiatrist. The local education authorities would need, therefore, to liaise with the hospital and finance such art therapy provision as was required.

Liaison with St Albans graduates begins

At a meeting on 31 August 1974, Maxwell reported that 'some discussion about art therapy had already taken place between the DHSS and the DES'. This was in connection with the St Albans' course, as the college was seeking DHSS approval for it and the DES had approached the DHSS concerning job prospects for graduates. (In the section on training, we

Beginning of organised activity

shall see how the issue of post-course employment played an important role in the approval or not of new courses under the regional advisory committee structure in the public sector of higher education.) BAAT sent a copy of their booklet, and so on, to the DHSS in view of these discussions.

In October, BAAT received a letter from the student representative of the remedial art course, suggesting a meeting to discuss the course and their association with BAAT. An informal meeting was held, BAAT being represented by myself and John Tagg, and the students by Pam Gulliver, Gayleen Preston, and Andrew Rennie. It so happened that those meeting found themselves in total agreement about their aspirations for art therapy: that is, that it should become a postgraduate profession, totally separate from OT; that art therapists should be first and foremost artists; that art therapy should be a radical force in the treatment of mental illness. Most of the working party members and the BAAT representatives had left-wing politics in common, and were active trade unionists. By that time, BAAT members, and particularly the council, were becoming frustrated by a seven-year campaign to try to improve art therapists' conditions through comparisons with an art education model, and the St Albans representatives were frustrated by low pay and status, and the 'medical model' of psychiatry taught at the college.

Gayleen Preston was invited to attend a BAAT council meeting on 23 November 1974, where she spoke about the working party set up by the student body. This group 'wished to be under the umbrella of BAAT and did not want a division in British art therapy. There was increasing awareness that the two bodies shared interests' (Minutes, 23 November 1974).

At the informal meeting, and at the council, the issue of BAAT's link with the NUT had been discussed at length and the reasons for BAAT being a Central Association of NUT explained. The students had suggested that a more promising link would be with the Association of Scientific, Technical and Managerial Staff (ASTMS), a union operating in the Health Service which had seats on the Whitley Council, a left-wing, TUC orientation, and had been negotiating for speech therapists who were in a similar situation to that of art therapists. Coincidentally, I had several friends working for the union, so agreed to make an informal approach. By this time it was becoming clear that the NUT was not in a position to further BAAT's cause, due to problems arising through cuts in adult education provision and their involvement with the Houghton Committee on teachers' pay. The NUT was, however, invaluable to BAAT in instructing the council on how to mount a campaign through both parliament and pressure on civil servants in relevant ministries.

Moving towards the NHS

BAAT begins to withdraw from the NUT

On 13 January 1975, Michael Edwards, then chair of BAAT, received a letter from Maxwell at the NUT. He had obtained a copy of the report of the Committee of Inquiry into the Pay and Related Conditions of Service of the Professions Supplementary to Medicine and Speech Therapists:

> As far as I can find, there is no mention in the document of Art Therapists and the way is therefore clear for us (the Union and the Association) to submit representations to the two Secretaries of State for Education and Science and for Health and Social Security.
>
> I am sorry that the pressures on the Union regarding the Houghton Committee's Report made it impossible for us to submit the formal evidence to the Halsbury Committee, but I have kept in touch as you know with the Secretariat of the Halsbury Committee.
>
> We must make the next move quickly to pre-empt PTA committee from making decisions as a result of the Halsbury Committee's Report.

In February the NUT proposed to raise the membership subscriptions of affiliated organisations by £1.25 per person. This represented a considerable increase and the council felt it would be resented by BAAT members. Since the NUT's failure to submit evidence to the Halsbury Committee (even though this tactic had been agreed in a lukewarm manner by BAAT) there were strong feelings in the council, noted in the February council minutes, that 'we have missed the boat... it was thought that BAAT's position needed to be clarified before the AGM on 26 April and concerning that Michael Edwards agreed to write to Edward Britten of the NUT'.

In the same minutes, a note appears about area reorganisations in the NHS, stating that paramedical staff would have their own representatives at meetings of area administration:

> Art therapists need to get their standing as paramedicals ratified by their district administrator otherwise there was a danger of them being categorised as 'link' therapists and unable to attend meetings in their own right.
>
> (22 February 1975)

This is the first acknowledgement in any minutes, or in any BAAT document, that art therapists might consider themselves as 'paramedicals'. There was no challenge to this term in the minutes, which suggests that, with the new support from the St Albans graduates' working party and the disillusionment with the 'educational' campaign, moves towards the NHS were becoming more attractive.

The NUT had recommended that individual BAAT members write to their MPs, drawing attention to the poor salaries and conditions of service

155

Beginning of organised activity

of art therapists generally. A letter which the MP for Warrington received from T. Alec Jones of the DHSS explained that the terms of reference of the 'Halsbury Report' applied only to the professions supplementary to medicine and to speech therapists, including only classes to staff already covered by the Whitley agreements, so no recommendations had been made for art therapists. However, the letter continued:

> We have fully accepted that the salaries of art therapists would need to be re-examined in the light of any agreements reached by the Whitley Council on the basis of the Committee's recommendations, and as Mr. Naylor (BAAT member) says, the Whitley agreement following the Committee's interim recommendations in the autumn was in turn quickly followed by an interim award to art therapists. Consequential improvements for art therapists are under urgent consideration and will be promulgated as soon as possible similarly backdated to May 1974.
>
> ((PO/H) 1476/4, 17 March 1975)

This was the most sympathetic letter received to date from the DHSS, albeit concerned only with salaries and not with the status of art therapy in the NHS.

A note on the state of art therapy training

Because art therapists had seen themselves as a postgraduate group, on the same level as graduates with Art Teacher's Diplomas, the question of admission criteria to the St Albans course had been a very central one. By 1975, it appeared that St Albans, too, was admitting mainly graduates and only a small number of nurses and occupational therapists. Two other art therapy trainings had emerged in the 1970s:

a) The Option in Art Therapy, run by Michael Edwards since 1969 in the School of Art Education, initially of Birmingham University and later of Birmingham Polytechnic. This was part of the postgraduate Art Teacher's Diploma course and catered for about twelve students who did some of their teaching practice in hospitals and special schools as well as having seminars and workshops in art therapy.

b) The Option in Art Therapy, run by Diane Waller at Goldsmiths' College as part of the postgraduate Art Teacher's Certificate. This had a similar format to the Birmingham option at first, but fairly rapidly began to separate itself from the ATC course and in 1975 plans were formulated for a full-time Diploma in Art Therapy.

The proposed Advanced Diploma at the Institute of Education of London University had never materialised.

156

Moving towards the NHS

All these developments will be discussed at length later, but need to be mentioned here because by 1975, there were approximately sixty art therapy 'graduates' per year emerging and seeking employment. Despite the fact that their training was part of an art teaching qualification, many of the Birmingham and Goldsmiths' students who had completed the options felt a strong allegiance to art therapy as opposed to art teaching, and indeed the options were recognised as 'qualifying programmes' by BAAT for many years. The fact that these students had a 'double' qualification was understandably a source of aggravation to St Albans staff and graduates, as was the fact that they received mandatory awards to do an ATC/art therapy course, whereas St Albans students were obliged to seek 'discretionary' awards.

However, the moves by Goldsmiths' to establish a discrete Diploma in Art Therapy did not appear to be welcomed by St Albans, due to factors ostensibly to do with post-course employment opportunities but probably also to do with 'ownership' of the profession, and threat to the college itself if a competitor should arise in the same region.

These training issues were developing at the same time as the campaign for improved conditions was being conducted and the two were closely linked.

Parliamentary action

In June 1975, BAAT representatives, including Gayleen Preston from the St Albans working party, met Messrs Jarvis, Macavoy, and Maxwell at the NUT. The NUT undertook to write to the Secretary of State for Education, Fred Mully, and to enlist the support of sympathetic MPs in order to have a question concerning the pay and conditions of art therapists asked in the House of Commons before the end of that parliamentary session.

On 7 August 1975, R.C. Mitchell MP asked the Prime Minister whether he was satisfied with the co-ordination between the DES and the DHSS and the Home Office in regard to the employment, conditions of service, and rates of pay of art therapists, and if he would make a statement. The PM replied that the pay and conditions of employment of art therapists were determined in accordance with their respective responsibilities in different services (*Hansard* 297, 7 August 1975). This was hardly a useful reply, but it served to draw the House of Commons' attention to art therapists, which was to prove beneficial in a later campaign.

On 21 August, the Secretary of State wrote to Fred Jarvis, enclosing the answer to the question and saying that the secondment of art therapists to hospitals by the local education authorities is 'entirely a matter for them and I am sure that you will understand that there can no question of my seeking to intervene'. This news, together with the suggestion from the

157

Beginning of organised activity

NUT that Central Associations should become Local Associations, meaning that BAAT members would have to pay full subscriptions to the NUT as well as to BAAT, caused considerable despondency in the council.

At the AGM in April 1975, a proposal had been put forward and carried: 'that members instruct the Council to explore the possibilities of affiliation with other Unions than NUT'. A member had also suggested that the council should 'investigate the possibility of BAAT becoming a professional association independent of a Union', and this had been agreed.

With the lack of progress all round in the campaign, internal dissent was growing.

Internal issues

The dissent that had been present from the earliest days of BAAT concerning the priority given to its different objects was never far from the surface. By 1975 it had perhaps polarised, with the two factions being: the 'political/union faction' and the 'learned society' faction. At the April AGM, at which I was elected chair (Michael Edwards having been in that position since 1971) there was much anxiety from a group of members, represented by a letter signed by three founder members, that in the process of working for a career and salary structure and 'recognition' of art therapy within the DES and DHSS, other objects had been neglected. The letter stated that it wished to call attention to 'certain matters which are causing considerable concern to the well functioning and ultimately the reputation of the British Association of Art Therapists'. These were, briefly, to do with content and style of *Newsletters*, content and style of the journal, and lack of a permanent address. They suggested that a twelve-month programme of events should be published in each *Newsletter*, that positive support should be given by the council to local groups who should be notified of new members and associate members in their areas, and that council members should give small exhibitions, lectures, seminars, and workshops for local art therapy audiences. In short, these members proposed a shift of attention from the 'political' campaign to the 'public relations' or 'learned society' functions of BAAT.

The result of this letter and the AGM debates was that the three signatories were invited to attend the council and asked to take on some of the suggested tasks; for instance, to form a panel to edit the *Newsletter*. However, the minutes of the following council meeting note that they were not able to attend.

The 'feeling' within the council was very similar to that of the late 1960s, when the officers felt criticised and unsupported by the members for carrying out the task they had been requested to do. It was clear that

158

Moving towards the NHS

there was a group of members, and these tended to be mostly 'founder' members, who had never felt happy about BAAT's union status and would have preferred to see more attention to publications, production of a 'learned journal' (instead of *Inscape* which, between 1969 and 1980, tended to carry mostly articles of a philosophical-political stance, rather than case studies or 'research' according to a survey conducted by Andrea Gilroy and the author in 1989), and more liaison with bodies such as the Royal College of Psychiatrists.

The new council of 1975 was therefore faced with a salary campaign which seemed stuck, a probable need to leave the NUT, and, if so, a proposal to make, to present to the members, on the future structure of BAAT, They had also undertaken to oversee training and standards of professional practice, which meant liaison with St Albans School of Art and the other two training centres, and any other colleges which might wish to start art therapy training. Morale among members was low, with dissatisfaction both from the art therapy 'graduates' who were experiencing abysmal pay and conditions in the NHS and the 'founder' members, whose needs were not being met by the union orientation of BAAT at that time.

As before, the officers set up sub-committees to try to address the various objects, and a series of seminars was arranged and co-ordinated by Diana Halliday on the theme of 'Concepts and Intuitions in Art Therapy'. The salaries and conditions campaign was being co-ordinated by myself, Mary Newton, and Gayleen Preston (now treasurer), and liaison between BAAT and the Royal College of Psychiatrists and other 'clinical' organisations was conducted by John Birtchnell. *Inscape* was being edited by Dan Lumley, *Newsletter* by Michael and Ros Edwards, and Michael Pope was liaising with the NUT over BAAT's future. Other members, new to the council, assisted with increased public relations activities.

A period of co-operation and co-ordination

Between the April AGM and November, several attempts had been made to contact ATTI with a view to ascertaining if a move to that union, which represented teachers in further and higher education, would be advisable. This proved impossible. In December, an informal meeting was arranged with ASTMS.

In the meantime, Colin Hunt, principal of Hertfordshire College of Art (previously St Albans School of Art), had agreed to meet BAAT representatives for a lunch 'to see if we can work together'. The lunch was attended by Colin Hunt and John Evans, then head of the art therapy department, and by myself, Michael Edwards, and Michael Pope. The outcome was that both parties agreed to prepare a resumé of their views

159

Beginning of organised activity

on art therapy and how they would like to see BAAT develop in the future. The views were to be exchanged by letter, then another meeting arranged to discuss the matter and what could be done to the advantage of both parties. By that time, some of the 'St Albans' graduates had joined BAAT and it appeared that these graduates and the 'political' wing of BAAT were forming a powerful sub-group within the organisation. The graduates of all three programmes had made a commitment of time, money, and personal involvement in art therapy and their priority was to be respected as professional workers (not lowly paid 'handmaidens' or volunteers) and to receive a salary commensurate with the responsibilities of the job (equivalent to further education teachers).

Parliamentary campaign continues

In December 1975, myself, John Birtchnell, Gayleen Preston, and Mary Newton met Gerard Vaughan and Linda Chalker at the House of Commons. (Dr Vaughan was a consultant psychiatrist at Guy's Hospital as well as MP for Wokingham.) The aim was to persuade a government minister to take up the art therapists' cause. The result of the (cordial) meeting was that the BAAT representatives were advised to choose which ministry they wished to come under, before they could proceed.

At the following council meeting, it was proposed and agreed that contact should be made with ministers at the Department of Education. In February 1976, a letter from the Chair to the council informed them that she had been in touch with the NUT, 'expressing our anger that we are virtually in the same position this year, just before the AGM, as last. Mr. Maxwell now informs me that he is taking the following actions':

1. Adding appendices to the existing BAAT–NUT document as follows:

    a) making a comparison between the salaries of art therapists in England and Scotland (where all were paid on Burnham rates);
    b) providing evidence which BAAT had submitted to Russell and Warnock Reports;
    c) giving details about existing training programmes;
    d) information about the way in which the junior training centres had been taken over by the DES as schools for mentally handicapped children as a possible precedent for art therapy.
2. He was sending the document to DES and DHSS by 27 February 1986. Furthermore, Maxwell said that he would try to arrange a meeting between BAAT, the NUT, and 'relevant government officials' before the BAAT AGM.

Moving towards the NHS

It was clear that BAAT was reluctant to sever its links with the NUT and that the NUT was prepared to continue to support BAAT's case even though the likelihood of it succeeding in its original aims was very slim.

Chapter eighteen

Struggles for control of art therapy in the context of a Whitley Council initiative

In the previous chapter I pointed out that there was considerable disillusionment with the strategies which BAAT had been using, in co-operation with the NUT, to gain recognition for art therapy and improvements in salaries and conditions. Moves had begun to reopen talks with the DHSS, even though there were many reservations about seeking comparable status with paramedical professions.

For some time the DHSS had been wishing to 'regulate' the employment of groups termed '*ad hoc*'. If a hospital wanted to employ, say, an art therapist, the hospital administrator had firstly to seek permission to do so from the DHSS, stating which part of the budget would be used to pay the employee. This was an unwieldy system, and administratively time-consuming. So in March 1976, the Management Side of the Whitley Council wrote to the Staff Side, proposing that the Council should consider a joint initiative to investigate the feasibility of allocating the '*ad hoc*' grades in the NHS to the General Whitley Council. Those grades which could be assimilated would then have their own career and salary structure laid down by the Council, and there would be no need for the DHSS to be involved at the time of employment.

The Whitley Council itself is a fairly cumbersome institution in the health service. It is the body which is responsible for determining pay and conditions of service for NHS staff and is, in practice, composed of two councils – Professional and Technical 'A', consisting of the professions supplementary to medicine (including occupational and physiotherapists), psychologists, speech therapists, biochemists, physicists (the so-called 'scientific professions'), and Professional and Technical 'B' (laboratory assistants, technicians, etc.).

PTA 'A' is further divided into committees A to E, committee C being concerned with the professions supplementary to medicine or 'remedial' professions as they were called for short. Each committee is composed of representatives of unions and professional associations in the form of numbers of 'seats' according to numbers of members. In 1976, the full Whitley Council comprised twenty-two staff-side seats, of which two

162

Struggles for control

were held by ASTMS, two by NALGO, two by the British Association of Occupational Therapists, for example. (The Staff Side of the Whitley Council looks after the interests of the NHS workers and the Management Side does the same but from the point of view of the DHSS and its advisers.)

The *ad hoc* grades which the Management Side proposed should be considered for allocation to the Whitley Council were:

a) industrial therapy helpers;
b) staff engaged in teaching and social training of the mentally handicapped and mentally ill, including supervisors and assistants;
c) teachers of handicrafts;
d) art, music, and drama therapists;
e) rehabilitation officers.

They suggested a programme of joint inspection visits and the preparation of a joint report.

The Staff Side agreed, suggesting that Regional Scientific Officers and helpers in Scotland should be included. Having agreed to undertake the exercise, the joint secretaries arranged a programme of visits to hospitals employing each of the above categories of staff, including both mental handicap and psychiatric hospitals. They visited twenty hospitals and one rehabilitation centre.

As far as criteria for allocation were concerned, these were not specified, apart from a group of staff appearing to be 'well established', in which case the working party could recommend that an allocation be made. The exact position within the Whitley Council (i.e. the *functional* council (either 'A' or 'B') and the *committee* to which the group of staff would be allocated (A to E)) would depend upon each side's assessment of the case. (The professions supplementary to medicine were mainly covered by committee C, the speech therapists by committee B.) The Staff Side would consider which placing would be likely to produce the best results for the *ad hoc* grade in question. Their assessment might also depend on the interests of the unions with substantial membership in those grades.

The brief to the secretaries of both Staff and Management Sides, in considering allocation to a functional council, included looking for the closest related professions for comparison. In the case of art therapy, this was said (by DHSS management) to be OT, and the secretaries were interested in finding out whether art therapists were working within OT departments or undertaking duties which might fall to such departments or to OT helpers.

This initiative by the Whitley Council was a very important development for art therapists and BAAT saw that it would be essential to have

163

Beginning of organised activity

some representation within the NHS negotiating machinery, if and when allocation was recommended, so that art therapists could have a say about in which committee (A to E) they should be included. The NUT did not, of course, have any representatives on the Whitley Council. If the Joint Secretaries' Report was to identify art therapists as an 'established group', BAAT would have a chance to negotiate for a career and salary structure and eventually a seat on one of the Whitley Councils. (In 1976, the full-time salary of a single-handed art therapist was between £2520 and £3201 per annum, the equivalent of a two-day per week lecturing post in higher education.)

Given this major development in the health service, BAAT council felt that the time had come to break with the NUT. At the March 1976 AGM, a proposal was carried that BAAT allow its NUT membership to lapse at the end of 1976. This statement was placed in the BAAT *Newsletter*, together with an explanation of the reasons for the decision.

Andrea Gilroy, a graduate from the Birmingham art therapy option, who was elected honorary secretary at that AGM, wrote to Jarvis at the NUT regretting the decision. The letter stated the reasons as follows:

> Our initial hope was that all art therapists would be paid on the Burnham Scale, art therapy being seen as an integral part of education. However, with the advent of full time health-service oriented Diplomas in Art Therapy, there is a split developing amongst art therapists as to their philosophical and practical orientation. In order to preserve unity and to prevent another association of art therapists being formed, it is necessary to leave NUT.

The letter also mentioned that the opportunity for submitting the joint BAAT/NUT document to either the Halsbury or Houghton Committees had been missed, and, since it seemed to be difficult to secure any subsequent appointments with appropriate civil servants of either the DHSS or DES, it was time to review the campaign. Local Association, as opposed to Central Association, status was not considered suitable for BAAT. The letter ended with grateful thanks to the NUT for its help and advice over the years.

By the end of 1976, then, BAAT would be 'on its own' as a small association, unless decisions about the future were made quickly. Much would depend upon the results of the Joint Secretaries' Report and upon exploratory talks with other unions which Andrea Gilroy and I had undertaken to pursue.

The Whitley working party reports

In October 1976, BAAT received the Report of the Joint Secretaries. Several BAAT members had been interviewed in their place of work, and

Struggles for control

visits had been made to both Hertfordshire College (for brevity called Herts College hereafter) and Goldsmiths' courses. The outcome was very encouraging to BAAT. In summarising the current position of art therapy, the report stated:

> Para 23: There is a whole time equivalent of about 100 art therapists in the NHS. The DHSS' main criterion is an art qualification of two years post A level study. There are a growing number of courses now in 'art therapy' as such, all within the art sector of further education. The first and largest is a one-year full time course at Herts College of Art and Design.

> Art Therapy is not confined to the NHS: art therapists also work for educational authorities, social services and prisons. We visited one of the other courses at Goldsmiths' College, London and it was clear from our discussions with the Principal and students that in this case the course was oriented towards special education. These courses are given no special salary recognition by the DHSS at present, other than a year's incremental credit in respect of the year spent on the course.

The function of art therapy, as perceived by the Joint Secretaries, was summed up as follows:

> Para 26: In broad terms the art therapy we saw was intended to perform one or both of two functions. The first was present in nearly all cases and might be termed 'rehabilitative' (encouraging sense of identity and helping to achieve behavioural change). The second function might be termed 'diagnostic': therapists performing such a function were generally anxious to disclaim any intention of 'interpreting' patients' work themselves in psychiatric terms, but did contend that a patient's art work could constitute useful diagnostic evidence for psychiatrists and could help them monitor changes in a patient's condition. This second function seemed the most marked where art therapy was strongest and independent of OT. At the less rigorous end of the rehabilitation spectrum was a third possible function which might be termed 'diversionary'. This was probably, and perhaps necessarily present in most if not all the units we visited, but in our view only in two cases did this arguably predominate.

The report went on to make a case for allocation to the Professional and Technical 'A' Committee:

> Para 57: For category (i) art and music therapists, the case is very strong. There is clearly a growing role for such staff, and the *ad hoc* grades applicable to them are well established. Some of the art therapists we met were working within OT departments, and as the McMillan Report suggested (para 33) it can be argued that staff not

165

Beginning of organised activity

trained in the therapeutic application of their subject are best used under the supervision of a member of the remedial professions. However, for those who have Herts or Goldsmiths' College training, such supervision appears to be unnecessary and apparently would be resented. We therefore recommend that we seek to negotiate for this category.

This was good news in that the Joint Secretaries had appeared to recognise the value of training. The note in Paragraph 57 concerning OT seemed to imply that separation from OT, in terms of clinical supervision at least, could be a possibility. An independent review had perceived art therapists as a 'well-established' group with a unity of aims and objectives.

The findings in Paragraph 26 were interesting in that apparently several art therapists had given the working party to understand that art work could 'constitute useful diagnostic evidence for psychiatrists and could help them monitor changes in a patient's conditions'. This function was seen to be strongest where art therapists were independent of OT. It might be that this was another strategy to achieve separation from OT by implying a 'partnership' with psychiatrists, as a higher status group, as many art therapists had tended to play down the 'diagnostic' role of art therapy, preferring to see the art-making process as therapy in itself.

Explorations with other unions

Having left the NUT, BAAT council felt it was essential to link with another union as soon as possible, and this time one with strong health service representation.

Discussions were held with the Confederation of Health Service Employees (COHSE) and with the National Association of Local Government Officers (NALGO). As the council minutes show, these were helpful and important meetings, but in so far as COHSE's membership was primarily made up of nurses, BAAT council felt that art therapists might get 'swallowed up' and their needs be of little import when compared with those of nurses. The same applied, to some extent, to NALGO, as very few art therapists worked in the social services, whose staff predominated in NALGO.

A further visit to ASTMS was made by myself and Andrea Gilroy, who met Donna Haber, a Divisional Officer. Donna Haber had been responsible for the negotiations which had brought both speech therapists and child psychotherapists under the Whitley Council. These were both small professions by NHS standards. There was, then, a precedent for this union understanding the needs of small emergent staff groups. On the basis of these meetings, BAAT council decided to recommend to its health service members that they should join ASTMS.

166

Struggles for control

The possibility of a new segment emerging

> Pockets of resistance and embattled minorities may turn out to be the heirs of former generations, digging in along new battle lines. They may spearhead new movements which swell back into power. What looks like the backwash, or just plain deviancy, may be the beginning of a new segment which will acquire an institutional place and considerable prestige and power.
>
> (Bucher and Strauss 1961: 333)

The comment in the Honorary Secretary's letter to the NUT concerning the 'preservation of unity' arose as a result of growing impatience on the part of the art therapy graduates of St Albans in particular, but also of students from Goldsmiths' and Birmingham, at the lack of progress in negotiations, resulting in poor salaries and status in the NHS. Another issue of irritation to St Albans was that the two art therapy programmes at Birmingham and Goldsmiths' were still situated in postgraduate Art Teachers' Certificate courses (although Goldsmiths' had in October 1976 allocated five places for art therapy studies under the umbrella of the 'Goldsmiths' Diploma in Art and Design'), whereas the Certificate in Remedial Art had been renamed Diploma in Art Therapy and was a full-time, discrete art therapy programme. There had been strong indications from St Albans that some of their staff and students wanted to form a new 'professional' association, admitting only its graduates and thus achieving a complete turn-about from 1970 when BAAT did not admit St Albans graduates to membership!

However, there was co-operation between BAAT officers and several of St Albans' graduates, as noted previously, and also between BAAT and the management of Herts College of Art following the lunch in December 1975. Suggestions both for training criteria and for maintenance of professional standards had been exchanged.

A working part on professional status had been set up by BAAT, which included John Evans from Herts College, Michael Edwards and Peter Byrne from Birmingham Polytechnic, the Chair and Vice-Chair of BAAT, and practising art therapists including three Herts College graduates. In the same way as the working parties at the NAMH in the 1950s, this group struggled to define criteria for a core course without really grappling with the fundamental question: what constitutes art therapy?

One member, an early St Albans graduate, had clear ideas on the way forward.

> A professional body must be set up, consisting of art therapists from the various areas in which art therapists practise. These should include subnormality, psychiatry, social services, Home Office establishments. Representatives from these varied fields should form a

Beginning of organised activity

committee which could also include the heads of the various colleges which train art therapists.

The criteria by which an art therapist should be judged competent to be a registered member of the professional body we feel are basically those that guide the St Albans course.

(Minutes of working party, 11 May 1976)

The details of these criteria will be discussed in the context of training in general in Part V, but a summary of the meeting of 30 October 1976 will give an idea of the issues which were predominating prior to the Extraordinary General Meeting of November 1976.

The main differences of opinion in the working party seemed to be around criteria for entry to training courses, with BAAT representatives considering that a degree in art or design was essential, and St Albans being prepared to admit nurses and OTs:

It was argued that only if art therapists can claim a common training background, such as a degree and therapy training – would they have a strong bargaining position. It was stated that the St Albans policy (of admitting OTs and RMNs) has the full support of all ex-students and the DHSS and in particular St Albans felt that negotiating strength should be a training as therapists not skill as artists.... Also giving opportunity to train OTs in art therapy is useful politically in that OTs regard 'creative therapy' as being within their professional sphere and in many instances have effective control in the hospital field. MN was concerned that the DHSS would see this opportunity to train OTs as the cheapest and easiest way of providing art therapists, effectively blocking art and design graduates. The problem appeared to be resolved when JE pointed out that the number of OTs and RMNs was small – 5 or 6 only, and he would be happy to set a percentage limit on the number of 'non-graduates' accepted.

(Minutes, 30 October 1976)

A proposal was then drafted to put to the EGM on the composition and purpose of an Art Therapy Registration Board. This was to consist of representatives from the three training courses, plus 'art therapists of at least three years work experience representing the range of art therapy situations', a psychiatrist elected by the Royal College of Psychiatrists, and two observers, one from the DHSS, one from the DES. The purpose of the body would be to draw up firm criteria for the registration of art therapists, based on the recommendations of the BAAT professional status working party, that would be 'acceptable' to the DHSS and other employing agencies. It would be empowered to determine its own constitution in relation to that of BAAT.

168

Struggles for control

BAAT officers were concerned by this proposal, as there was no guarantee that the 'art therapists' would be BAAT members. Indeed, the 'determining of own constitution' paved the way for a new body to be formed, outside BAAT but with powers to determine the future of art therapy in terms of training and membership criteria. BAAT could, therefore, be left with little function other than public relations and some services to members, as it was not a union nor part of a union any longer. The Chair decided to add an amendment to the proposal to put to the EGM, stipulating that the 'art therapists' should be BAAT members.

The phrase 'acceptable to the DHSS and other employing agencies' was also problematic, the main anxiety of BAAT council being that such a new 'professional association' would draw art therapy away from any 'radical' aspirations it still had as a result of the strong critical stance towards 'traditional' psychiatry, and away from its roots in trade union activity. The fact that a new association would have 'registration' as one of its functions would also give it considerable power. As Johnson pointed out:

> In the case of professionalism the occupational association is the registering body and it develops effective sanction mechanisms for controlling not only occupational behaviour but also non-occupational behaviour.... The association will also attempt to impose a uni-portal system of entry to the occupation in order to ensure that shared identity is reinforced by the creation of similar experiences of entry and socialisation.
>
> (Johnson 1972: 54)

The council of BAAT felt that if anybody were to take on this role it should be BAAT, which had had its union link through the NUT and was seeking new and perhaps stronger union affiliations in order to counterbalance the 'elitism' which was suggested by the notion of 'professionalism'. BAAT still, however, wanted to maintain control over entry to the profession, by excluding non-art graduates, the assumption being that art-trained people would bring a more radical and less 'medical model' orientated approach to training than would be the case with nurses or OTs. The council did not want art therapy to become polarised into two opposing areas: 'the professional' and 'the union' but wished to maintain these functions under the same umbrella, i.e. BAAT. (See Ozga and Lawn 1981: 22–33 for comparison with teacher-union activity.)

The extraordinary general meeting of 20 November 1976

This was an extremely important meeting in the history of BAAT, in that it marked a major change of tactics in the campaign for a career and salary structure, which was to be orientated towards the health service rather than

Beginning of organised activity

adult education. It also marked a new phase in BAAT's internal structure, from being a Central Association of the NUT to being a 'professional association' in the form of a non-profit-making company limited by guarantee.

In her report, the Chair made the following observations:

At a meeting which I attended last Friday at the DHSS, I was asked to put forward the views of the BAAT on training and qualifications for art therapy. The DHSS admitted that their qualifications for entry to art therapy posts were out of date. They were concerned that the training for art therapy was non-medical (in comparison with OTs, they said). I put forward a strong case for the necessity of a serious full-time commitment to art, to degree level, as an important requirement for training, to be followed by a professional art therapy course. Their psychiatrist adviser seemed to be in agreement.

The Chair also gave the results of a questionnaire which had been circulated asking members to state whether they were in favour of campaigning with the health service or with education. Replies were as follows: in favour of health service: 46; of education 18; don't know: 8. Only 72 replies had been received out of 200 to date.

The Chair summed up the reasons why the council had recommended such a change of emphasis, from their previous arguments that those art therapists who worked in hospitals should be part of the education service and paid on Burnham, to their current recommendation that art therapists should be employed by the health service:

During our later negotiations with NUT, there was pressure in the education field for everyone to be qualified as teachers. When we entered NUT in 1967 this was not so. We felt that the Union were hampered in their attempts to negotiate for us by this, and the more so since they had no contact with DHSS or Whitley Council. An increasing number of our members who work in hospitals felt that they were therapists and not teachers. And, very importantly, the severe cut backs in education and particularly in adult education have led to greater insecurity for those people employed on further education scales and seconded to hospitals. Indeed, in a DES document entitled *The Education of Patients in Hospitals* it states: 'Hospital authorities have got wise to the fact that they are paying a lot more for art therapists through reimbursing LEAs than if they were to employ them direct.'

Consequently, as financial cutbacks lead to a narrowing philosophy in education, those of us who held perhaps a rather idealised view of the scope of education find our ideals more and more at variance with the practical realities of our work as art therapists. Chances of success-

Struggles for control

ful negotiation with the DES fade rapidly. So we have had to change tack.

(Chair's Report, EGM, 20 November 1976)

A sad note followed, as the Chair read out a letter of greeting from Adrian Hill, the President, then seriously ill in King Edward VII sanatorium in Sussex, where he had started his 'career' in art therapy.

For the first time, a BAAT EGM was attended by staff from Herts College and a number of their current and ex-students. In view of the rumoured 'new' art therapy association, there was considerable tension in the meeting as proposals central to the future of BAAT and art therapy were debated. The Chair and Honorary Secretary had allocated a specific time to each proposal and the meeting ran from 10.30 a.m. until 4 p.m.

The first two proposals were to raise members' subscriptions and to have the chair nominated from the council every two years, instead of the vice-chair automatically becoming chair. The third concerned the future status of BAAT, and it was proposed that: 'BAAT should become an incorporated non-profit making company limited by guarantee.' BAAT's lawyer, Barry Stead, attended the meeting and spoke to the proposal, which was accepted by the members, unanimously.

After lunch came the proposal which was considered to be critical to the issue of 'power and control' of the profession: it came from the professional status working party:

That an Art Therapy Registration Board be established (with membership as specified) and with an amendment proposed by the Chair to read *'art therapists who are full members of BAAT'* with three years working experience.

As stated previously, the unamended proposal would have given control of 'registration' to non-BAAT members. Two votes were taken, one of the *whole meeting* (including, of course, the St Albans students and staff) and one of full BAAT members. The proposal and its amendment were passed with a huge majority by both.

The following proposal was that: 'Full members of BAAT should be members of a recognised trade union.' This was passed unanimously, leading to a discussion on unionisation, led by Andrea Gilroy, Mary Newton, and Linda Knott, which resulted in a recommendation that all health service art therapists should join ASTMS. This again was passed with a large majority.

The atmosphere after the meeting was euphoric. Decisions had been made and with the agreement of the majority, not only of members but of the one-time 'enemy'. The mission seemed to be shared, and the means of achieving it clearer, as a result of the future link with ASTMS. The Joint Secretaries' Report had given hope that art therapy might actually

171

Beginning of organised activity

be on the road to becoming 'a profession' and art therapists seen on a level with other health service professionals.

Anxieties about becoming enmeshed in health service bureaucracy and hierarchy, which had preoccupied many art therapists, had got submerged, temporarily, in this phase of art therapy's *perestroika*.

Events following the EGM: setting up a limited company and exploring possible links with other unions

Following the membership's decision that BAAT should become a limited company (or a 'professional association', as some members saw it), Barry Stead began negotiations with the Board of Trade (BoT) to achieve limited company status.

Having drawn up a constitution which was similar in format and identical in its aims and objects to that of 1964, this was submitted to the BoT for approval. BAAT was then asked to justify the use of the title 'British' Association, and to demonstrate that it represented the interests of the majority of art therapists in England, Wales, Scotland, and N. Ireland. The officers were obliged to obtain data from the three training courses and from the DHSS and other employers on the number of art therapists practising, and to determine whether or not the majority were in BAAT. As a result of the November EGM's decisions, BAAT's membership had almost doubled, and clearly represented the majority of known art therapists in England, Scotland, Wales, and N. Ireland, so the title 'British' was able to be justified. There were, though, very few art therapists outside England – about seven in Wales, five in Scotland, and three in N. Ireland, and the position is not much improved, possibly due to lack of training courses being established in these countries.

On 26 August 1977, Barry Stead wrote to the Chair saying that the British Association of Art Therapists Limited had been duly incorporated on 24 August. The internal organisation of BAAT remained much the same as before, with a chair and other officers being elected every two years and council members every year.

The first officers of the new BAAT were:

Chair: Diane Waller (then Senior Lecturer in Art Therapy at Goldsmiths' College and part-time art therapist at the Paddington Centre for Psychotherapy);
Honorary Secretary: Andrea Gilroy (then art therapist at Joyce Green psychiatric hospital in Kent);
Vice-Chair: Terry Molloy (art therapist at Brookside psychiatric adolescent unit);
Treasurer: Lynda Knott (art therapist in a hospital for mentally handicapped people in South Ockenden, Essex).

Struggles for control

The subscribers, who initially formed the Association, consisted of the above four together with Michael Edwards (Senior Lecturer in Art Therapy at Birmingham), Britta Warsi (art therapist in a psychiatric hospital), Diana Halliday (art therapist/psychotherapist in a child guidance clinic), and the first elected members of the Council of Management were all the above plus Jill Pickersgill (art therapist from Wiltshire), Annette Wolfenden (deputy headmistress and art therapist working within special education in Hertfordshire), Peter Byrne (lecturer in art and art therapist), and Robin Holtom (art therapist in a psychiatric hospital in London).

So, ten years after BAAT had become a Central Association of the NUT, it had changed its structure to a Limited Company but retained the same wide mixture of objects, giving it a union, learned society, and 'professional association' function (in setting itself the brief of determining training and standards of practice), and having a council and officers who were all actively engaged in the practice of art therapy and identified themselves in that role.

It was a time of high morale in the association, and this was reflected in the Chair's report which contained the following optimistic note:

> This year (1977) then, we have made a determined effort to establish art therapy as a profession in its own right. For the first time ever we have had direct and most encouraging contacts with civil servants from the DHSS. The Joint Secretaries of the Staff and Management side of the Whitley Council set up a working party to investigate *ad hoc* grades in the NHS and their report was most favourable to art therapists as a group with an identifiable philosophy. We continue to receive dozens of enquiries about art therapy each week, from school leavers to postgraduate students and other professionals as well as universities, colleges and careers officers, and the existing courses in art therapy are much over-subscribed.

> (Diane Waller 5 November 1977)

However, this exhilaration was shortly to be disturbed by the emergence of a new group, formed out of a small organisation called SESAME, which was involved in drama and movement in therapy, and which proposed to re-establish itself as the British Institute for the Arts in Therapy.

The disturbance surrounded the initial aims for the new organisation, which included setting standards for the training and practice of all the arts therapies, including visual art therapy, thus taking on one of BAAT's main objects under their new constitution. As BAAT had gone to considerable lengths to have its constitution and objects approved by the Board of Trade, and to justify entitlement to the use of the term 'British' there was anger and indignation that another group, who were not primarily art therapists, should appropriate this object. The name, as first proposed, was

173

Beginning of organised activity

also similar to BAAT's and it was felt that this would cause confusion. As a result of representations to SESAME, the name was changed to the British Institute for the Study of the Arts in Therapy, and the objects were modified to be complementary with rather than clashing with BAAT's.

BISAT was formed in 1977, and described itself thus:

> The British Institute for the Study of the Arts in Therapy (known initially as the SESAME Institute for the Arts in Therapy) was established early in 1977. It is the first association in Great Britain to represent Arts therapists in all of the major fields (the visual arts, music, drama, movement/dance and writing) and its work – which is primarily concerned with professional standards, training and research, has gained support both in this country and abroad. The Institute's panel of Consultants includes many eminent psychiatrists and psychotherapists, and among its members are several of the men and women who have pioneered arts therapy in Great Britain. Any interested person may become an Associate Member of the Institute.
>
> (BISAT Seminar Report 1978)

BAAT was not convinced that much could be achieved by an association claiming to represent the 'arts therapies' when neither art nor music therapy, which had been practised since the 1940s and had established training courses, had yet secured a career structure in the NHS. Drama and movement therapy were being practised but were not organised to the same extent and there were at that time no full-time training courses in Britain. BAAT also felt that each of the 'arts therapies' had its own specific theoretical and clinical models, and that an attempt to put these diverse disciplines under one umbrella, merely because their title included an art form, was spurious. In fact, they considered that the failure of the proposed Institute of Education course to get off the ground in the early 1970s had been mainly due to this mistake.

Another problem was the composition of BISAT's Council of Management, which consisted mainly of non-art therapists. It was also a charity and thus was considered 'elitist' by the BAAT council. During the time of BISAT's formation, there were many discussions between representatives of BAAT and SESAME, and eventually objectives were drawn up which enabled the two organisations to have a cordial relationship.

BISAT's objectives

At the first seminar of BISAT, the primary objectives of the Institute were presented as follows:

1. To support organisations such as BAAT, the Association of Professional Music Therapists of Great Britain, and SESAME, in

Struggles for control

their efforts to establish and maintain the highest standards in training and professional conduct, and to investigate the advisability of recommending additional training requirements for those wishing to engage in the psychotherapeutic application of the Arts.

2. To engage in research, in co-operation with people from the fields of health and education, and to create closer liaison between Arts therapy and medicine.

3. To design and promote comprehensive multi-disciplinary programmes in Arts Therapy.

4. To carry out education programmes for interested arts therapists and, upon request, for others who are using the Arts with sick and handicapped people.

The report pointed out that the term 'arts therapy' had been applied to work which was carried out on many different levels. There appeared to be a need for greater clarification of these levels and recognition of the different professional training requirements for each of them. The institute considered that it could be of particular assistance by encouraging and supporting carefully planned studies into the full implications of arts therapy. It noted:

> Other associations could fill a very important need by focusing upon the more general interests of professional therapists, but it was the belief of those who had been working closely with the Institute that one of the ways in which it could be of greatest service, both to the patient and the professional, would be by continuing its policy of concentrating upon research, training and standards.
>
> (Lynn Eskow, July 1978, p. 3 of BISAT report)

The institute received a grant for two years from the Carnegie Trust. BAAT was debarred from receiving grants because it had as one of its objects to 'protect and promote the interests of its members', but otherwise its objects, drawn up in 1964 and restated in the new constitution, were echoed by those of BISAT – except that BISAT included all the 'arts therapies'.

Because of its 'learned society' orientation, BISAT met the needs of those art therapists who had missed this in BAAT. By organising seminars (some in conjunction with the Champernowne Trust) and opening these to other professions, BISAT was able to provide an opportunity for dissemination of information about the 'arts therapies' and for exchanges of ideas and theoretical positions.

By 1981, though, BISAT had run into serious financial difficulties. It had few members, despite its multi-disciplinary orientation, and was not self-supporting. It had to maintain an office and part-time secretary. The

Beginning of organised activity

situation had become so grave that a working party of its council recommended that only full membership should be offered in future.

Like BAAT, BISAT started life with very ambitious objects. However, unlike BAAT, it did not represent one group of people who had a very strong desire to achieve reward and recognition for the job that they were identified with. The issues surrounding recognition as disciplines and as professions were very complex and different for each of the 'arts therapies', and while it was important to have a place to share ideas and contemplate the possibilities inherent in each discipline, it did not attract sufficient numbers to ensure growth. It had no clearly perceived function of its own; rather it appeared to duplicate the work already being initiated by individual associations. For example, art therapists, who were by far the largest group of 'arts therapists', were forming their own networks of discussion and debate through the BAAT regional groups which had been established by Michael Donnelly, who was to become chair of BAAT in 1981. Art therapists were engaged in setting and maintaining their own professional standards through the Registration and Training Sub-Committee (later the Training and Education Committee). These were 'grass roots' networks, paid for entirely from the members' subscriptions and from money raised through BAAT publications and events. BAAT did not have an office and paid staff to maintain, all duties being carried out voluntarily by officers and council, with occasional clerical assistance.

In 1984, after strenuous attempts to fund raise and to simplify the structure and objects, BISAT folded.

BAAT strengthens its trade union function

One thing that the liaison with BISAT revealed was the strength, by 1977, of the trade union orientation of BAAT. At the same time, it had begun to formulate 'core course' proposals for training, paying particular attention to entry requirements for candidates. In speculating about the 'ideal ingredients' for training courses, BAAT members were trying to create art therapists of the future, who would make a radical input into the NHS and hence an improvement in mental health care. They felt that, in order to attract people with sufficient qualifications and determination to take on the challenge of working as art therapists, it was necessary to offer salaries and conditions which would at least equate with the higher grades of the Burnham Scale. Long association with the trade union movement had removed the barriers to demanding and expecting to achieve decent pay and conditions for a high standard of work. On the other hand, other paramedical and nursing professions (consisting mainly of women workers, as with art therapy) were still seen as trapped in the position of low-paid 'carers', rather than as professional workers.

176

Struggles for control

Summary

In this part of the book, I have tried to show how organised activity among art therapists began in working parties sponsored by the National Association of Mental Health in the late 1940s and how it developed to a point where a professional association was formed (BAAT) in 1964. BAAT had complex objects, which gave it trade union, professional, and learned society functions. Between 1967 and 1976, BAAT was a Central Association of the National Union of Teachers and strategies were worked out between BAAT and the NUT to have art therapists employed by and paid by local education authorities on the same rates as adult education lecturers. These strategies did not succeed for several reasons, one of which was the changes in adult education funding ('the cuts') which put art therapy, as a fringe discipline, in a vulnerable position. Another reason was the development of a health service-orientated course at St Albans School of Art, some of whose graduates were motivated to co-operate with BAAT to devise alternative strategies for gaining improved conditions of service and salaries in the NHS. BAAT left the NUT in 1976, became a limited company but retained all its former objectives, and sought an allegiance with a health service union in order to devise further strategies for establishing art therapy in the NHS – but separate from occupational therapy. It also set up a Registration and Training Sub-Committee, with membership representing all the existing training courses and practising art therapists. This committee was to make recommendations about entry criteria and training for art therapy to BAAT Council and AGM. Thus, the control over entry to art therapy was still in the hands of BAAT.

Part IV

The campaign to establish art therapy in the NHS

Introduction

In this part, I shall describe the campaign which was mounted by BAAT in co-operation with the Association for Technical, Managerial and Scientific Staff (ASTMS), a union which represented a wide range of NHS staff, including doctors, psychologists, and speech therapists. We shall see that art therapists referred to themselves as 'a profession', and that they wished to be perceived as an 'autonomous' profession, not a subsection of or linked with any other occupation or profession (especially not occupational therapy).

In *Professions and Power*, Johnson makes a point (1972: 32) that may be relevant here. He refers to 'professionalism' as sometimes being a 'successful ideology', that is, an ideology espoused because the group has little chance of achieving control over their own occupational activities: art therapists were trying to convince 'the State' (as represented by the DHSS) that they should be regarded as a 'profession', and one which was comparable, first, to psychologists, and later to speech therapists, both of whom had gained a considerable measure of control over their own professions (the psychologists through the British Psychological Society and the speech therapists through the College of Speech Therapists). Certainly one form of practice of art therapy, that closely allied to 'psychotherapy through art', could claim similarity to clinical psychology through manner of practice, but another, and perhaps more prevalent, model in the mid to late-1970s (and still fairly popular today) was perhaps closer to the arts and crafts activities provided by occupational therapists. This was the so-called 'open group': art therapy took place in large, open studios and the therapist (or therapists) took on a role similar to that of a benign art college tutor. The emphasis was on the patient's relationship to their art work and only marginally on their relationship with the therapist and other patients. Although the therapists would encourage the patient to work spontaneously and to express their feelings through the art work, from the outside it appeared a very similar process to occupational therapy.

181

Establishing art therapy in the NHS

In order to claim comparability with either psychology or speech therapy, BAAT had to demonstrate that art therapists' training was at a similar level and standard. This was hard to do on the basis of options or a one-year course, but if the one-year course was synthesised with a four-year art training, which BAAT council believed was correct, then the picture looked different. But the DHSS had to be convinced that it was necessary to approve a higher level training for art therapists, for as long as the requirement for working as an art therapist was 'two years' art training post-A level', art therapists could be left under the supervision of occupational therapy.

The strategies used by BAAT and ASTMS during the period 1976 to 1982 to identity art therapy as a discrete occupational group (and in the eyes of art therapists themselves a 'profession') will be explored and discussed in the following chapters.

182

Chapter nineteen

BAAT and ASTMS: joint negotiations for a place on the Whitley Council for art therapists

We have seen that, at the BAAT EGM in 1976, members approved a proposal recommending that all health service art therapists (and any others who were in a position to do so) should join ASTMS. We have also seen that there was a shift in tactics away from linking art therapists with adult education lecturers in the hope that they could be paid by LEAs and seconded to hospitals to trying to negotiate a place on the Whitley Council. Some of the impetus for the latter had come from the positive findings of the Joint Secretaries' Report and some from pressure from Herts College students and staff to negotiate directly with the DHSS.

In this chapter I shall discuss the joint BAAT–ASTMS campaign for a career and salary structure in the NHS, in which they drew on support from psychiatrists and other NHS staff as well as from other unions and the Staff Side of Whitley. They also used parliamentary pressure, through lobbying MPs and arranging for questions to be asked in the House of Commons.

BAAT links with ASTMS

The results of the EGM vote were conveyed to Donna Haber on 14 December 1976, and from that time negotiations with the Whitley Council were conducted by myself, Andrea Gilroy, and Donna Haber in consultation with the council and membership of BAAT and ASTMS.

The first step they took was to send a questionnaire to BAAT members asking them to list all their qualifications and to notify their place(s) of work. They also asked which union members belonged to and if they would be prepared to join ASTMS if relevant.

There were 169 replies (April 1977), representing approximately 60 per cent of members and the results were as follows:

183

Establishing art therapy in the NHS

Qualifications held by members

(Total replying: 169)

First degree or equivalent in art or design	108
St Albans' Certificate or Diploma	38
ATD from Birmingham or Goldsmiths'	9
Other ATDs	16
No qualifications at all	8
No first degree or diploma	5
No postgraduate training	38

Members *fully qualified in terms of the current BAAT criteria*: i.e. a degree or equivalent in art plus a postgraduate teaching qualification *totalled 47*.

Unions

Members who would definitely join ASTMS or who felt they could be persuaded:	123
Other art therapists, working in education and social services, and members of the NUT or NALGO or other unions	46
Art therapists working in the NHS and belonging to NUPE, COHSE, and NALGO	6

These findings were sent to Donna Haber with a letter from the Honorary Secretary apologising for the poor response to the questionnaire:

> Apart from apathy the reason behind this could well be that these persons are no longer involved in art therapy (there is a very high drop out rate, primarily because of the poor salary, lack of career structure and lack of professional recognition). However, despite the poor response, I think ASTMS has a reasonable base for representing art therapists.
>
> (Andrea Gilroy 20 April 1977)

In a letter of 9 May 1977, Donna Haber asked whether BAAT wished ASTMS to negotiate for all art therapists to be brought under the NHS – including those working in social services and education, in which case ASTMS would approach the Secretary of State for Health and Social Services. After consultation with the BAAT council, the Honorary Secretary replied that for those employed by adult education authorities and seconded to hospitals, the answer would be yes, given the same pay. But for the rest it was difficult to say. A change to NHS employment for art therapists working under various job titles in the social services could mean that they might lose their jobs, as there was no establishment for art therapy at all in the social services, and the institutions might be reluctant to create a new post. Those art therapists working in prisons were usually

The Whitley Council

employed by the LEA or the education department of the prison and, as such, their position was insecure and might be improved by a change to the NHS. Art therapists in special education were in a different position. There are few whose job title was art therapist, most being employed as teachers and spending a proportion of their timetable as art therapists. They were receiving good salaries. However, some might wish to change so that a clearer distinction could be made between their roles as teacher and therapist.

It is doubtful whether at that time all art therapists could have been brought under the NHS and seconded to different institutions. In retrospect it might have been worth attempting, as the situation today is still problematic, with no formal establishment in either social services or education. Individual art therapists negotiate their own pay and conditions, and, although there are now (1989) many precedents for full-time art therapy posts in social services, a BAAT working party is having to undertake a similar campaign to that conducted with the NHS. At that point, the officers felt that they needed to take one step at a time and focus on NHS art therapists and, somewhat ironically, those employed by LEAs – representing a total change of tactic.

Discussions with the DHSS

On 22 October 1976, Andrea Gilroy and I had written to the DHSS to enquire about the Department's policy on art therapists. We wrote again in February and received a reply on 30 March 1977. The DHSS could not give any definite advice on how things were proceeding following the Joint Secretaries' work on the *ad hoc* grades, but gave the DHSS's current view on art therapy.

This was, first, that the Department would consider authorising the appointment of art therapists providing they had completed a 'formal course of training, recognised by the educational authorities, of at least two years duration and above GCE A level standard' (this, as stated previously, was based on the old Intermediate Certificate in Art, which had been phased out in 1964!). The DHSS did not at that time 'recognise' the courses at St Albans or Goldsmiths' for the purposes of salary.

Second, there were two salary scales of which the higher one was for an officer working without the professional supervision of another art therapist OR occupational therapist, and the lower one for an art therapist under such supervision. At that time the scales were:

Single-handed: £2520–3201
Under supervision: £2115–2625.

This compared with starting salaries of approximately £6000 for full-time lecturer II posts. As we can see from the questionnaire replies above, many BAAT members had qualifications which would have enabled them to be

Establishing art therapy in the NHS

employed in art colleges (and indeed many were, or had been, lecturers). The working week of an art therapist was thirty-six hours, and annual leave entitlement was four weeks plus statutory holidays.

According to the DHSS, the Whitley Council was 'considering' whether it would be right for art therapists to be brought within their purview for negotiating purposes. If that was successful, then there would be opportunities to discuss 'a number of issues relating to salaries, etc.'. However, the Department could not give any indication of when that might happen.

Following the receipt of this letter, a request to visit both Herts College and Goldsmiths' art therapy courses was made to the respective institutions by the following: Staff Side secretary of the Whitley Council; DHSS officer from the Finance Department; DHSS officer from the General Whitley Council. The visits were felt by BAAT and the two colleges to have been useful and to have given the opportunity to discuss at length the issues surrounding training and career/salary structure. There was some suggestion that OTs might wish to incorporate art therapy within their own structure, but the officers seemed to consider that art therapists needed to have their own structure.

By August 1977, there was still no further development in the position of art therapists following the Joint Secretaries' Reports and the visits to the colleges. ASTMS research department had drafted a document on the basis of information given by BAAT, which was to be forwarded to the DHSS, to draw their attention once again to the problems.

The document listed the qualifications required by the DHSS as against those required by BAAT, and proposed that the DHSS was 'undervaluing' art therapy. The following gave a clear definition of an art therapist's skills:

> Qualified (BAAT) art therapists have a considerable understanding of art processes, are proficient in the area of non-verbal communication and are able to provide a trusting and facilitating environment in which patients feel safe to express strong emotion. By virtue of their training, they have a sophisticated understanding of psychopathology which enables them to understand the nature of the patient's communications. They have a general understanding of psychiatry and can work with other members of a hospital team. It is now recognised that art therapy, properly practised, is important in the treatment of the mentally ill and mentally handicapped.

This statement makes a strong claim for the 'psychotherapy through art' approach of art therapy, and BAAT is claiming that art therapists have skills over and above those of the 'craft work skills' of occupational therapists (which were often referred to as 'art therapy' by medical and paramedical colleagues).

186

The Whitley Council

The document made a comparison of art therapists' salaries with those of teachers on Burnham rates, the starting salary of a Grade I teacher being approximately £600 below that of the top of the single-handed art therapist scale.

The single-handed scale was only 94 per cent of the Senior II OT scale and, as art therapists were classed as 'helpers', they did not enjoy the same holiday provision as OTs. There was no opportunity for progression on to higher salary scales, therefore no chance of career progression. Hence, there was a high drop-out rate. (On the basis of a survey conducted by BAAT, the average length of stay in art therapy was four years post-course.)

The root of the problem was that, because the DHSS did not officially recognise that postgraduate qualifications existed, art therapists were not treated as therapists in their own right but only as adjuncts to OT (where a two-year post-A level art training would be sufficient). Yet art therapists employed in the NHS, many of whom had undergone training, were bearing a considerable amount of responsibility in their jobs; this, however, was not recognised in their salaries or conditions of service.

If the DHSS recognised that art therapists needed a higher level of qualification, there would be pressure from the unions (and the Staff Side if they were assimilated to the Whitley Council) to pay them appropriately – in the same way as the other graduate professions.

ASTMS and BAAT decided to use speech therapists as a comparability group, as it was considered more effective to use another NHS profession with similar qualifications (for example, a three- or four-year degree in speech sciences) and mode of clinical practice, rather than teaching or adult education lecturing. They drafted a similar career and salary structure and began to formulate arguments to link art therapists with speech therapists in the hope that they would be placed in the same functional Whitley Council ('A') and Committee (B).

Relationship between therapists and the medical profession

In September 1977, BAAT received a copy of a DHSS Circular HC (77) 33 Amended. The document had first been issued fifteen years before, but was still pertinent because it discussed the relationship between the doctor and the 'remedial therapist'. Although it did not refer to art therapists, it served to highlight some of the 'clinical' reasons why art therapists wished to be independent of OT.

The DHSS Circular specified: '2. 1... the patient is the responsibility of the doctor and in referring the patient for therapy he is not handing over his overall control of the patient.' The doctor had the responsibility of instructing the therapist not to carry out certain forms of treatment if he ir she thought it might be harmful to the patient, and the therapist likewise

Establishing art therapy in the NHS

had the responsibility of discontinuing treatment which was either not helping or possibly damaging to the patient. For example, certain forms of physiotherapy might be harmful to a patient with a weak heart, and some forms of OT not appropriate for highly anxious or phobic patients. Such judgements were perhaps more easily made about 'directed' forms of therapy than about art therapy which might imply an approach nearer to psychotherapy. Art therapists who were not part of OT departments had been accustomed to receive referrals direct from a consultant psychiatrist or registrar. Sometimes these referrals were appropriate, sometimes not. But the art therapist did have a direct line to the doctor. In cases where art therapists were part of an OT department, the referrals were made to OT and these were often patients who needed diversionary activities or work-orientated rehabilitative approaches. These were often not suitable for, nor did they wish to undertake, art therapy.

Sometimes art therapy could liberate angry feelings or enable depressed patients to express their sadness through prolonged crying, etc. – whereas previously they may have been mute and withdrawn, but apparently more 'stable'. Unless a head OT was particularly understanding of art therapy and either 'allowed' the art therapist to attend the ward rounds or reported accurately to the team themselves, there was a danger of the art therapist's work being regarded as 'harmful' on occasions, leading to the patient being suddenly withdrawn from treatment without consultation. Such actions could affect the art therapy service quite adversely, as numerous letters of complaint to BAAT had shown.

The claim for being recognised as a separate discipline from OT and having direct access to the medical staff was, then, based on theoretical and clinical foundations as well as on considerations of professional status i.e. on art therapists' wish to be viewed as a graduate profession.

From the point of view of OT, however, whose career progression was based on the 'head count' (that is, salaries for senior staff were based on the number of staff managed by them), it was financially desirable to have art therapists under the OT department. It could also be clinically desirable, as the art therapists were usually well qualified and enthusiastic about their discipline, and had the possibility of working with patients whom other professions had 'given up on'.

The linking of art therapy with occupational therapy was, then, based partly on an administrative convenience and partly on the similarity between the 'open group' model of treatment to arts and crafts activities offered by OTs. It was not based on common theoretical or clinical models. Art therapists continued to stress this point and still do so today.

188

The Whitley Council

The Joint Secretaries propose allocating art therapists to the Whitley Council

At a meeting with Donna Haber on 15 October 1977, Andrea Gilroy and I heard that the Joint Secretaries' Report had recommended that art therapists be allocated to the PT 'A' Whitley Council. ASTMS asked BAAT to draw up a proposed career and salary structure, and again asked if BAAT wished all art therapists to be brought under the NHS. No firm decision appears to have been made on this issue.

Andrea Gilroy and I drew up a structure based on previous drafts, again modelling the grades and career structure on those for speech therapy. ASTMS also alerted BAAT to the fact that it should provide justification as to why art therapists should be graduates, and particularly art graduates.

BAAT officers deliberated and came up with the following reasons: that graduate training guaranteed a certain level of intelligence and maturity, and that the question was comparable to that of 'should doctors/psychologists/music therapists be graduates'. They claimed that art therapists should normally be art graduates because they would have the following attributes:

an aptitude for handling and understanding materials and a general background in art techniques and workshop practice;
an understanding of fantasy and imagination, communication and problem-solving;
ease with and sensitivity to pictorial and other non-verbal communications;
ability to relate positively to, and be accepting of, the emotional and irrational in art.

The training should be postgraduate in order to include the basic elements as described in the Registration Advisory Committee's recommendations for a core course (see Chapter 24 for further details), although it was to be emphasised that the postgraduate year was something like a foundation for art therapy.

Given that the majority of art therapists were working single-handed and unsupervised, with a wide range of patients, BAAT officers stressed that basic training at postgraduate level was essential to safeguard patients' interests and give the best possible service.

The Honorary Secretary wrote to Donna Haber enclosing the draft career structure together with the justifications above, adding a note:

However, one thing which we have assumed is implicit in the negotiations for a complete new career and salary structure for art therapists is that we be quite separate from the OTs. I thought it best not to actually state that in the letter to the DHSS as it is not clear in the Joint

Establishing art therapy in the NHS

Secretaries document whether or not the DHSS is making the same assumption!

(Andrea Gilroy 24 October 1977)

Donna Haber forwarded the documents to the DHSS, mentioning that BAAT had felt the work of art therapists to be fairly described in the Joint Secretaries' Report and adding that the only persons who should be designated art therapists in the NHS should be those eligible for full membership of BAAT, with protection for those already in post, and that they should be responsible either to senior art therapists or to medical practitioners rather than to nurses or OTs: 'They [art therapists] have a unique role in the treatment of patients.'

(Note Bucher and Strauss's point about the 'sense of mission' among specialities:

It is characteristic of the growth of specialties that early in their development they carve out for themselves and proclaim unique missions. They issue a statement of the contribution that the specialty, and it alone, can make in a total scheme of values and, frequently, with it an argument to show why it is peculiarly fitted for this task. The statement of mission tends to take a rhetorical form, probably because it arises in the context of a battle for recognition and institutional status.

(Bucher and Strauss 1961: 326))

In Donna Haber's statement, a claim for the unique qualities of art therapists is explicitly made. As we shall see, both BAAT and ASTMS made use of rhetoric in letters and documents sent to the DHSS and at meetings and in instructions to members during the campaign against the DHSS's Consultative Document, which is described in the next chapter.

Donna Haber also had to remind the DHSS there was an approved training at the Birmingham Polytechnic, within the PGCE course. This was followed up by a letter from the Head of the School of Art Education at Birmingham to the DHSS, regretting the omission of Birmingham from the Joint Secretaries' Report. A reply was sent from the DHSS, saying that the decision to visit St Albans and Goldsmiths' was no reflection on Birmingham but was necessitated by the need to keep to an itinerary.

This issue is mentioned here because it was to reflect the growing ambivalence within BAAT about approving training programmes which were part of another profession's training. By that time (autumn 1977) Goldsmiths' had started a small Diploma in Art Therapy course and was about to separate from the ATC. St Albans had always been 'unhappy' about the recognition of anything less than a full-time art therapy course. BAAT Council wanted to continue to support Birmingham, however, due to its long and active involvement in art therapy, including having a mode

The Whitley Council

of the MA Art Education devoted to art therapy, and the possibility of a separate diploma starting there.

The key word for art therapists (at least the activists on council and among the membership) seemed to be 'autonomy' – from art education and from OT and they hoped that the Joint Secretaries' Report and their liaison with ASTMS would help them to achieve this.

Meeting with the British Association of Occupational Therapists

Despite the desire of art therapists to be recognised as separate from OT, both sides were aware that good working relationships existed in practice. It was therefore considered important by BAAT to try to establish some regular contact with BAOT, so that each association could clarify its position alongside the negotiations for art therapy to be brought under the Whitley Council. A meeting was arranged for 17 March 1978, at the BAOT office in London. It was attended by the Chair and Honorary Secretary of BAAT and John Evans, Head of Art Therapy at Herts College, and three officers from BAOT.

The meeting was friendly, and it was clear that OTs were recognising the aspirations of art therapists for a separate structure. The outcome was as follows:

BAOT urged unity among the arts therapy groups and between them and OTs, for it was suggested that any negotiations within Whitley would need the backing and support of OT.

They suggested that BAAT consider state registration, which would provide a link between a government body and BAAT. OTs were part of the Council for the Professions Supplementary to Medicine which meant that their training was inspected every four years, any changes having to be approved by the PSM and BAOT.

They felt a distinction should be made between the 'artist' in hospitals and the 'art therapist', and that the 'artist' could be on the grade of Technical Instructor and remain under OT.

They saw BAAT's main problem when negotiating to be in acquiring a separate budget. At that time (and often now) art therapy budgets were incorporated into OT budgets, and it was felt by BAOT advisable to leave it so, otherwise the budget would be very small and limited in scope.

BAOT suggested that, when the art therapy career structure was drawn up, a useful starting point for an art therapist would be the equivalent to the Senior OT grade, and that a requirement should be built in for 'untrained' people to be eligible for secondment to courses within a specified period of time.

The BAAT officers made it clear that they felt the issue of 'budget holding' to be important in determining the structure and scope of the art

Establishing art therapy in the NHS

therapy service, but they recognised that it was unlikely that a small emergent group would be granted its own management autonomy, even if it succeeded in gaining some clinical autonomy.

The meeting was felt by BAAT to have been useful and the council decided to investigate the possibility of art therapists joining the council of the PSM. They were cautious about this, given that speech therapists, with whom they felt some allegiance in terms of clinical practice, had withdrawn from negotiations to join the CPSM, feeling that the council was too prescriptive concerning, for example, training course syllabuses and examinations. They did not want a body outside their own College of Speech Therapists to have this degree of control of their occupation.

The DHSS's document on the use of art in hospitals

Shortly after the meeting with BAOT, BAAT acquired a document prepared by a DHSS adviser on art in hospitals. It was dated January 1977, meaning that it had been prepared after the Joint Secretaries had reported, but it did not take into account the findings of the report.

In brief, the document suggested four categories in which art could be used as a therapeutic activity for physically handicapped, mentally ill or mentally handicapped people, and identified the likely provider and the skills that would be required of the provider.

The categories were: life enrichment; development of potential skill; to achieve specific remedial results; the use of projective techniques.

The categories of provider listed included: artist, OT, helper, volunteer, doctor, nurse, social worker. There was no mention of art (or music) therapist.

The first two categories (life enrichment and development of potential skill) were felt not to require professional medical knowledge, but the other two (to achieve specific remedial results and the use of projective techniques) should, the author thought, be carried out by OTs. The document noted:

> Artists can make a valuable contribution and could contribute on (3) [to achieve specific remedial results] with additional knowledge. In all categories the provider should be part of the OT service.

This document caused consternation in the BAAT council as it had seemed to ignore those parts of the Whitley's own Staff *and* Management Sides' working party findings, which had been published in 1976, and which related to art therapists and their role. It was all the more astonishing as the BAOT had appeared to take note of these findings, yet the document had been prepared by the OT adviser. BAAT was not sure whether or not the document had been superseded by the Joint Secretaries' Report, or if it represented a 'forward plan' on behalf of the DHSS. The Honorary

192

The Whitley Council

Secretary wrote immediately to the DHSS, requesting a meeting between herself and the Chair and DHSS officers, to discuss the training and professional standards of art therapy. They stressed that they were not intending to try to negotiate a future status in the NHS prior to the Whitley's own deliberations, but to clarify ideas of a 'purely professional nature'. A draft copy of BAAT's Registration Advisory Committee's Report was included (April 1978).

A reply was received from DHSS on 14 August, suggesting a meeting on 24 October at the DHSS.

Art therapists' conditions and pay at this time continued to be calculated as a proportion of OT salaries. The rate in April 1978 was:

Single-handed: £3252–£4040
Under supervision: £2970–£3375.
For technical instructors (under OT) they were:
A grade: £3375–£4212 (equivalent to single-handed)
B grade: £2892–£3540 (equivalent to under supervision), (BAOT Salaries Bulletin L/78/AH).

Typical of the kind of letter that BAAT and ASTMS were used to receiving at that time was the following from a member in the Bristol area:

> There were two art therapist members of ASTMS paid as OT aides. They received £2241 per annum, the salary of 'helpers under supervision'. They had university degrees and the Diploma in Art Therapy from St. Albans. Their hospital manager had refused to acknowledge the existence of the various government circulars specifying rates of pay for art therapists (*ad hoc* grades) and had asked the members to prove that there was a special rate of pay. The members had filled vacant OT posts on three-month contracts.
>
> As a result of BAAT/ASTMS intervention, the members were transferred to the correct art therapy salary scale.
>
> (10 August 1978)

Such examples were a spur to the BAAT officers to maintain pressure on the DHSS and Whitley representatives.

In July 1978, Andrea Gilroy, Donna Haber and I attended the PTA Staff and Management Side of the Whitley Council, where there was a favourable response to art therapists being seen as a separate occupational group, with a proviso that those 'qualified' with a degree and a postgraduate art therapy training be termed 'art therapists' and those without should be called 'artists' and remain within the OT structure.

The Staff Side agreed to recommend to Management that:

a) Art therapy be seen as a separate group; and
b) PTA Committee 'A' should be asked whether art therapists could be accepted onto Committee 'A' which covered psychologists,

Establishing art therapy in the NHS

biochemists, physicists (the 'scientific' professions). (It was felt that this was somewhat unlikely, and that a more reasonable option would be Committee 'B' which covered speech therapists, whereas Committee 'C' covered OTs, physiotherapists, remedial gymnasts, etc.

A working party was formed to look into a possible career structure for art therapy.

Meeting with the DHSS

In October 1978, the long-awaited meeting with the DHSS took place with representatives from the training section and DHSS advisers.

The minutes of this meeting stated that the DHSS believed that:

> To look first in detail about ideas for training and qualification for art therapists was putting the cart before the horse. Other issues needed considering first, which included assessing the need for 'creative therapies' for different patient groups, and assessing how best their contributions could be co-ordinated into a rehabilitation group.

The DHSS considered that:

> A number of groups had worthwhile contributions to make: OT helpers, art teachers and volunteers, and that the Department believed there was a need to define and draw together the above issues and seek opinions on them from a wide range of NHS and other professional interests concerned, and as a result, to issue some definitive general guidance.

They felt that it was necessary to define the required job before discussing the training process (even though a job was already being done and had been seen to be done by the Joint Secretaries and training was actually in process, with the blessing by that time of the Council for National Academic Awards and to some extent the DHSS, at St Albans!).

BAAT officers agreed with the DHSS that BAAT 'could not act in isolation' and that there was 'a need to clarify the art therapist's role and how it could be developed'. They stated that it was their opinion that BAAT was already doing the job that the DHSS had not yet begun to do, which was to define the role of an art therapist and assess the best way to present the service to the patients.

BAAT's letters and recommendations were discussed at this meeting, especially the stated need for graduate entry to art therapy training, when OTs and physiotherapists did not have this. The officers were asked to explain how the role of the art therapist would interrelate with the work of the volunteer with 'artistic skills', the art and handicraft teacher, and the OT who sometimes used media for specific treatment.

The Whitley Council

They replied that there was an important distinction between arts and crafts provided for the purpose of 'life enrichment' (to quote the adviser's own document) and the work of an art therapist who was not using art for 'diversionary' purposes but as a therapeutic agency, and backed this up with examples from clinical practice.

All were able to agree on the need for therapists to work closely together in the 'best interests of patients' and that a clear referral system would be required to select appropriate patients for specific treatment. BAAT officers commented that they saw 'No reason why art therapists might not work independently and report directly to the consultant'.

(I have already mentioned that direct access to consultants was seen as important, so that the method of approach of the art therapist and likely effects of the process on the patient's behaviour could be understood and appreciated. I also mentioned in Chapter 17 that establishing a 'partnership' with psychiatrists might have been a strategy to achieve separation from OT and 'status by association' with the medical profession. Such a position presented problems for the view of art therapy as a 'radical' treatment, opposed to the medical model of psychiatry.)

The DHSS representatives concluded by repeating the Department's view that it was necessary to obtain 'a wide range of views on the main issues' and that he understood that a Consultative Paper would be produced shortly and BAAT would be included in the consultations.

In the BAAT council minutes following the meeting at DHSS, it was reported as having been 'difficult' in that it seemed that the Joint Secretaries' Report had not been much welcomed by the DHSS, in that the report had perceived art therapy as a 'unified discipline' and had mentioned that art therapists were performing specific duties apparently to the satisfaction of the medical team and their employers. Andrea Gilroy and I felt that the adviser's document of January 1977 had carried more weight in the DHSS, and that there was an attempt to group art therapists with 'artistic volunteers' and put them onto an OT helper grade. They saw their task as needing to make a very clear distinction between 'qualified' (in BAAT terms) art therapists, performing specific treatment-orientated tasks, and 'artists' who were engaged in 'diversionary' (or 'life-enriching') tasks.

They would use the findings of the Joint Secretaries' Report and the DHSS adviser's document as a basis for arguing a separate structure for art therapy: one which would separate them from the other staff and volunteers engaged in 'creative activities' in hospital. How to do that, yet to maintain the art base of the art therapy qualifications, presented a problem, in that much would rest on their skill at synthesising the 'know-how' from the art degree with that of the art therapy training, to provide a five-year training package.

195

Establishing art therapy in the NHS

In this respect, the work of the BAAT Registration and Training Committee was to prove vital, and this will be discussed in the last part of the book.

BAAT, then, had to pay attention to the 'public image' of art therapy and art therapists, and to 'relations with other professions'. Art therapists had rejected the image that the DHSS seemed to have of them, and had to engage in tactics to project their own image not only to the DHSS management but to other professions, particularly psychiatrists. This became extremely important during the campaign to counteract the recommendations in the Consultative Document, which I shall discuss in the next chapter.

Also important is the issue of 'synthesising' their art training with therapy training. (See Ben-David and Collins's discussion of scientific roles created by 'role-hybridisation', in which they refer to psychoanalysis and bacteriology:

> Freud attempted to maintain his status by trying to raise medical practice into a form of scientific research and as a result created psychoanalysis. Similarly, Pasteur gave rise to bacteriology by maintaining his theoretical perspectives after moving into research on wine fermentation, and elaborated his discovery into a new specialty.
>
> (Ben-David and Collins 1966: 459–60))

Art therapists had to find a way to convince the DHSS that they could produce a synthesis of four years of art education and the one-year art therapy training to produce the discipline of art therapy. This issue will be explored further in Part V.

Chapter twenty

The DHSS Consultative Document on art, music, drama, etc., therapy and the subsequent campaign by BAAT and ASTMS to change its recommendations

As the DHSS had indicated at the October meeting with BAAT officers, it was ready to issue a consultative paper concerning the above groups in the NHS. BAAT received a copy of the Consultative Document (referred to subsequently as 'the Document') on 20 November 1978, forwarded by Mr M. W. Perry at the DHSS. Comments were due by 21 February 1979. The accompanying letter stated that the DHSS would consider whether, in the light of comments received, a health circular on the subject would be helpful.

The Document mentioned the 'widespread acceptance of the value of art and other creative skills in making a valuable contribution to rehabilitation and improving the life style and preventing deterioration in the abilities of long-stay patients'.

The Document included much from the adviser's document of January 1977, in restating the categories of art activities and the providers, adding under (c) 'employment of staff termed art and music therapists etc., who are practised in the skills of their art and in some cases have had training in the therapeutic application of art'.

The Document recommended that:

> development in the use of creative media in therapy should continue, and that art therapists as at present employed will continue to provide a valuable part of the total pattern of services. The Department believes, however, that any movement for art therapy to develop as an organisationally separate NHS profession would be both unnecessary and undesirable in terms of the needs of the service; that it would run counter to the general policy of integration of the remedial professions; that it would add to the problems of co-ordinating rehabilitation programmes; that it could result in disputed responsibilities with OT departments, many of which already extensively use art media and the services of art practitioners of various kinds, and might lead to undesirable confinement to the scope and responsibility of OTs. Similar

197

Establishing art therapy in the NHS

independent status might well be sought by music and drama therapists and others, thus bringing further splintering.

The conclusion was that the DHSS should continue to appoint art therapists where there was agreement by consultants and OTs, and that for management purposes they should come within OT, to whom they would be accountable for referrals and budget.

Receipt of the Document caused extreme concern and anger among art therapists who saw their own recommendations, and those of the Joint Secretaries' Report apparently ignored in the interests of administrative convenience and cost and on the basis of flawed arguments about the nature of art therapy and its relationship with OT.

Immediately a campaign to quash the recommendations was mounted by BAAT and ASTMS, which was to be conducted through lobbying MPs, other trade unions, other professional associations and Royal Colleges, and the DHSS itself.

In December 1978, BAAT sent out a letter to all its members, enclosing a copy of the Document, the minutes of the October meeting at the DHSS, suggested questions for members to ask their MPs, and a postal motion for ASTMS branches. They were urged most strongly to write to their MPs and to go to ASTMS branch meetings to enlist support.

In the meantime, the officers, together with the BAAT Registration and Training Sub-Committee, set about replying to the Document, arguing against each recommendation. They referred to the Joint Secretaries' Report, and to the DHSS's own Working Party Report on the Remedial Professions of 1973, quoting a paragraph to support the idea of trained art therapists being directly responsible to consultants. They strongly disputed that OTs were qualified by their training and experience to supervise art therapists, basing their contention on an examination of 75 per cent of prospectuses from OT training centres.

The passage in the Document concerning integration was challenged.

We do not regard the Document's proposals as being about genuine integration but as an attempt to incite a large established group of staff to submerge and stunt the development of a smaller emergent group.

An attack was also made on the DHSS's criteria for 'art therapist':

BAAT strongly advises the DHSS to dispense with the irresponsibly outmoded two years post-A level requirement for art therapists which causes the very problem that DHSS is trying to avoid, namely small groups of unqualified staff calling themselves therapists. DHSS should accept the criteria for a qualified art therapist as stated in the Registration Advisory Committee Report and Recommendations, sent to the DHSS on publication in 1977.

198

The DHSS

BAAT included an analysis of the academic and professional qualifications of members, based on a survey of 150 registered members, showing that 117 had degree-level qualifications and 98 had an art therapy qualification recognised by BAAT. The majority of other members had another professional qualification (SRN, Certificate in Education, etc.). Eight had master's degrees and three had PhDs.

In February 1979, ASTMS sent their reply, pointing out the contradictions between the Document and the Joint Secretaries' Report and strongly protesting at the issuing of such a Document when negotiations were proceeding in the appropriate Whitley context. This was seen as an attempt by DHSS to pre-empt the negotiations.

But, in March 1979, BAAT received a letter from the Psychotherapy Section of the Royal College of Psychiatrists, enclosing a letter from the Council of the Royal College to the DHSS, which had been sent without consultation with the Psychotherapy Section. It stated that in the view of the college the Document was 'sensible and well prepared', and especially the part with special emphasis on the need to integrate the arts therapies into the hospital rehabilitation programme 'under the overall control of doctors'. The college agreed with the DHSS that art therapy should be organised by OT and be an integral part of OT. They commented:

> The fact that the majority of art and music therapists are not subject to any special training requirements and disciplinary procedures applicable to the Professions Supplementary to Medicine is an important factor in bringing them into the general rehabilitation programme. It was desirable for art therapists to be properly trained and important that these 'linked therapies' should not be given independent status but fully integrated.
>
> (Ref. C 7/79 EFCC 74/78)

At the request of BAAT, the Psychotherapy Section, which had previously been supportive of art therapists' attempts to gain separate status, agreed to send their own response.

The British Association of Occupational Therapists 'broadly agreed' with the Document, but suggested that new criteria be established by the DHSS so that the term 'therapist' was applied only to those who had taken a training in art therapy. They were keen to see a comprehensive therapeutic and rehabilitation service, with shared opportunities for education and training. 'OTs do, however, recognise that postgraduate experience and training are essential elements in the development of their own expertise in these areas.' They foresaw a situation where OTs would take a one-year art therapy course in order to use the skills and techniques of art therapy, but they would not be defined as 'art therapists'. This had already been identified as a problem by BAAT back in 1970, on the formation of the St Albans Course, which was prepared to accept OTs.

199

Establishing art therapy in the NHS

They did recognise, however, that for staff who were 'qualified and experienced in the therapeutic application of technique' it might be experienced as restrictive to be under the 'umbrella' of OT, and that it might not be necessary for all referrals to go through OT.

The response from Herts College of Art in April 1978 drew attention to the fact that the Council for National Academic Awards (CNAA) had validated its postgraduate Diploma in Art Therapy, and that a high level of competence had been declared by its Health and Medical Services Panel through a rigorous validation process. They had stated that:

> The level of knowledge achieved in psychiatry, clinical psychology and psychotherapy is at least as high and arguably higher than that achieved by OT – that view being confirmed by the number of OTs at senior level who had completed the course.

Furthermore, the CNAA had asked the OTs on the course what was provided there which was not provided within OT training. They had been informed that the course covered the use of art and art therapy in a 'very special way' and gave a better understanding of operating in a therapeutic team. They felt they could reach the same end point as the art graduates, due to their greater experience in therapy. This was strongly disputed by BAAT, given that art graduates normally had a four-year immersion in art practice prior to art therapy training, and OT basic training covered a very wide area and did not include psychotherapy.

The Herts response concluded that:

> Only those persons who are full members of BAAT should be called art therapists and be recognised in the same way as OTs, physiotherapists, etc. It is unacceptable for another professional group to control and supervise referrals and treatment; no other precedent exists for one professional group to control the practice of another.... For clinical purposes, the medical consultant is responsible for treatment and there should be direct access to that person.

Herts reference to 'professional' groups does somewhat beg the disputed question as to whether art therapists could be identified as a 'profession': there was considerable doubt in the minds of the DHSS as to whether or not art therapists even formed an occupational group!

BAAT members were very active in writing to and discussing the Document with their MPs, and as a result MPS wrote in large numbers to the Health Minister, who stressed the 'consultative nature' of the document.

Unexpected support for BAAT's case was provided by SCOPE, a group of OTs who were interested in promoting 'creative therapies in the NHS and other settings and to encourage their general use by OTs as well as by specialists in the field'.

200

The DHSS

Although SCOPE 'welcomed' the Document, they considered that there was:

No adequate recognition of specialism in creative therapies and in particular it showed no regard for the training and membership of the professional associations. It largely overlooked the distinction between those who had specialised and those who had no training. It nowhere mentioned that creative therapies had achieved erudition and authority in their field.

They did not agree with amalgamation, which they felt would secure nothing but 'rifts, resentments and disharmony'. There would be no problem of co-ordination as this already existed, and the Document had exaggerated possible disputes over areas of work:

Commonly OTs value the skills of creative therapists and regard them as a resource and not as a threat. Likewise creative therapists acknowledge the contribution of OTs trained to work in this area. Expertise should be complemented and nurtured.

They went as far as to recommend the establishment of creative therapy departments, and that trained and professionally recognised therapists should have independent status and work closely with other therapists. Untrained assistants should be responsible to trained counterparts in their own field.

Although a small group (about 130 members) SCOPE represented a fairly strong voice within OT. SCOPE members tended to be young, more politically aware, and somewhat dissatisfied with their own professional training and position. Their response was a considerable contrast to that of the BAOT council.

BISAT responded with comments similar to those of BAAT. It expressed itself

saddened by the DHSS' approach, in that it ignores the increasing body of knowledge concerning the application of arts therapy which has been built up through the pioneering work of the past 30 years.

BAAT received more than 100 copies of documents from individuals and groups of staff, and professional associations, responding to the Document. A fairly typical response was from one area paramedical committee, signed by a head OT, a senior psychologists, and a music therapist, which refuted the Document's claims. They felt that it was obscure and lacked understanding of the breadth and variety of employment situations, and furthermore was inaccurate in its presentation of the basis of art therapy which was not in OT but in psychoanalysis and psychiatry. It added, 'OTs do not profess to possess the level of skills in art or music attained by properly qualified arts therapists.'

Establishing art therapy in the NHS

It was clear that the DHSS was particularly concerned at the possibility of small professions emerging and demanding separate career and management structures, which was contrary to the move towards larger units.

A letter from Eric Deakin, Minister of Health, in February 1979 to one MP gave further insight into the DHSS view:

> Concern has been expressed at the possible risk of a proliferation of new therapy professions involving the grafting of therapy training onto previously acquired artistic skills and at the danger that rehabilitation services might become too diffuse if each new therapy develops in an independent way within each hospital. The Consultative Document outlines these dangers and puts up proposals for bringing the various therapies together as far as possible so they can be coordinated within an established department (the OT department is suggested as an appropriate link but other possibilities exist) whose roles and activities are already well known to other professional staff.... The real benefit to the NHS comes when people trained in art – not necessarily to degree level – are taught how to apply that training in a therapy context to particular types of patient. At present most available training in art therapy as such is of only one year's duration whereas the OT, whose training includes training in art therapy as well, undergoes a three-year course geared to the needs of the NHS.

Here we have a clear example of attempted state control of professions and an assumption that a huge, abstract entity like the NHS could have 'needs' which could be met through training. The DHSS's officers seem to be concerned lest there be a proliferation of small groups, which would be difficult to manage and 'uneconomic'. (Art therapists were inclined to think that the power of the *medium* of art therapy, with its emphasis on evoking unconscious material through images, was also responsible for the DHSS's wish to keep it under OT, and hence 'under control'.)

The replies from the health ministers to the various MPs became gradually slightly more defensive as the campaign mounted. They stressed that the views of art therapists were being taken into account, and a letter to Michael Marshall MP in February 1979 stated:

> This is just a consultative document and cannot be regarded as a firm statement of the NHS or departmental policy.

Another (to Hugh Jenkins) said

> No slight to art therapists is intended, since it is recognised that many are very skilled in their work and performing a valuable specialist function within the NHS

and

The DHSS

We appreciate that in many cases the OT would have received less specialised training in art than an art therapist who has completed one of the 1 year courses, but she would be better equipped than the art therapist to determine which form of therapy was most beneficial in a given set of circumstances.

A senior OT from Hertfordshire argued, however, that the Document

can only be seen as a retrograde step for these professions... OTs and art therapists work well together... the Head OT should not really be expected to be clinically responsible for therapists of specific training other than her own.

Articles and letters appeared in various therapy journals and newspapers, revealing considerable dissent within the OT profession about the Document and their own relationship with art therapists.

The campaign to correct the facts in the Document and to defeat its recommendations occupied the Councils of both BAAT and the music and drama therapy associations fully between November 1978 and April 1979 (for although drama therapists were not yet organised in terms of training or numbers, they looked to the future, and in this respect the DHSS was correct). It was mainly the efforts of the council and members of BAAT and the Association of Professional Movement Therapists, who had by then also linked with ASTMS, in conducting the campaign which had some effect in getting the DHSS to modify its stance.

Discussions with the Council for Professions Supplementary to Medicine

In view of the advice given by BAOT at the joint meeting with BAAT before the Consultative Document was issued, and as a result of the Document itself, BAAT asked for an informal discussion with the CPSM. This was agreed for 26 June 1979.

The CPSM had strict guidelines for accepting professions on to its register:

1. that the profession had reached maturity, and had an established and recognised governing body;
2. that it was based on a systematic body of knowledge, which may or may not be wholly scientific in character, which was compatible with the body of knowledge for the time being attributed and acknowledged to be the basis of contemporary medical practice;
3. that the profession had a mutually accepted relationship with the organisations taken to represent practitioners of contemporary medical practice; and that such medical organisations were willing to

Establishing art therapy in the NHS

nominate medical practitioners who were prepared to serve on a board of the new profession;
4. that the profession had a recognised course of training over a substantial period;
5. that its examinations were adequate and properly conducted, with particular reference to the appointment of recognised external examiners or assessors, for example by the universities or Royal Colleges;
6. that a minimum standard of education was enforced for all entrants although special provision may be made for the acceptance of mature students;
7. that the applicant organisation should have an appropriate and acceptable code of conduct regulating relationships with patients and members of other professions or be able to satisfy the Council that the members of the profession were willing to be governed by such a code.

The CPSM was responsible for identifying and accrediting the component professions and for registering them. The PSM Act of 1960 did not limit employment or professional services only to those who were registered, but there had been attempts to make it an offence to use the common title (dietitian, etc.) without being registered.

After an exploratory meeting, BAAT decided that membership of the CPSM at that time could bring too many restrictions without necessarily any advantages. The status 'supplementary' to medicine did not appeal, nor did the statement in the CPSM's letter accompanying the guidelines that the Occupational Therapy Board would be consulted should BAAT wish to pursue an application.

Had BAAT proceeded, an extension of the act of 1960 would have needed to be approved by Parliament. It was at that stage that speech therapists had withdrawn their application.

Meeting with the Occupational Advisory Committee of ASTMS

In March 1979, I asked Donna Haber if she would attend a meeting of the above, in order to put the facts about art therapy training and standards to the committee as the DHSS had extended their deadline for receipt of responses to the Document and BAAT wanted the OAC to support BAAT's case for art therapy to be recognised as a postgraduate profession – as equivalent to clinical psychology, for example.

I attended a meeting on 11 July 1979. There was general sympathy with art therapists, but the psychologists were hesitant about agreeing art therapy training to be on a similar level to their own. The biochemists strongly disagreed. There was, however, support on a 'union' basis for art therapists to be seen as a separate professional group.

The DHSS

By this time there had been no further development from the Joint Secretaries' recommendations and art therapists were in a kind of limbo as a result of waiting to see how the DHSS would respond to the replies to the Consultative Document and waiting for the Whitley Council to act.

However, these matters were to remain unresolved due to the government's setting up a commission to look into the pay levels of the PSM grades, speech therapists and helpers – and also the *ad hoc* grades, to which art therapists still belonged. This was under the chairmanship of Professor Clegg, with a secretariat provided by the Office of Manpower Economics.

Chapter twenty-one

The Clegg Commission

The last major review of the pay and conditions of the Professions Supplementary to Medicine had been undertaken in 1974, under the chairmanship of the Rt. Hon. Earl of Halsbury. The Halsbury Committee had reported in December 1974 and recommended pay increases backdated to May 1974. On 14 March 1979, the Staff and Management Sides of the Whitley Council submitted to the Secretary of State for Social Services a jointly agreed document, setting out the case for a comparability study for the PSMs, on similar lines to the study then envisaged for nurses and midwives. This document states that since Halsbury the pay of the PSMs had declined, and that the precise shortfall could only be properly established by an 'independent and impartial consideration of all the relevant factors'.

The Commission was established under the chairmanship of Professor Clegg to look into the pay levels of all the professions covered by the PTA Council, including the *ad hoc* grades which were being considered for assimilation into Whitley. Evidence was received from several different sources, one of which was a firm of management consultants, Hay MSL Ltd. Hay employees analysed the content of a sample of the jobs of the grades involved, and advised the Commission of their opinion as to what salaries those jobs would command outside the NHS.

Hay sent questionnaires to about 100–125 people, and the answers formed the basis of job descriptions. A proportion of those sending in questionnaires were interviewed. Evidence was also received from the Staff Side of Whitley and from unions.

Working with ASTMS Research Group, Andrea Gilroy and myself prepared some responses to the Hay questionnaires, which were organised under 'Know How', 'Problem Solving', and 'Accountability'.

On the basis of the questionnaire, art therapists scored high in all areas and were rated by ASTMS Research Group as comparable with clinical psychologists and with lecturers in art at colleges of further or higher education as an 'outside NHS' comparator. They were similar to the latter in that they determined individual relationships and responses, and at the

The Clegg Commission

same time carefully monitored the development and progress of the subjects.

However, in comparing their pay with these two groups, the result was as follows:

Clinical Psychologist: Basic rate £3486 rising to £3915
Art Lecturer Grade I: £3480–£5988
Art Therapist: £3041–£3679.

On basic rates there was not much difference, *but* the art lecturer could rise to a maximum of £9639 as a principal lecturer and the psychologist to over £10,000, whereas the ceiling for art therapy was £3679.

ASTMS submitted evidence for BAAT, and the Hay researchers interviewed two art therapists in psychiatric and mental handicap hospitals in Surrey and Kent.

ASTMS prepared a document, to which BAAT submitted a chapter on art therapists, entitled *The Forgotten Professions*. This was widely reported in the press. *The Times* social services correspondent wrote:

Representatives of 26000 highly skilled health service employees described as belonging to the 'forgotten professions' have called for substantial pay rises in evidence submitted to the Clegg Commission on Pay Comparability. At the same time Britain's top 350 nurses have put in a large pay claim to the Whitley Council to bring them into line with other senior health authority staff.... The Clegg Commission has heard from ASTMS that speech therapists, radiographers, technical instructors, art therapists and chiropodists should receive pay increases of between 30 and 150 per cent... the union's divisional officer, Miss Donna Haber, said that people were drifting away from these professions because of the poor pay: 'Some women are leaving because they are making a lot more money as secretaries'.

(The Times 15 September 1979)

Meeting at the DHSS

On 22 October 1979, I received a letter from the DHSS, inviting Andrea Gilroy and me to have an informal talk with the training section. This was useful as it allowed us to stress the developments going on in BAAT's training sub-committee towards presentation of a core-course syllabus.

In February, Mr Perry from the DHSS wrote to myself and Julia Robbins of BAOT, who had agreed to co-ordinate a joint BAAT–BAOT working party as a result of the Consultative Document responses. The letter said that the DHSS had heard from the Royal College of Psychiatrists that they were unable to present a 'college view' on the Document.

Establishing art therapy in the NHS

From the comments that had been received from other individuals and groups, it appeared that the following were most pertinent:

1. that there should be as much flexibility as possible in local arrangements for employing art therapists;
2. that there appeared to be a need for a clear distinction between creative therapists with appropriate qualifications in the therapeutic application of artistic skills and those with solely art qualifications, and the term 'therapist' should only be applied to the former;
3. clinical accountability of creative therapists with appropriate therapeutic qualifications should be decided locally;
4. there was no need for a separate managerial and administrative structure for this field of activity.

Perry reported that the DHSS was considering what action might usefully be taken by the DHSS, and that nos 1 and 4 were affected by the wider implications for management in the NHS which were contained in the new government White Paper *Patients First*.

The Report is published

BAAT eagerly awaited the publication of the Clegg Report, which came out in March 1980. However, its results were very disappointing. Under the heading 'Helpers and the *Ad Hoc* Grades', Paragraph 57 stated:

> The evidence concerning handicraft teachers is even more slender than that for helpers and technical instructors and the posts evaluated for art and music therapists could not be regarded as representative of the pay grade. Accordingly we propose to leave those grades, along with other grades not investigated by the consultants, to be fitted into the new salary structure at the appropriate points.
>
> (Report No. 4 PSM: 16)

This statement, following the submission of so much evidence prepared in co-operation with a professional research group, and the completion of lengthy, complex questionnaires followed by in-depth interviews, caused fury among BAAT members and considerable consternation to ASTMS who had submitted the evidence. They speculated that the art therapists who had been interviewed had come out higher on the Hay scale than occupational therapists at the same level.

Another campaign had to be mounted, but this time in co-operation with other NHS grades who were disputing the findings of the Clegg Commission. It was organised by ASTMS. On 21 March 1980, I wrote to all BAAT members, enclosing a note about emergency action which had

The Clegg Commission

been arranged by ASTMS in response to the Clegg Report. This was to include a march and lobby of parliament.

Letters of protest were sent to MPs, including Patrick Jenkin, then Secretary of State for Social Services. The Commission's methods and results were challenged by a wide body of professional workers, including psychiatrists. An editorial in the *Guardian* (13 March) went so far as to suggest that the government had issued instructions to Clegg to contain his findings within certain specified guidelines, and art therapists felt that this was the main reason for their exclusion.

ASTMS rejected the Clegg Commission's recommendations on several grounds:

1. any increase in the working week was totally unacceptable;
2. even if full recommended salary levels were to be paid, on current working hours they would be too low;
3. the recommendations for emergency treatment duty payments were 'an insult';
4. *Ad hoc* grades, such as art and music therapists, had been ignored;
5. Clegg had debilitated the career structure of PSMs by failing to recognise the skills of members.

ASTMS also questioned the independence of the Clegg Report.

A lobby and meeting was arranged to take place in the House of Commons Grand Committee Room on 27 March. It was attended by many art and music therapists, and representatives from other health service professions, including psychiatrists and psychologists, who supported the PSMs.

As part of their contribution to the lobby of Parliament, art therapists prepared a statement about their level of qualification and the nature of their work, ending with 'We demand a decent level of pay appropriate to the skills and qualifications of art therapists.' This was distributed during the lobby and march, and at the meeting attended by Dr Gerard Vaughan, then Minister for Health. This gave an opportunity for art therapists, and the other health service groups present, to vent their frustration vocally to a health minister who, until recently, had been a consultant psychiatrist in the NHS.

Further action was agreed at the ASTMS Disputes Committee at the King's Fund Centre in London on 1 April, including one-day stoppages. It was the first time that art therapists had considered taking strike action, but they agreed to join other ASTMS members. Donna Haber was to arrange an 'early-day' motion in parliament to reject the Clegg recommendations. BAAT members were to contact their MPs and lobby where possible.

Establishing art therapy in the NHS

On 21 April, I wrote to Patrick Jenkin, expressing the 'grave concern and disappointment' that Clegg failed to make any recommendations about art therapists' future career structure or rates of pay:

> We were led to believe that the Clegg Commission would make recommendations which would then facilitate our entry onto the Whitley Council, but despite the most carefully prepared and extensive written evidence submitted by ASTMS and BAAT, only two art therapists were interviewed and we learn from Clegg that these were not considered representative of the pay grade. How was this decision reached and on what evidence? Why were more art therapists not interviewed if this was the case?

A meeting was requested at the earliest opportunity, and BAAT officers duly met Jenkin at the House, where he showed considerable sympathy with their case and pointed out that the proposals contained in *Patients First* would affect management structures in the NHS. To BAAT's suggestion that art therapists should manage themselves, he replied that art therapists had every possibility of becoming managers, if they so wished, but pointed to the problem of small professions managing themselves in terms of overall budgeting. (*Patients First* was issued in December 1979. The bases of the proposals were to abolish the Area Health Authorities, to give more emphasis to local arrangements, and to give more power to Regional Health Authorities. They were passed into legislation in 1982.)

In the House of Commons on 29 April, an oral answer was given to a question concerning art and music therapists asked by Ian Mikardo, MP. Gerard Vaughan replied that their salary levels were determined by the DHSS in relation to those of OTs, and

> Now that the Council had agreed on a settlement of the Clegg Award to OTs, new salary levels for art and music therapists will be fixed with effect from 1 April and they will be announced shortly.

He added:

> I should like art and music therapists to be formally allocated to a Whitley Council so that their pay and conditions can be properly negotiated between NHS management and the staff organisations concerned.

MP Janet Foulkes asked about speech therapists, but Vaughan replied that art and music therapists were related to OTs and technical instructors (and not to speech therapists).

It was clear from the response both of Clegg and Vaughan that the government had made up its corporate mind that art therapists should be linked to OT despite the copious evidence from the Consultative Docu-

The Clegg Commission

ment replies, including those from many OTs and independent professionals who had questioned this link or actively disputed it on historical and theoretical grounds. The art therapists interviewed by Hay MSL, who were considered by Clegg to have been 'untypical', had contradicted the government's 'view' of art therapy. However, instead of arranging to interview other art therapists at random, or paying attention to the Joint Secretaries' 1976 findings, the Commission appeared to have colluded with the DHSS. If the two art therapists were 'untypical' then where had the criteria for 'typical' art therapists come from? This was a question that art therapists were asking, with considerable anger and bitterness at that stage.

On 22 May, Vaughan wrote to BAAT, expressing his sympathy with art therapists' frustrations. He pointed out that the new rates of pay for PTA 'A' staff were exactly equal to OTs instead of being 98 per cent of them, at the basic grade and Senior II level. He added that, after 1 June 1980, any new art therapy appointments would be approved only for candidates who had a qualification in art therapy from Herts College of Art, Goldsmiths' College, or Birmingham Polytechnic (as recommended by BAAT). New appointments under the old regulations would be at instructor level, with lower rates than for art therapists.

Vaughan stressed that he wanted to see art therapists allocated to a functional Whitley Council so that their pay, conditions of service, and grading criteria could be negotiated between NHS management and the staff organisations concerned. Referring to the issue of separate management for art therapy, he said that this was affected by wider implications for management in the NHS resulting from the recent consultation paper *Patients First*.

This letter gave some slight cheer to the BAAT members who had fought two major campaigns in two years, and who were still struggling with difficult working conditions and low salaries.

True to Vaughan's word, in May 1980 the DHSS published a Personnel Memorandum, limiting the employment of art therapists to those with:

a qualification above GCE A level standard in art or music and a further qualification obtained on a course of at least one year's full-time study in the therapeutic application of their art or music skill, such as the Diploma in Art or Music therapy.

(PM(80)17)

Salary scales were then:
Single-handed £4500–£5300
Under supervision £3800–£4500.

The new rates were an improvement and were no longer a proportion of OT rates, but they were still *ad hoc* and appointments could be approved

Establishing art therapy in the NHS

only by the DHSS. The definition had failed to stipulate possession of a degree in art or music or other subject prior to therapy training, which would have given a better chance of a claim to postgraduate standing, on the same level as psychologists.

However, the requirement for training, as recommended by BAAT, was seen as a step forward.

Struggle for a Whitley place

In August 1980, Donna Haber received a suggestion from the Management Side of Whitley that art and music therapists be termed: 'Remedial Instructor II', if under supervision, and 'I', if single-handed. They were to be firmly under the OT department and would have limited responsibilities therein.

This proposal was strongly rejected by BAAT, ASTMS, and the Staff Side of Whitley. ASTMS notified Whitley that proposals for a career structure would be produced by BAAT/ASTMS and submitted for consideration.

There were difficult issues to resolve concerning pre-therapy training requirements. The DHSS already approved nurses and OTs taking art therapy training at Herts College as well as those with a degree in art or art education. However, they did not sanction this for graduates with other degrees. BAAT, Goldsmiths', and Birmingham wanted to limit entry to graduates in art and design or art education in order to make a foundation to rest the one-year training upon. This will be further discussed in the training section, but is mentioned here as it was an internal problem to art therapy as an occupational group and had grown from philosophical and ideological positions concerning the nature of the discipline.

The DHSS was prepared to accept: a degree in art or psychology, a teaching qualification with a specialism in art, a nursing or OT qualification. They felt that social work and degrees in other arts would render candidates 'borderline'. They would not accept people with 'other degrees' even if the colleges had accepted them and advised colleges who wished to accept 'special cases' to contact the DHSS first.

By August 1980, nearly four years had gone by since the Joint Secretaries' Report and there was still no decision about assimilation of *ad hoc* grades. The Personnel Memorandum of June 1980 gave an important boost, however, in requiring an art therapy training for art therapists instead of the previous two years' post-A level art, which meant that they could be separated out from art instructors, who, like technical instructors, were to remain under OT. There were, of course, a large group of TIs who were more useful to the head count system of calculating OT salaries than art or music therapists. BAOT recommended that art and music therapists 'can be treated quite separately from the other *ad hoc* grades'.

212

The Clegg Commission

Following a meeting of BAAT officers with the DHSS's medical and OT advisers, and with ASTMS, in June 1980, it was decided to relate the art therapy career structure to that of the other PSM grades. Speech therapists were used as a comparator. A draft proposal was to be considered by the Management Side in January 1981, after which, if approved art therapists would have to be allocated to a committee. The proposal was, however, not approved, so a meeting was called with DHSS advisers to try to resolve the problems.

In June 1981, BAAT, APMT (music therapists), ASTMS, and Management Side representatives met to try to finalise the proposals. I had already been in contact with the DHSS who were concerned that the structure should be in line with those of other NHS employees (notably OTs).

Donna Haber opened the meeting by giving the Staff Side view of the most appropriate grading structure for art therapy, which was based on that for speech therapy. She noted that Management had turned this down and proposed a link with OT. The structure had been duly prepared as follows:

1. Art therapist (often known as 'basic grade'). This was not intended to be used initially, but reserved for the future as a possible 'probationary' grade.
2. Senior II
3. Senior I
4. Head IV
5. Head III.

In view of the very small numbers of art therapists, it was not thought necessary by the Whitley Council to include grades above Head III (promotion to which was determined by the number of practitioners in the department), but that an allowance should be made for an art therapist who advised at district level.

It was the view of the working party which discussed the grading structure that most practising art therapists who were already on the 'single-handed' scale would be assimilated on to the Senior II grade. This left the problem of criteria for promotion to Senior I to be determined. In the Whitley Handbook, such criteria for OT included provision of 'advanced techniques'. In the case of art therapy, these might include: provision of an out-patient service, family therapy, advising and educating other professions on the use of art and music therapy, working with groups of patients regarded as having special difficulties (e.g. drug addicts).

Management Side suggested forming a joint staff-management working party following assimilation, so that all applications to promotion above Senior II level could be scrutinised with a view to determining criteria for the future. This was to be considered by BAAT, APMT, and

213

Establishing art therapy in the NHS

ASTMS together with the definition of 'highly skilled and specialised' work. They agreed to submit a paper for another meeting in July.

The issue concerning pre-therapy qualifications was still not resolved, and the DHSS was pressed to dispense with any reference to '2 years' post-A level art' as a prerequisite. A definition offered by Staff Side was: 'A qualification for entry to the grade of art therapist would be an appropriate university degree or equivalent plus successful completion of a one-year full time or two years half time postgraduate course'. This was passed to Management for consideration.

At the following meeting on 17 July, it was agreed to set up a joint panel to define Senior I posts and to agree a set of criteria for 'highly skilled and specialised' as these terms related to art therapy. Both health authorities and individuals should be able to refer to the panel, which would consist of representatives from Staff and Management of Whitley, and art and music therapists. It would have a maximum of eight and minimum of four members.

A letter from the DHSS to Donna Haber of 17 August noted that their aim was to circulate the draft career structure to both sides of Whitley in time for consideration at the next meeting on 17 September. The draft was turned down. On requesting the reasons from the DHSS, it appeared that Management Side were not in favour of the 'art therapist' (basic grade) being reserved for future use only. They also felt the definition for Senior I to be too vague, and did not feel the note concerning advice at district level to be appropriate.

BAAT officers arranged to meet representatives from Whitley in November, to go through the document again. Despite some last minute misgivings on the part of Herts College, who felt that inclusion of the Birmingham option and Goldsmiths' diploma might cause the DHSS to set the salary scales, etc., lower than if only Herts' CNAA-validated diploma had been included, the planned career structure was presented to the full Whitley Council on 19 November 1981 and was agreed.

The DHSS circulated a draft of a proposed 'advanced letter' (or Personnel Memorandum) concerning art and music therapists, attaching a note recently circulated by BAOT, explaining aspects of the agreement to those OTs who were then managing art therapists.

The art therapy courses were notified and asked to comment. Herts College noted that they did not feel the Birmingham course met core course requirements, and requested BAAT council to pressure Birmingham for a proposal for a full-time art therapy course. There was disappointment that the career structure was at the same level as that for OTs. BAAT requested that the approved courses (Birmingham, Goldsmiths', and Herts) should be listed separately, with the full name of the course included. The question of pre-therapy training criteria was to be

214

The Clegg Commission

left up to the colleges concerned, with the proviso that these should normally be at graduate level.

Most of the suggestions were incorporated into the advance letter, and, in March 1982, the DHSS issued PM(82)6, confirming the previous draft document. Art therapists had, then, achieved a separate career and salary structure, and some ability to negotiate their terms and conditions under Whitley. However, they were not considered numerically large enough to warrant a seat on the Council, so were dependent on ASTMS to represent them. They saw their next major task as acquiring a seat and gradually improving their conditions and salaries.

The issue of separate management had still to be resolved and the DHSS would make no firm recommendations on this, preferring to leave management arrangements at local level.

The news about the assimilation was received with much enthusiasm by BAAT members, though tinged with disappointment that the structure was limited and linked to OT. It produced a sense of having 'arrived' as a 'profession' and an end to '*ad hoc*' days.

Part V

Training in art therapy

Introduction

One of the requirements for registration as a profession under the Council for the Professions Supplementary to Medicine, when BAAT explored this possibility in 1977, was that the profession had a 'recognised course of training' over a substantial period, and that its examinations were 'adequate' and properly conducted, and that a minimum educational standard should be enforced for all entrants to training.

Dyne, in his paper on problems in training for psychotherapy (1985), draws attention to the two forms of statutory control of professions which are intended to protect the public and to regulate activities. 'Functional' control prohibits practice for fee or reward by unregistered persons and controls the function of the profession in society. 'Indicative' control protects the name by which practitioners practise, and makes it an offence to call oneself by these names and thereby to claim membership of the profession. Dyne suggests that each has its problems, but that indicative control is more workable because practice is firmly based in public academic studies, trainings are conducted in public institutions variously accountable to government and profession; and practice is hedged by many legally enforceable regulations (e.g. building regulations and restrictions, for architecture, and the right to prescribe drugs, for medicine). 'Thus although these professions are indicatively controlled de jure, de facto they closely match functional control. With certain exceptions, the field of psychotherapy has no such bases or limitations' (1985: 93–4).

Inclusion on the CPSM Register would have given both forms of control, but, as previously explained, it is doubtful whether BAAT could have defined the function of art therapy clearly enough to succeed in joining the CPSM, even if art therapists had wanted this.

BAAT certainly did want art therapy training to take place in the public, and therefore the regulated, sector, however, rather than in private institutions. From its earliest days, BAAT had set itself the brief to devise programmes of training for art therapy and to set standards for practice, anticipating that if art therapy was to become a discrete occupational group and acquire a career and salary structure which met the aspirations

Training in art therapy

of its members, it would be necessary to introduce training courses which would contribute to the formation of art therapy's identity in the eyes of the relevant ministries.

In the following chapters I have attempted to put art therapy training into a context alongside training for some other professions, such as nursing, occupational therapy, and art teaching, and have traced the development of the first art therapy courses.

To demonstrate that there were several critical factors which led to training being established in some institutions and not in others, I have also briefly discussed instances where proposals for art therapy training were put forward (to BAAT and even to the Council for National Academic Awards) but did not gain approval. Bearing in mind Ben-David and Collins's discussion of the way that new ideas are taken up at certain times and in certain places (1966: 452), it will be interesting to consider that the 'adoption' of art therapy training by certain institutions may have been in large part a result of their need for diversification and role change following governmental pressures on higher education, and that this opportunity was seized by those art therapists who happened to be in the right place at the right time and had the potential to develop the courses.

Chapter twenty-two

Some contextual background and early views on training

The literature

There is little critical literature concerning art therapy training emanating from British authors, except by the author herself (1987: 200–2) and incorporated into more general articles on the theory and practice of art therapy (Birtchnell 1976, 1980). There is currently a major review by BAAT's Training and Education Sub-Committee of training taking place and this is the first since the 'core course' was introduced in 1978. In 'Art therapy and adolescence', I have suggested that current art therapy training may expose students to contradictions similar to those of social work students (Cannan 1972: 248), resulting in confusion and apparently 'adolescent' behaviour in the profession. Birtchnell has persistently challenged the dominance of art graduates in the profession, believing that they exaggerate the importance of art in art therapy and use such expressions as 'the therapeutic value of art'. He believes that the insistence of the professional association on art-graduate status is nothing more than political expedience (1977).

There is some descriptive literature in *Inscape*, one issue, 3 (2) 1979, being devoted to training, with articles by John Evans, describing the training at Hertfordshire College of Art, myself, describing Goldsmiths', and two students giving their impressions of these courses. In the following issue, 4(1), Peter Byrne describes training and research at Birmingham Polytechnic, and another student gives her response to the training issue, deploring the 'competitiveness' which she experienced between students trained at different colleges. The deliberations of the BAAT Registration and Training Committee were published in *Inscape* 1978 2 (1), together with recommendations for a 'core course' of training. (This will be discussed in detail in Chapter 24.)

Training in art therapy

Some comparisons with other occupational groups

As the accounts of 'pioneers' of art therapy training within the British higher education system demonstrate, establishing such training was a slow and painful process, as is the case with most new disciplines. Art therapists did not, however, go along the same path as psychotherapists in establishing training primarily within the private sector, possibly because this would have been in conflict with the trade union orientation of BAAT, and may have served to keep art therapy 'on the margins' rather than integrated into the education and health services. The training of psychotherapists has tended to take place in private institutes, has been very expensive and not subjected to the stringent regulations and validating processes that universities and polytechnics are bound by. (More recently charitable foundations have offered low cost psychotherapy, and training has begun to be offered in the public sector.) Even Champernowne, who had piloted short courses of art therapy training at Withymead, was convinced of the need to establish full scale training within the public sector, and preferably the universities.

This was in contrast to other professionals, or occupational groups, such as nursing and occupational therapy, whose training during the 1970s was still concentrated in nursing schools and OT colleges funded by the DHSS, rather than in universities and polytechnics, where it has since developed. Students spent much of their time as 'apprentices' in hospitals, in a hierarchical system which did not encourage questioning and criticism, or expose students to the range of opinion and diversity of teaching styles normally found in universities, polytechnics and art colleges (the latter containing a fair number of staff and students with 'radical' opinions or at least prepared to question the status quo – Madge and Weinberger 1973 discuss this.

Salvage, in *The Politics of Nursing* (1985), a critique of nursing practice and training, draws attention to this important difference in the status of student nurses as opposed to 'ordinary' university students and the effect it has on their subsequent attitude and practice. (See also Melia 1983; Baly 1980; Waller 1987, for elaboration of this point.)

Early views on training for art therapy

The question of what constituted a suitable training for the practice of art therapy had perplexed various individuals and committees from the late 1940s on. The emphasis tended to be on content and entry requirements.

Marie Petrie, in discussing the value of art for children with emotional and behavioural difficulties, made the following comment:

222

Early views on training

To trained eyes, definite symptoms of whatever psychic difficulties, fears or inhibitions the child is suffering from will here emerge, documented not only by the choice of subject, by the content or absence of content of the drawing, painting or model, but as much or more by the general handling or by the means employed. I hasten to add that these trained eyes do not as yet really exist, or exist perhaps only in a few isolated cases, for any really reliable diagnosis would demand not only the experience of the trained child psychologist but also that of the trained art teacher.

(Petrie 1946a: 77–8)

Petrie felt that if the psychologist was an artist, able to understand the language of the art used in analysis, she might be able to utilise the children's drawings as diagnosis. On the other hand, the art teacher, who had stimulated the drawings and thus the means to understand the child, might be the best person to help to eradicate the child's problem:

though she should act with the full support of doctors, parents and colleagues.... The understanding art teacher, knowing the difficulties facing the individual child compared with his more normal class mates, familiar with child-psychology as I assume her to be and with the laws and methods of art, should be able to apply the laws and methods as a well-thought-out course of therapeutic treatment.

(Petrie 1946a: 82–3)

Petrie expressed views which were supported by Naumburg and Kramer in the USA in the 1940s (see Naumburg 1947, 1950, 1953, etc.; Kramer 1958, 1971, etc.).

In discussing the role of OT in sanatoriums and psychiatric hospitals, she noted:

I believe the time has come to enlarge the field (of OT) even further and to include the practice of the visual arts more especially in the media employed by occupational therapy, or, better still, to form a distinct new branch, art therapy, requiring a separate training.

(Petrie 1946a: 87)

Given that her book was prepared in 1944–5, Petrie was ahead of her time in suggesting that art therapy should have its own training, and her ideas were subsequently taken up by the first working parties held at the NAMH.

One of the difficulties was, as has been previously pointed out, that art therapy meant very different things to different members, and the early discussions about training reflected this. The main topic of debate at the first Conference for Art Therapists in Hospitals and Clinics, chaired by John Trevelyan in 1950, was whether or not occupational therapy could

Training in art therapy

encompass the field of art therapy. There was no agreement on this point, but Champernowne felt that, due to the force of emotion which could be released from the unconscious as a result of image-making, the personality of the art therapist would be of vital importance as they would be in the position of receiving and containing this force. She therefore considered analysis to be an essential ingredient of training.

Trevelyan felt that a 'real' educationalist would be able to be in complete sympathy with the patient, and favoured the establishment of a multi-disciplinary centre, rather like Withymead, where people could train in art therapy. Many people expressed the view that art therapists should be first and foremost artists, whereas others disputed this, considering that 'art students lacked the necessary personality and experience of human relationships to make good therapists'.

Neither the conference nor the following working parties were able to agree on the nature and content of training for art therapy, and it was not until the formation of BAAT in 1963 that the matter received serious, organised attention.

The position of the visual arts in the 1960s

In Chapter 4 I drew attention to the state of the visual arts in the 1940s and in particular to the lack of career opportunities for artists, other than in commercial art or teaching. In the mid-1960s there was a major change in the organisation of art education, following the Coldstream Report of 1961, in that the National Diploma in Design and its preliminary, the two-year Intermediate Certificate in Art and Design, were replaced – in certain approved institutions only – by the Diploma in Art and Design, a degree-equivalent qualification.

MacDonald comments on this change:

The Coldstream Report of 1961 and the subsequent activities of the National Council for Diplomas in Art and Design (NCDAD) resulted in a swing away from vocational, useful, and specialised design education, indeed away from the needs of society and towards a 'liberal' type of art education dominated by high art and tall talk. One accidental cause of this swing of the sixties was the large proportion of Colleges recognised by the NCDAD for Dip.AD in Fine Art, compared with the number recognised for Design areas. Naturally students applied for and expanded the recognised departments, thus more and more Fine Art staff were appointed, affecting the future structure of the Colleges. By the session 1969–70 there were 2,987 students following Dip.AD courses in Fine Art, more than twice as many as in the Three Dimensional Design or in Textiles/Fashion and nearly twice as many as in Graphic Design.

(MacDonald 1973: 97)

224

Early views on training

Macdonald felt that there were problems in this situation because the NCDAD had not recommended that every student carry out practical design work on the new diploma (this had been enforced under the previous system). He felt that liberal studies staff lectured increasingly on communication with society, that the practical work had less and less to do with everyday events, and it was possible for a student to pass through the course without ever 'designing and completing any artefact in general use'.

Even though the majority of fine art graduates became teachers post-course, Macdonald felt that this should not influence the training.

> Christopher Cornford writes that art students 'could be encouraged to think of teaching children as an admirable and interesting kind of job' instead of 'an absolute last ditch'. True but the hostility towards, and fear of society, which motivates dislike of teaching, of any other 'ordinary' job, even of society itself, is what needs to be banished. Instead it is often deliberately encouraged.
>
> (Macdonald 1973: 97)

At the time of BAAT's formation, art therapy was not the career option it is today, but, as has been shown earlier, many art graduates of the NDD system found themselves 'teaching' in hospitals as an alternative to schools. Dip.AD courses, with their compulsory 'complementary studies' programmes, began to change the emphasis of art education in the colleges from a mainly practical base to a more philosophical one, due to the inclusion in the programmes of communication theory, psychology, philosophy, history, and sociology of art.

A government survey on the employment of art college leavers (HMSO 1972) does not list art therapy as a possible future career, which is hardly surprising since the students surveyed came from 1967–8 art and design courses. Graduates at that time tended to enter art therapy 'accidentally', whereas all career guides concerning art and design today contain information about art therapy as a career.

There is evidence that there was some awareness of the existence of art therapy, however, in that in 1966 Adamson presented an exhibition of patients' work at the Ashmolean Museum, Oxford, and talked to the Ruskin fine art students about his work. The Ruskin might have been exceptional, however, in encouraging an interest, as most art therapists interviewed report very negative responses on behalf of art school tutors (especially in the 1970s) to their consideration of art therapy as a career.

The term 'art therapy' was also used perjoratively about students' art work. For example, Madge and Weinberger include some comments from tutors' notes on their students. One tutor said:

225

Training in art therapy

> Jackie is a nice girl, a serious girl, even. Her work is diabolical and I tentatively suggest that it is bad because it is art therapy only. The distancing process needed to discipline the therapy side of art does not seem to exist in Jackie's work.
>
> (Madge and Weinberger 1973: 154)

The tutors' notes often contained references to the personality of the students:

> Diana is a very neurotic girl, her tenseness is a handicap because it is difficult to have a conversation with her without her getting defensive. Her work is turgid and unresolved but there may be some outcome from her recent puppet project.... Unless she resolves her neurosis there is little hope for her career in fine art.

> Joe is erratic in his working procedures and allows the more frivolous and self-indulgent aspects of his personality to obtrude into his work sphere.... However there is probably some sensibility and intelligence behind his buffoon–like persona.

> Dave is an intelligent student with an interesting mind which is sometimes hidden by a deliberate act of inarticulate yobbish-ness.
>
> (Madge and Weinberger 1973: 151, 167, 177)

Most of the comments are, in fact, ones which would be considered negative and intrusive, and suggest that the tutors were making links between the students' personality and the type of art produced – but in a judgmental way. The justification for such behaviour, which Madge and Weinberger found to be common among staff, was that students needed to be tough enough to withstand a career in art (especially fine art). These attitudes were experienced by many students coming to interview for art therapy training and were felt to be unnecessarily punitive. However, the fact that 'personality' of the art student was considered important enough to note at some length suggests that some tutors saw themselves rather like art therapists (that is, they considered the relationship between image-making and personality, the manner of producing the image, the intention of the student), but they expected the student to produce 'art' rather than 'art therapy'.

Thus the change from Intermediate/NDD, which were practically based courses dominated by painting from life and still-life and the study of the history of art, to the new Dip.AD, with its emphasis on stripping students of preconceptions about art, was a profound one. (See Madge and Weinberger 1973 for further information.)

226

Early views on training

BAAT's role in the promotion of training begins

In 1965, BAAT's training sub-committee began to have discussions with the child psychology and art education departments of the Institute of Education of the University of London, where Adamson had been a visiting tutor on an in-service special education course. A proposal was formulated for an *arts* therapy course to be established within the advanced diplomas in education structure. The course was to cover visual art, drama, dance, and drama therapy, and applicants would require graduate or equivalent qualifications, plus five years' teaching or related experience. This was in accordance with BAAT's view of qualification for art therapy being dependent on an art-teaching background, and it met with the approval of the other arts therapists involved (Sue Jennings (Hickson), drama therapist, Marion North, Director of the Laban Centre for Dance and Movement, Julienne Brown, music therapist). Most of the officers of BAAT between 1965 and 1971 were involved in discussions to try to establish the course, but it failed to start. Possible reasons for this failure were, it appears:

a) economic: the course was very complex and required a high staff–student contact, making it expensive to operate;

b) structural: it was multi-disciplinary and required sophisticated time-tabling and total co-operation between several different departments;

c) definition: art therapy was loosely defined, and the arts therapies were at different stages in organisation and in establishing their identity;

d) territory: it was not clear which discipline would be in control of the course;

The proposal was eventually, in 1972, offered to Goldsmiths' which declined to take it on, for all the reasons above but primarily due to its complexity and high cost at a time when education cuts had begun to take effect.

As pointed out in Chapter 15, the negotiations for starting the course at the Institute gave BAAT and the NUT impetus for their campaign to have art therapy taken over by local education authorities within an educational framework. It also gave opportunities for art therapists to have regular discussions with the other arts therapists, particularly music therapists, with whom they were to negotiate jointly with the DHSS from 1976 onwards. The proposal also set the level which was to be aimed at subsequently for art therapy training – i.e. postgraduate, post-experience. It gave impetus to others in their moves to establish training, or at least some art therapy education in other art teaching areas, e.g. Hornsey School of Art where Margarita Wood ran an option in art therapy within the ATC course in the late 1960s and early 1970s, Brighton School of Art where

227

Training in art therapy

Joy Schaverien ran a similar option in the ATC, Birmingham (Michael Edwards from 1969 on), Goldsmiths' (Diane Waller from 1974 on).

In the next chapter, I shall discuss both these options, using the Goldsmiths' option as a 'case study' to illustrate some of the institutional constraints of the period which caused the option to move through several different phases before it emerged as a full-time art therapy training.

Chapter twenty-three

Art therapy training within an educational framework

I have pointed out the importance to BAAT of art therapy training being situated within an education framework in order that art therapy could be viewed primarily as educational and not as paramedical (1963–75 approximately) and that art therapists could be provided with a career and salary structure equivalent to those of adult education tutors. BAAT therefore supported linking art therapy training with that of art teachers, and two of these initiatives were eventually recognised by BAAT as qualifying art therapists.

Art therapy at Birmingham

The earliest of these was developed by Michael Edwards after his appointment to the School of Art Education at the Birmingham School of Art (now Birmingham Polytechnic) in 1969. Michael Edwards had spent many years at the Withymead Centre, following his training in art and art education. He subsequently worked with adolescents at the Tavistock Clinic, where he had Kleinian supervision, at the same time working at the Ealing child guidance clinics. He was appointed as a lecturer in the School of Art Education because of his experience in art therapy, and was encouraged to develop an option by Lucy Burroughs, Head of Department. Byrne comments that

> Prior to his [Edwards's] appointment as Lecturer and Tutor in Art Therapy and Art Education in 1969, the College had employed Lea Elliot, a specialist in remedial and therapeutic art education. She made valuable links with many schools, hospitals and clinics in the Birmingham area, and her teaching on the post-graduate Art Teacher's Diploma course embodied a growing social awareness on the part of artists and art educators which was, and still is, a feature of the Birmingham School of Art Education. This emphasis, combined with rapidly changing attitudes to madness, deviance and therapy, created an atmosphere

Training in art therapy

> in which it was possible to pull together some of the rather vague ideas about art therapy which were floating about in those heady days.
>
> (Byrne 1980: 4)

Edwards says of these early days:

> I had inherited the informal opportunity for art education students to do something outside teaching, including art therapy. I believe Hornsey had been doing something similar too. My appointment, as an experienced art therapist, was clearly to build on this small beginning and when I joined the staff in 1969, I immediately began putting the art therapy element onto a much more professional footing. Several of my first art therapy option students went on to become art therapists. As I was elected to the BAAT Council in the Spring of 1970, during my first year at Birmingham, and became Chair the following year, an office I held for four years, what we were doing at Birmingham was obviously closely monitored, in an informal sense, by prominent BAAT colleagues. Because BAAT was at the time *politically* committed to an educational stance it did not seem anomalous at that time that art therapy training should be offered in an art educational context.
>
> (Edwards, letter of 3 August 1985)

The option had a similar structure to the ATD course, in that students spent a proportion of their year on practical placement, but in hospitals instead of or as well as in schools. Students taking the option had to do more practice, in order to complete the statutory number of days of teaching practice. In addition, they had psychology and art therapy lectures:

> It was a climate which really encouraged the students to think for themselves. It had a strong philosophical input. I think the conceptual analysis was strong there. It is still strong. Even though the students were in a double role, they were forced to think about that very carefully and to clarify exactly what that meant... that fitted in with BAAT's philosophy of the time.
>
> (Edwards in interview)

In the mid-1970s, art therapy was incorporated into the post-experience Diploma in Art Education, which became the MA in Art Education. It included a mode in art therapy and, by 1979, two students were supported by the Social Science Research Council for three-year projects in art therapy.

Throughout the 1970s, then, Birmingham's School of Art Education actively taught and promoted art therapy theory and practice and encouraged research into the discipline as a result of its master's and research degrees. To date, each training centre employs a senior lecturer who

Training and education

qualified at Birmingham. Although, as mentioned above, art therapy options were taught at both Hornsey and Brighton Colleges of Art, they did not develop to become 'recognised' by BAAT, probably due to the fact that the initiators left and there was insufficient basis to continue them without such stimulus.

The Goldsmith's option: a case study

(In this section I shall be examining my own influences and role as the person responsible for starting art therapy training at Goldsmiths', as well as the institutional context in which it developed.) The next option to develop was at Goldsmiths' College, within the Art Teacher's Certificate Department in 1974. Goldsmiths' ATC had, like Birmingham, employed distinguished art educators with a strong involvement in child psychology. Anton Ehrenzweig, author of *The Psychoanalysis of Artistic Vision and Hearing*, had been a senior tutor in the department, as had Seonaid Robertson (whose book *Rosegarden and Labyrinth* emphasises the role of art education in developing the child's personality), and Charity James, who founded the Curriculum Development Unit at Goldsmiths'. This gave fertile ground for the development of an art therapy option, at a time when teacher training was in the process of 'diversification' due to government policy of cutting the number of institutions offering training and the number of student places within them. Following a postgraduate degree from the Royal College of Art and a year in the Balkans researching into the role of art education and traditional arts in a rapidly changing society, I was employed for two days a week at Goldsmiths' to start and run an option in art therapy. For the rest of the week I was employed at Paddington Centre for Psychotherapy as an art therapist.

In *Inscape*, I said about the option:

> It seemed wildly over-ambitious: students spent two days a week on teaching practice and two days in a hospital or special school or prison, and tried to cram in a mass of clinical theory as well as educational studies and their own art work. All concerned worked flat out, and of the first nine students who completed the option, two have returned to full-time training in art therapy, three sought additional training in psychotherapy and are now art therapists and the others went into teaching and community work.
>
> (Waller 1979: 9)

The second year of the option continued in the same form, but more students wished to take it, and a network of placements was established, in the same way as at Birmingham. However, unlike the situation at Birmingham, the combination of art teaching and art therapy was not viewed so positively:

231

Training in art therapy

It was obvious that a more satisfactory and less exhausting way of running the option would be for those students who applied for and were accepted for the option to be together in one tutorial group and to do their art therapy practice in a block and likewise their teaching practice. In this way they would not be confusing their roles and we could usefully explore the boundaries between teaching and therapy. The option continued in this way for three more years.

(Waller 1979: 9)

Whereas Byrne stated that at Birmingham:

It is part of the philosophy of this school to consider art therapy and art education within a common context. This does not imply a blurring of roles or an attempt to equate art therapy with art teaching, but on the contrary, it is believed that a comparative and critical study of these partly related but different concepts can lead to a clarification of values and objectives.

(Byrne 1980: 6–7)

In 1977, due to pressure from students and myself, five places were allocated by the Dean of the School of Art at Goldsmiths' for a year of individual postgraduate study in art therapy, leading to the college's diploma. It was policy only to accept students who had spent at least a year out of art school and who had some experience of hospital or community work for the ATC option. This was extended to the diploma students:

the mix of ATC students studying art therapy and these graduates was a very stimulating one and led to wide-ranging debates about, for example, the nature of creativity, the importance of art in children's emotional and physical development, the relationship of the teacher to the child and how this was different from the therapist's, and so on. The intensive study of group dynamics enabled the ATC students to cope with and understand the large and small groups of children they were asked to teach in inner London schools.

(Waller 1979: 10)

Establishing a discrete diploma was, however, a major problem at Goldsmiths', due to the existence, in the same Region (SE) of Herts' Diploma in Art Therapy. Proposals were turned down several times by the Regional Advisory Council and the DES, the reason given being that there were 'no jobs', or that the job market in art therapy was already being catered for by the Herts Course. There was no pressure forthcoming from Goldsmiths' as an institution to establish an art therapy diploma, as by the mid-1970s diversification problems had been largely solved, so it was left

Training and education

very much in the hands of the small group of art therapy staff to fight their own battle.

They were caught in a very difficult situation: on the one hand, there was pressure from the BAAT Registration and Training Committee (1977 on) for discrete training in art therapy to be set up, especially from Herts' representatives; on the other, because of Herts' Diploma, the RAC and hence the DES would not approve a course in the same region at a time when art therapy had no career structure of its own in either the NHS or education.

The option was, however, proving very popular among students and my part-time contract had been increased to almost full time, giving more scope for negotiating within the college. I was appointed to a full-time post in 1978. A way round the problem was arrived at through discussion with the Special Education advisers at the DES, who felt that Goldsmiths' could draw on its educational expertise to mount a specialist course in art therapy for in-service teachers. However, the term 'art therapy' was disliked by special education staff, so the diploma was entitled the 'Therapeutic Application of Art Processes in the Education of Children and Young People'. This course gained approval from both the RAC and the DES, starting in 1979 with eight full-time teachers participating. The programme was identical to that being followed by the five Goldsmiths' diploma students, except that the latter were doing their placements mainly in psychiatric hospitals with adult patients, and the twelve ATC option students. This made a total of twenty-five students, and during the session 1978–9 the college agreed to establish an autonomous section of the school of art under the title of the Art Therapy Unit. Andrea Gilroy, then Honorary Secretary of BAAT, was employed part time in 1979, becoming full time in 1980. From 1979, the ATC option was discontinued, and with it the mandatory awards to students, leaving intending Diploma in Art Therapy students competing for ever-diminishing discretionary awards from their local education authorities, and teachers for rare secondments. The unwieldy title of the in-service course, plus the increasing frustration of the unit staff in not being able to name accurately what they were teaching, led to further discussions with the RAC and DES, and in 1981 the DES agreed to a Diploma in Art Therapy being established at Goldsmiths' with two modes being formed out of the existing programmes:

Mode 1: Clinical (art graduates with working experience in the NHS, etc.)
Mode 2: Educational (for qualified art teachers only).

The strategies employed by the unit staff to maintain the art therapy programme under a variety of different titles, although frustrating, had

233

Training in art therapy

succeeded in establishing art therapy as a discipline within the college for long enough to enable Goldsmiths' to play a part in countering the Consultative Document and to make a case to the DES that the training was established and graduates were getting jobs. This was easier after the DHSS required a training in 'the therapeutic application of art' from June 1980 on.

It also enabled the unit to gain resources and a firm base within the college, albeit with considerable struggle and recourse to a large group of consultant psychiatrists, the 'Clinical Advisory Committee'. However, the further development of art therapy at Goldsmiths', in terms of higher degrees, was hindered for some years by the fact that Goldsmiths' was seeking to become a full school of the University of London, instead of an institute with recognised teachers offering university-validated degrees. The college also offered CNAA-validated degrees in fine art and textiles, thus making it a rare 'mixed economy' institution in the 1980s. Until such time as the issue of school status was resolved, further initiatives (such as the Master's in Art Therapy) were halted. (In 1986 Goldsmiths established an Advanced Diploma in Art Therapy and in 1989 an MA, validated by the University of London.)

The fate of the options

Given the fact that both options were within well-recruiting ATC courses, and that both Goldsmiths' and Birmingham were subject to similar diversification pressures, it is significant that at one (Goldsmiths') the option fairly quickly separated out into a discrete diploma, whereas at Birmingham this did not happen.

Edwards pointed out that he had prepared a plan for an art therapy qualification which would incorporate both the ATD and a certificate or college diploma, so that students who had completed the art therapy option would get both. This did not receive support. It is possible that such a combination, which would have had to be presented to the Council for National Academic Awards (CNAA) which validated courses in the public sector, might have been turned down; or that combining art therapy with a mandatory teacher training course would have been seen to 'dilute' the latter. The issue of loss of mandatory grants, which had already been faced by St Albans and was to be faced by Goldsmiths' in 1979, may also have influenced the polytechnic against diverting student numbers into art therapy training.

Byrne summed up the situation at Birmingham in 1980 thus:

> It is very difficult at present to envisage any development at Birmingham involving the expenditure of money. We will have to use what staff we have and we will probably have to continue to operate within

234

Training and education

the format of the CNAA course validation: in other words it would be very difficult to set up an independent art therapy department à la Goldsmiths'. But within the present structure ideas can be explored and advantage can be taken of our unique position in a large Art College... and that Birmingham is a multi-racial city where cross-cultural phenomena can be examined... and of the growing amount of knowledge and research available on the premises of the School.

(Byrne 1980: 7)

Another factor influencing developments in the two options may have been timing, as the Goldsmiths' option started just before BAAT began discussions with the St Albans' students and the moves towards separating from the NUT began. As chair of BAAT at the time, I was, of course, centrally involved in these discussions as well as being course leader at Goldsmiths'. I was also working as an art therapist in a centre for psychotherapy, employed by the ILEA but at a time when adult education institutes were beginning to trim 'marginal' activities, such as art therapy. When tested against the reality of teaching practice in secondary schools in inner London, the idealistic views of education which had prompted the philosophical linking of art therapy with art education had rapidly faded. It is certainly the case that after two years of combining the option with the normal ATC timetable, I had decided to push for a separate art therapy training, the structure being similar to that of the ATC, 'alternative course' which a group of us had formed in 1973–4, culminating in a booklet entitled *In Pursuit of Change in Education and Society*. The theoretical and practical programme of study which was submitted first to the Board of Studies of the School of Art and later to the college's academic board was influenced by my work as an art therapist at Paddington Centre for Psychotherapy and emphasised critical analysis of models of psychiatry, psychotherapy, and institutions, and group dynamics. (At that time, the centre was in turmoil, due to an experiment in large group psychotherapy stemming from Ezriel's approach, which led to an enquiry and the subsequent demise of the day hospital. The art therapy department was independent of the day hospital, but served its patients, and it was thus witness to the 'tyranny of the therapeutic, in which naked power replaced the ideals of a therapeutic community designed to eliminate hierarchy and bureaucracy' (Baron 1987, in *From Asylum to Anarchy*, a analysis of that period based on her participant observation).)

This course thus envisaged was to be aimed at art graduates or art teachers with working experience and part of its agenda was to carve out a place for art therapy as a radical form of psychotherapy in the NHS and elsewhere. (This is obvious from early course programmes, notes, and documents which I had prepared, and from the style of teaching which was modelled on student participation and joint decision making,

235

Training in art therapy

stemming from my involvement with the social psychiatry and therapeutic community movements but somewhat overshadowed by the events at Paddington Centre.)

The details of the institutional constraints which led to a Diploma in Art Therapy being started at Goldsmiths', despite lack of wholehearted support from the college, and not at Birmingham which had initiated study of art therapy within the ATC and MA courses warrant a separate research project and book. The outcome for Birmingham was, though, that approval was eventually withdrawn by the DHSS in 1985, owing to the lack of a full-time and discrete art therapy training being offered. In the early 1970s, both options were encouraged by BAAT for the same reasons as the Institute of Education proposal. This led to conflict with the then St Albans School of Art.

The Certificate in Remedial Art at St Albans School of Art (now Hertfordshire College of Art and Design)

I have already pointed out that the Herts course caused considerable concern to BAAT on its formation in 1970. In his article about art therapy training at Herts, John Evans reviewed the (then) eight years of the course's existence from 1971, when it was titled the Certificate in Remedial Art of the St Albans School of Art.

Evans suggests that the name reflected the lack of confidence on behalf of the DES in the term 'therapy' as applied to an educationally funded course, and it was not until 1975 that the name was changed to the Diploma in Art Therapy. Evans says:

> Even in 1975 this agreement was by no means easy, since practitioners in the Health Service are and always were called 'art therapists'. The word 'therapy' seemed to generate a fear and suspicion, amongst many, particularly within art schools, where there was and still is a strong desire to have art considered as academically respectable (it had only recently been established that art qualifications were of degree status) and the notion that art could be therapy was seen as insulting to the serious pursuit of Fine Art.
>
> (Evans 1979: 6)

Evans felt that even in the art school at St Albans, this suspicion was evident. He maintained:

> For a small college attempting to mount a training in art therapy, the first of its kind in the country and needing the approval of the establishment within the DES and DHSS, academic respectability was important... thus the title 'Remedial Art' was felt to be more acceptable

Training and education

than therapy... it was necessary that the work of the course had the sanction of named psychiatrists to give it credibility.

(Evans 1979: 6)

Evans acknowledges the 'rift' and lack of communication between the college and BAAT, already discussed in Chapter 15. He confirms that the problem was that BAAT was part of the NUT and seemed to be clearly identified with the art education movement, and that it was seen as somewhat anti-psychiatry in its outlook.

For a college needing the approval of orthodox psychiatry to survive, it was not surprising that it should not identify too closely with this image. Other problems existed, the College's policy of admitting health service professionals was seen by BAAT as a sellout to the NHS who quite naturally at that time, given their professional status, regarded OT as senior to Art Therapy. Also, I think the course seemed to pose a threat to a group of artists whose therapeutic skills were informally and individually acquired.

(Evans 1979: 7)

In 1973, Christine Walker, Honorary Secretary of BAAT, wrote an article for the Central Youth Employment Executive's Bulletin, mentioning the Birmingham option and the Herts course. The Principal of Herts, Anthony Harris, wrote a letter objecting to the contents. The substance of his complaint was that he felt therapy had been confused with teaching and that the Herts course had not been acknowledged sufficiently:

Reference to the Departments of Education and Science and of Health and Social Security would have established that the *only* course at present approved is the post-graduate Certificate in Remedial Art offered by this college.

(Harris, 27 November 1973)

The CYEE wrote to BAAT querying the 'claim to ownership' and asking for clarification. Christine Walker replied, stating that there was 'some ambiguity in the present situation concerning the training of art therapists'. She said that BAAT did not consider the terms 'art therapy' and 'remedial art teaching' to be synonymous. By 'remedial art teaching' BAAT was referring to specialist art education with the handicapped, or to remedial classes in normal schools, while 'art therapy' was used both as a collective title for a range of art activities directed towards the alleviation of emotional stress and also to describe a more specific non-directive primary therapy, usually in clinical settings. Walker said that 'remedial art teaching' might include elements of art therapy, and, since many art therapists might also be trained teachers, it could be seen

Training in art therapy

that there were areas of considerable overlap, leading to confusion in terminology. She added:

> It may be that the decision of St Albans School of Art to award a 'Certificate in Remedial Art' for completion of a course in art therapy may have introduced a further ambiguity into the situation.

Walker outlined BAAT's position on promoting art therapy, pointing out that the Association had defined a professional procedure distinct from art teaching and occupational therapy, and at the same time had taken into account 'that education in its broadest aspects concerns itself with facilitating the development of human potential'. She drew attention also to the fact that many art therapists were employed by local education authorities to work in psychiatric hospitals, paid on the Burnham Scale, and by contrast, art therapists employed within the terms of the Whitley Scales were in a much less fortunate position. It was for that reason that BAAT had looked 'more hopefully' towards the DES rather than the DHSS. Walker concluded that, while progressive thinking in education might offer substantial support for the theoretical base in art therapy, neither BAAT nor any of its members would reject the relevance of psychological and psychiatric models within their work. She regretted the lack of communication between BAAT and Herts College, ending 'However, members of his staff and both present and ex-students are members of our Association and have been actively involved in it' (Walker, 17 December 1973).

This example serves to illustrate how both BAAT and Herts were using strategies to promote views of art therapy which, although differing in certain philosophical elements, were not entirely opposed. For example, BAAT had linked with the NUT and sought comparability with teachers and adult education lecturers to avoid being pegged on the DHSS's *ad hoc* paramedical grade. Comparability of art therapy training with postgraduate teacher training was part of the strategy, and seen as a way of getting art therapy into the higher education system. Herts had developed an art therapy course, drawing in Adamson (who had only recently ceased to be an officer of BAAT) as consultant art therapist, and called the course 'Remedial Art' as a device to avoid possible censure from the DES, which might have resulted in the course being closed. They admitted a small percentage of paramedical staff in an attempt to facilitate relations with the DHSS.

Yet neither part appeared to want to recognise these strategies for what they were, at least for another two or three years. (I have already explored some of the possible causes for the continuation of the rift in Chapter 15.)

An art therapist who trained at Herts in 1971 recalled the rift and the attempts of some of the students to heal it:

Training and education

> I was one of two people that were already members of BAAT. There was one other member who had worked as a sessional tutor... there were only two members in the entire year. I was a full member because I was working as a nursing assistant-cum-art therapist full time. As students, I and others invited the Chair of BAAT down to talk to us and I think a few other people did join after that. But we had to do that as a student body in the evening in a pub. It was under the table, as it were.... I can't remember the details but it must have been something trivial that caused the rift.

Another student said:

> I know we became more involved in the political side, but I suppose in those days there was quite a lot of rivalry going on and I think that what was happening was that BAAT was seen as a Goldsmiths' allied thing and there was a lot of mythology around about what this ruckus was all about... and BAAT suffered because of it, so I think it was quite important.

The decision by BAAT to cease being a Central Association of the NUT and to link with ASTMS as its union, together with the development of the Goldsmiths' option away from an educational model, and the work of the BAAT Registration Committee, were factors which Evans considered to be helpful in establishing a good relationship with BAAT.

The Diploma in Art Therapy at Herts was validated by the CNAA Board of Health and Medical Services on 1 September 1977. It was heralded by BAAT Registration Advisory Committee as 'a validation of art therapy as such'. (An MA in art therapy was validated in 1982.)

The validation by the CNAA, a national body, happened just after the publication of the Joint Secretaries' Report and before the DHSS issued the Consultative Document on Art, Music, Drama, etc., Therapies. Evans says of the validation:

> We called it a College Diploma in Art Therapy, and with the support of people like the College HMI, we went forward. I think it was a very courageous move by the CNAA to do what was unique in the system, that was, to validate an institution which wasn't till then doing any CNAA work. The institution had to be validated, and along with it, the course – as a postgraduate course, not an undergraduate course. That had never been heard of. There was no degree work (at the College) and no advanced work other than art therapy at that time. There was a foundation course and a range of part-time courses.... By then we had a team of people – Kim James, John Henzell, Felicity Weir, Peter Wey and myself who were quite articulate and formed a good team who could argue coherently for what they were doing. It made sense, and

239

Training in art therapy

it was on that basis that it got validated. That was a major step forward, I think.

(John Evans, in interview)

Evans felt that the major problem the course faced in the late 1970s was the threat of almost total cutback of discretionary awards, the withdrawal of Training and Opportunities (TOPS) grants, and the increase of overseas fees to £3000 per annum. He felt that establishing a two-year part-time course might provide a solution, although he thought that in the long term the DHSS should provide finance, for at that time they did not contribute anything towards the costs of art therapy training although they paid the full costs of OT training.

The issue of course content

In an article in the same *Inscape* in which John Evans's article appeared, Alison Goldsmith gave an account of her experience as a student on the Herts Course. She raises the issue of the charges made by BAAT, the two options, and many of the Herts students themselves, that the course was 'too clinically biased':

The formality of this occasion (the final exam on 'terminology') came as a blow to most of us who had initially seen the course as a 'friendly' affair. This exam, together with weekly seminars on psychiatry and psychology gave rise to one of the most frequently voiced complaints that the course was too clinically biased. I think that this feeling reflected a wider issue concerning the role of the Art Therapist in hospitals.

The main argument against the clinical bias was that Art Therapy should offer an alternative to standard psychiatric practice and therefore more time should be devoted during the year to other alternative therapies such as bioenergetics. Some students felt that the clinical content was an attempt to force the art therapist into a conforming role and consequently threatened the independent and sometimes the 'abrasive' nature of the art therapist in a hospital.

(Goldsmith 1979: 8)

Alison Goldsmith disagreed that this characteristic of the art therapist was threatened by course content and felt the course was trying to equip the student with a 'reasonable vocabulary without which his independence could turn to isolation'. She was happy with the balance between academic and practical aspects of the course.

The question of course content was one which had to be addressed by BAAT urgently, given that, of the existing training programmes in the mid–1970s, two were in the form of options and one was a full-time

Training and education

course, yet all were considered to be contributing to the development of art therapy as a discrete discipline. John Evans says about the joint BAAT-Herts discussions in 1975:

> The most crucial effect of these discussions was the decision to have a core syllabus... because that was something outside, to sound off against... it was always clear that if there was to be the 'profession of art therapy' it was going to be vital for the options to become something different... to take off in their own right... whether in the same model as here or in some other model... I could always see that. While they were options in teacher training, you couldn't do anything. The fact that there was a free standing course here meant that there was a big effect on the options and how they saw themselves.
>
> (John Evans in interview)

In the next chapter I shall discuss the role of the BAAT Registration and Training Sub-Committee from its formation at the BAAT EGM of 1976 to its subsequent recommendations on 'core course' requirements in 1979.

Chapter twenty-four

The BAAT Registration and Training Sub-Committee and its contribution to the debate on art therapy training during the 1970s

One of BAAT's aims, given in its constitution, both of 1964 and 1977, was:

> (e) To encourage suitable persons to enter the profession, to devise and establish courses of training for such persons and to see that proper standards of professional competence are maintained by Members and Associates.

In previous chapters I have noted that the DHSS's criterion for working as an art therapist was the possession of a two-year post-A level qualification in art, which remained until June 1980 when a requirement for a qualification in the therapeutic application of art was added. BAAT's own criteria were for many years similar to those for qualified art teachers: namely a degree or equivalent in art or design followed by either a postgraduate teacher training including an art therapy option (from Birmingham or Goldsmiths') or, after 1975, the Certificate in Remedial Art (later Diploma in Art Therapy) from Herts College.

It was vital to BAAT, and to the professional aspirations of the art therapy movement as a whole, that only training courses at postgraduate level were mounted, to maintain comparability with graduate teachers, lecturers, speech therapists, and psychologists rather than with technical instructors or OT aides (the last two seeming to be the comparator which the DHSS would have preferred to see). Early discussions with the Institute of Education set the level to be aimed at and the introduction of an art therapy option at postgraduate level at Birmingham School of Art Education gave art therapy some representation within higher education. The Certificate in Remedial Art, however, caused concern in BAAT because it was felt to accept lower educational standards, and to move art therapy towards the 'medical model' of psychiatry in taking psychiatric nurses and OTs rather than all art graduates. As mentioned in the previous chapter, this seemed to have been a somewhat exaggerated concern at the time as the numbers were very small.

242

Training in the 1970s

Conflicts over training in the early 1970s almost caused a rift in the movement, but according to Bucher and Strauss such conflicts are not uncommon.

> Probably the areas in which professionals come most frequently into conflicts of interest are in gaining a proper foothold in institutions, in recruitment and in relations with the outside. Here there are recurrent problems which segments and emerging specialists have with their fellow professionals. In order to survive and develop, a segment must be represented in the training centres.
>
> (Bucher and Strauss 1961: 331)

Establishing a new academic subject is no easy task, as Goodson (1981) points out in relation to geography. Arriving at agreement by all parties concerned as to the nature and content of the training is also problematic, as comparison with psychotherapy shows.

Khaleelee makes the following observation, just as applicable to art therapy as to psychotherapy:

> Probably every profession has been through this phase in the process of becoming established – that is – of acquiring statutory authority to practise. The individual practitioner in addition to responsibility to his client or patient, has to accept the obligations of membership to a professional body which is accountable to society through the state. Accountability implies regulation of training and the right to practise. A boundary is drawn between legitimate and illegitimate practitioners. Regulation is the price to be paid for safeguarding an exclusive right to practise.
>
> (Khaleelee 1982: 1)

Hinshelwood, in his article 'Questions of training', points out that such consensus has not yet been achieved as far as psychotherapy is concerned (though a Standing Conference has been addressing the issue for several years).

> Entry to most professions is automatically restricted through a recognised training resulting in a certificate of competence. One of the curiosities about the psychotherapy profession is that it lacks such a rite de passage... this is one of the major obstacles to achieving a traditional professional status for psychotherapy.
>
> (Hinshelwood 1985: 7–8)

By 1979, however, representatives of the art therapy movement in Britain had reached a consensus, on paper, at least. In 'Art therapy in adolescence', I suggest:

243

Training in art therapy

In the case of art therapy, a driving force for unity seemed to be a firm belief in the value of the visual arts generally, and specifically in their potential to provide a means of expression and communication not usually available within hospital or other 'clinical' settings. A powerful identification with the role of 'artist' and perhaps 'outsider' in the face of the medically dominated and hierarchical structure of the NHS may have also played a part.

(Waller 1987: 191)

The consensus may have been on paper rather than borne out in practice, bearing in mind the fundamental disagreement between the training courses about pre-training qualification and experience – still unresolved today (1989). (See Bucher and Strauss's discussion of 'spurious unity and public relations' (1961: 331) for elaboration of this issue.)

As far as the art therapy movement was concerned, though, the 'enemy outside' which stimulated internal cohesion was the DHSS, and the 1970s was a period in which there was a struggle between BAAT (in co-operation with Birmingham, Goldsmiths', and Herts College) and the DHSS to determine the level and content of art therapy training. The events leading up to the 'consensus' of 1979 will be explored in this chapter. The fact that these three centres of further and higher education had embraced art therapy at all was seen as useful ammunition in the campaigns described previously.

The structure and content of training prior to the establishment of the BAAT Registration and Training Sub-Committee in 1976

The courses at Birmingham, Goldsmiths', and Herts had several common features:

(a) They were all one year full-time, or part of one year full-time courses;
(b) they were at postgraduate or post-experience level;
(c) they were cited within schools or faculties of art and design;
(d) they admitted primarily art graduates (Birmingham and Goldsmiths' 100 per cent);
(e) they required a period of practical placement similar to teaching practice and emphasised the relationship of theory to practice;
(f) they included some 'experiential' work – i.e. students were required to participate in art therapy groups;
(g) they encouraged students to continue their own art work.
    The differences were:
(a) Birmingham and Goldsmiths' had options within another profession's training;
(b) the theoretical element of each course differed, with Herts including the study of psychiatry encompassing psychiatric terminology and

Training in the 1970s

psychology, and having formal examinations in these subjects, whereas these areas were covered only in a brief and critical way at Birmingham and Goldsmiths'. Especially at Birmingham, there was emphasis on art, aesthetics, iconography and symbology, and at Goldsmiths' on child development, the influence of culture on imagery, social psychiatry and, in particular, groups;

(c) Herts included 'media studies' for non-art graduates and offered all students access to art studios, whereas at Goldsmiths' students tended to do their art work in their own time. Birmingham's position within the School of Art Education enabled the option students to use the studios freely;

(d) Birmingham and Goldsmiths' students had to undertake teaching practice as well as art therapy practice, making a heavy demand on their time and a need to differentiate between the roles of teacher and of therapist.

(This information is based on syllabuses from the options and the Herts Course in 1975.) Acknowledgement of the similarities as well as the differences was the first step in the preparation of the 'core course' requirements.

Following the meeting of Herts and BAAT representatives in 1975, there was an exchange of ideas concerning the structure and content of training between BAAT, Birmingham, Goldsmiths', and Herts College. The BAAT working party included representatives from the three colleges, plus practising art therapists from different 'camps' and John Birtchnell, as a consultant psychiatrist.

In January 1976, Herts suggested the following entry requirements for art therapy training:

Persons entering a course of training should be mature, creative, flexible people who have experienced the value of the visual arts and have some previous work experience within psychiatry. Such a person would have a degree level qualification and consequently all courses offering a qualification in art therapy should be post degree level.

Suggested content included: skill in using media; experience in using specific art therapy techniques with individuals and groups; the study of psychiatry, clinical psychology and sociology; study of the nature of art, its psychology, the nature of visual imagery as it relates to art therapy.

There was to be a clinical placement, including psychiatric hospitals together with social services day centres, etc., for a minimum of ten weeks as a member of a team.

Training in art therapy

Self-awareness was to be encouraged through formal art and group therapy as important to the development of students' awareness of the dynamics of therapeutic relationships.

The course was to have external examiners.

These suggestions were put to the BAAT working party, which was also looking at the American Art Therapy Association's registration criteria, based on a credit system, with a view to determining whether or not such a system could operate in Britain.

Training and registration

The position in the USA was that a variety of levels of training operated in both universities and private colleges, at undergraduate and graduate level. The American Art Therapy Association had established its own criteria for recognising 'qualified' art therapists, based on points accumulated for training and practice. For example, a master's degree in art therapy gained 10 points, as did a graduate-level in-residence placement equivalent to the master's degree. Whereas a bachelor's degree in art therapy gained 6 points, and an association arts degree in art therapy 3. In addition to training, an applicant for registration had to work for a period of 1200 hours, cumulative or consecutive, for which they gained 2 Professional Quality Credits per each 1200 hours.

Outstanding contributors to the field of art therapy, as judged by the Standards Committee of AATA, could receive up to 5 points. Registration needed 12 Professional Quality Credits.

In summary, registration, or 'qualified' art therapy status, was dependent not on training but on a mix of training and post-training experience.

At its initial meetings, the BAAT working party studied the American system, as it was felt that a credit system might get over the problems of the 'options' as opposed to the 'full-time' course. At a meeting in September 1976, both John Evans and Michael Edwards suggested a credit system, which included the possibility for practising therapists of long standing to be registered. Other members produced the criteria on which the St Albans course was based, including a strong recommendation for the study of psychiatry, clinical psychology, and sociology to be assessed by a written examination, either in a college or set and examined by the professional association, and that a period of 1800 hours of supervised practice should be completed prior to registration:

Courses should be validated by the professional body guided by the above criteria and a credit system should be devised related to the various elements of which they are composed. Attending one of the

Training in the 1970s

validated courses should be essential as the major factor in forming the basis for recognition for membership of the professional body.

(Working party minutes, 11 September 1976)

I, on the other hand, was opposed to a credit system, feeling it to be unworkable. I thought the training should last for two years, that it should be for art graduates, and that it should concentrate on providing in-depth therapeutic skills. The first year should include group dynamic experience and the second specialisation in a particular area of fieldwork. The course should integrate theory with practice throughout.

All agreed that a 'creative arts' qualification was necessary for acceptance onto an art therapy course: 'otherwise the profession of art therapy is in danger of being regarded as an adjunct or addition to other professions, a skill easily acquired without any necessary depth of knowledge.' Fieldwork placements were also considered essential, together with the ability to establish a 'therapeutic relationship' and work in a multi-disciplinary team.

These were very general and somewhat vague suggestions, given the number of models of clinical practice which prevailed. There had been a considerable shift away from Adrian Hill's model of involvement in art as a form of therapy in itself, towards Champernowne's acknowledgement of the role of both art and therapist in the treatment process. There was considerable difference of opinion concerning the necessity to study 'psychiatry' and 'psychology', given the magnitude of the field and the reluctance of some members to have art therapy identified in any way with traditional models of psychiatric treatment (e.g. chemotherapy, ECT, and so on). There was already anxiety that the DHSS would see art therapists as 'handmaidens' of psychiatrists, instead of as professional workers in their own right. To some extent, this problem had occurred with nurses, as Salvage points out in a discussion of nursing education:

Although nurses controlled the patient's environment through housekeeping duties, they were also expected to act as medical assistants, and much of their formal training took the form of lectures from doctors.... Doctors have also had a powerful influence on the occupation through their membership of nursing committees, statutory bodies and even selection panels, an arrangement which for the most part is not reciprocated.

(Salvage 1985: 63)

Salvage suggests that, nowadays, more people recognise that the nurse is able to survey the entire spectrum of health care – assessment, diagnosis, treatment, rehabilitation, nutrition, etc., and that the medical approach is only part of the solution to the problems of preventing and treating illness and maintaining good health. 'But on the whole, training is still dominated

Training in art therapy

by the medical model of illness which sees the body primarily as a collection of organs to be serviced ('cured') when something breaks down' (1985: 63). There is a problem, though, in emphasising the need for nursing, as opposed to medical, knowledge, for Salvage feels that there is no consensus yet about what nursing knowledge actually is. However, there is growing agreement that the medical model is only of limited use in patient care and that and understanding of the social, economic, and environmental factors which affect the health of the population is becoming recognised as an equally vital aspect of a nurse's knowledge.

These social and environmental considerations, especially as they affected mental health, were felt to be essential ingredients in art therapy training by many members of BAAT and its working party. There were arguments about the question of teaching 'terminology', with some members feeling this was important if art therapists were to be able to discuss clients with members of the clinical team, and others feeling that to teach and examine psychiatric terminology was to collude with 'labelling' patients. In other words, there had to be a difference between learning the vocabulary and absorbing the ideology. They felt that the area should be approached critically, if at all.

The BAAT Registration Advisory Committee visits

At the November EGM 1976, the working party was re-established as the BAAT Registration Advisory Committee, with one of its major briefs being to define a core course of training.

At a meeting on 1 March 1977, it was proposed that in order to discover what was being taught and how at the three existing training centres, four members from the RAC should visit each centre. Each member compiled a list of the areas to be looked at, and the predominant points were:

1. placements – time, variety, supervision;
2. the psychiatric and psychological theory taught;
3. the students' response to the course;
4. the entry criteria and the type of assessment at the end of the course;
5. the aims of the course;
6. the facilities for students' personal art work;
7. number of hours spent in each study area;
8. experience gained in groups and interpersonal relationships.

The visits were scheduled to take place between March and May, and each member was to write up their findings for discussion by the RAC at its May meeting.

248

Training in the 1970s

On comparing the reports, there were found to be more similarities than differences in both content and style; all three centres divided their programme into three parts:

(a) placement;
(b) theoretical study;
(c) students' personal art work/experiential learning through art therapy workshops.

There was little evidence to show that the options differed overmuch from the full-time course, except that they included some teaching practice, but the style of teaching and the subsequent identity of the students was towards art therapy. All three centres were seen to encourage students' personal learning and involvement in the therapeutic process, rather than presenting material in traditional lecture format. This approach to teaching appeared to reflect the fact that the training took place within art schools where there was a 'culture' of 'learning through doing' and of a tutorial system, rather than in medical or nursing schools, where the lecture format was usual.

On the basis of the reports, a decision was made for each member to produce his or her own recommendations for a core course of training for subsequent discussion and with the aim of producing a recommendation to put to BAAT Council and the AGM.

In October, the issue of entry requirements was discussed. This was a contentious matter, owing to commitment on the part of some members to art graduate entry and by others to post-experience or other graduate entry, as well as art. The following was agreed:

> With regard to entry criteria the selection of candidates for art therapy training will depend upon evidence of personal maturity and/or appropriate pre-course experience. Academically, intending students will also normally require a first degree or its equivalent in the visual arts. In cases where applicants have an alternative qualification a substantial and developing experience in art will be expected.

A synthesis was then made of the recommendations of each member of the committee and a draft drawn up for a core course.

This reflected current practice in seeking a balance between theoretical, practical (clinical), and experiential work. The range of subject areas to be studied was left very wide, in the expectation that different centres would opt for their own preference:

> It is strongly urged that a catholic selection of fundamental concepts be presented to the student:

249

Training in art therapy

(a) An introduction to and study of relevant theories and models – psychological, behavioural, medical, psychoanalytical, developmental, educational, biological, anthropological, social, political, philosophical, semiotic, aesthetic and artistic.

Quite clearly it would have been an impossible task to cover most or all of these either superficially or in depth during a one-year course. However, their inclusion avoided the need to pin down groups of people with strong ideas about training, and left each centre to follow its own nose.

Suggestions about placement were more specific, with sixty days being the recommended time 'in appropriate institutions under the supervision of persons with responsibility for the clinical application of art therapy'. This followed closely the teaching practice model for the ATC courses. It was not specified whether this was to be in blocks or continuous. The importance of art therapy workshops and other forms of training groups was stressed and inclusion of this aspect of training considered essential. (See the Appendix for a copy of the Core Course Requirements as published in *Inscape* 2 (1) January 1978.)

The proposal was adopted by BAAT, together with recommendations for a probationary period of work following completion of training.

It will be the responsibility of the student to obtain such employment and to inform the RAC of the probationary employment. To obtain their agreement it must satisfy certain minimum requirements.... In most instances 15 hours per week would be taken as a minimum for part time work. It would, however, be at the Registration Committee's discretion to give approval to alternative probationary arrangements.

The document stated that all current full members of BAAT would be considered registered art therapists, and others who had lapsed could re-apply by 1 March 1978. Interim arrangements for registration were suggested, as the core course requirements could apply only to students having commenced 'recognised' courses of training in 1978 and applying for registration in 1980 at the earliest. It was recommended that, in the interim period, 'BAAT recognise the courses of training at St Albans, Goldsmiths' and Birmingham'.

In fact, the probationary period was never put into practice due to the impossibility for BAAT of 'policing' post-course work experience, so it was dropped, with much reluctance as it put the onus for qualifying art therapists onto the colleges, and made it difficult for the officers of BAAT to justify to the DHSS and others a 'professional' training of one year only.

In November 1981, Herts College sent a letter to BAAT entitled 'Statement concerning the relationship of Hertfordshire College of Art and Design to BAAT'. They pointed to the fact that, in the absence of a

250

Training in the 1970s

group of courses of similar level and nature, the core curriculum had been drawn up as a basis for training, together with a probationary year, after which students may be registered with BAAT. They pointed out that since 1977, when the Registration Advisory Committee had produced its report, there had been many changes in the courses and the idea of the probationary year had been dropped. They felt reluctant to continue to be party to the interim agreement, owing to the fact that Herts College was the only one to be 'nationally validated', i.e. by the CNAA. They were concerned that Birmingham still had an option and that Goldsmiths' art therapy training was taking place under the umbrella of the Diploma in Art and Design.

In fact, the Goldsmiths' Diploma in Art Therapy had been approved by the DES several months before Herts' letter, in its two modes, educational and clinical. It was not CNAA-validated due to Goldsmiths' then current negotiations to be admitted as a full school of the University of London, so the diploma was validated by the Delegacy, the governing body of Goldsmiths' and an organ of the university.

Goldsmiths' strongly objected to the suggestion that its diploma was not of the same level and, following letters and meetings, the issue was resolved between the two colleges. Birmingham, however, was in a difficult position as the art therapy training was still within the PGCE. Michael Edwards had taken up an Associate Professorship at the University of Concordia in Montreal, and Peter Byrne had to contest the challenge from Herts about the status of the course.

Herts College were anxious that the inclusion of an option (and an 'unvalidated' diploma) would cause problems in the negotiations for assimilation to the Whitley Council. Birmingham replied with a satirical document which challenged the whole basis of 'professionalism' and attacked the 'scientific' model of art therapy alleged to be in operation at Herts.

Andrea Gilroy and I, being centrally involved in the Whitley consultations, were in a position to see that neither the 'scientific' professions nor the DHSS were about to admit art therapy to its 'postgraduate' banding, as a jump from 'two years post-A level art' to 'postgraduate status' would severely disturb the *status quo* of NHS professions. Nor would the DHSS or the Whitley Council negotiate directly with a college. Despite considerable personal antagonisms, which in some cases were never completely resolved, the issues around the core curriculum were submerged when the DHSS issued its Personnel Memorandum PM (82) 6 in March 1982, giving art therapists their own career and salary structure, equivalent to that of OTs. The memorandum listed the courses at Birmingham, Goldsmiths', and Herts as approved, and this list remained until 1985.

Training in art therapy

(The core course recommendations as agreed in 1978 have not yet been superseded, although a current BAAT Training and Education Sub-Committee has been addressing the need to update them in line with current practice and perceived needs of the art therapy service. This committee now consists of representatives from Herts, Goldsmiths', and Sheffield University, which introduced a Diploma in Art Therapy in 1985, and representatives from different areas of art therapy practice.)

Summary

During the 1970s, then, BAAT, in co-operation with three colleges of higher education, had succeeded in its mission to have art therapy training established within the public sector at a level equivalent to art teacher training. As a result of the consensus arrived at through debate in the BAAT Registration Advisory Committee, a core curriculum had been devised which was broad enough to avoid irresolvable conflict concerning course content and philosophy. Likewise, entry requirements had been established which ensured that the majority of entrants to art therapy training would be visual art graduates, but they were flexible enough to allow 'applicants with an alternative qualification' to be admitted, provided they had 'a substantial and developing experience in art'. All had to provide evidence of 'personal maturity' and 'appropriate pre-course experience'. Art therapy training had received national validation through the CNAA and was established as a postgraduate diploma in a university institution. Master's level teaching was introduced at Birmingham in the mid–1970s, albeit under the MEd structure, and at Herts in 1981.

In the next chapter I shall discuss those proposals for art therapy training which did not come to fruition, with the exception of the Institute of Education course which has already been discussed in the context of the formation of BAAT's overall policy on training in the 1960s.

Chapter twenty-five

Attempts at training which failed to materialise

I have pointed out in the previous chapter that, between 1965 and 1971, BAAT had many and lengthy discussions with the Institute of Education over a proposal to establish an art therapy training within the advanced diplomas in education structure. This course did not begin, although the discussions were valuable to BAAT in themselves because they set the level and style which BAAT would subsequently aspire to.

Other tentative proposals had been put to BAAT Council in the early 1970s, mostly from colleges of education wishing to diversify. Despite initial encouragement, firmer proposals did not emerge, possibly because of the difficulty in establishing a vocational training in an area which could guarantee no clear job prospects or career structure.

Some centres did, however, proceed to submit detailed proposals to BAAT, requesting advice and assessment. In this chapter I shall briefly discuss these proposals and suggest reasons for their demise. To avoid possible embarrassment to the colleges, I have used letters to identify them.

College A

At its June 1978 meeting, the RAC received a proposal from College A, a college of further education, outlining a two-year part-time course. It was described as:

> Open to all who are interested in art as therapy in their personal experience or in their working situation. It has, therefore, particular interest for those who, in their work, are concerned with other people, in the fields of health or education.

The college was prepared to accept people with wide-ranging qualifications, from 'art therapists requiring further experience' to 'medical ancillary workers'.

253

Training in art therapy

The college had been running the course as a one-year introduction to art therapy, but wished to expand and offer a course which would deem its graduates eligible for full membership of BAAT.

The RAC asked two of its members to visit the college, to meet staff and discuss the course content and especially the entry requirements. The college wanted to have the approval of BAAT and of its own academic board.

Following the visit, it was decided that BAAT could not support the course because of the level of entry and because there seemed to be a confusion of aims. For example, it was not clear whether the course was intended as a training in art therapy or for students' personal interest. The time allocated, one day per week for two years, was also felt to be inadequate.

The college did not press its case and it appears that the initiators of the proposal did not receive much support from their own institution. The course continued (and still does) as an introductory, or 'foundation', art therapy programme.

Perhaps there was, too, a reluctance to support an art therapy programme which did not insist on graduate or equivalent entry, and which was sited in an FE college.

College B

This was a polytechnic in the process of diversifying some of its art education programme. The initiator of the proposal, with the support of the college, sent a detailed proposal to BAAT in 1976, at a time when the RAC was considering 'core course' requirements. The academic board requested an 'official' adviser, and I was asked to take this on. With other members of the RAC, I paid several visits to the college and advised on the course content. The course was to be called 'Post-Experience Diploma in Remedial Art (Art Therapy)', following a precedent established by Herts College. College B hoped for CNAA validation.

The idea for the course had originated in 1974 as a result of discussion between the Faculty of Art and Faculty of Education. Several of the college's art graduates had been working as unqualified art therapists, and the college had identified many psychiatric hospitals and clinics in the area which had expressed interest in co-operating in a course.

The background to this proposal was not unlike that of Herts, in that the college had undergone structural change and it had identified a possible area for exploration. The college was in a region which was poorly resourced in terms of health care, and the staff hoped that an art therapy training would stimulate provision of art therapy posts.

The proposal, in BAAT's terms, looked promising. The entry criteria conformed, the syllabus included art activities, contextual studios, and

Unresolved training

personal psychology – the last being based round a model of 'co-counselling'. The assessment criteria were clear and adequate, and attention had been paid to the role of examiners.

However, the CNAA did not approve the course and it appeared that the elements which had caused the rejection were those which BAAT had queried: namely placement and 'personal psychology'. Regarding placement, this was dependent on the student's own work place and it was felt that this could be limiting, given the nature of the institutions available. The model of 'personal psychology' favoured, in particular co-counselling, was seen as too narrow. The CNAA had by that time validated the Herts course, so had a comparator which included discrete placements, unrelated to work situation (in its full-time course at least), and an eclectic approach to psychology. The college was given the opportunity to restructure the proposal but did not do so. (I wonder whether it may also have been the case that the college would have needed to employ a full-time art therapist to conduct the course and, by the late 1970s when educational cuts were taking place, this may not have been a priority.)

Given the lack of a training course in the North, this college could have provided a useful base for development.

College C

This was a one-time college of education which was in the process of diversification. The college put forward a proposal to BAAT in 1976 for a Diploma in *Arts* Therapy, which had been presented to their Regional Authority, and which the college hoped would be validated by a neighbouring university. The university's academic board appointed two RAC members as advisers, and they visited the college to meet staff and discuss the syllabus.

Although the entry requirements conformed more or less to those of BAAT, there was a difficulty similar to that of the Institute of Education course, in that the course was to cover art, music, and drama therapy. Despite the inclusion of practical placement, theoretical and experiential components, and an adequate assessment scheme, it was felt that the initiators (none of whom were art, music, or drama therapists) did not have a clear enough view either of each of the arts therapies, or of their relationship to one another. Given that there was at that time no agreement between BAAT and the DHSS on art therapy training, nor any such on music or drama therapy training, nor was there a career structure for any of them, the merging of the three together appeared unmanageable and unwise. The advisers could not support the course and the college did not pursue it.

Training in art therapy

In reflecting on the possible reasons for the demise of these proposals, it seems that the difficulties were not impossible to overcome, and indeed they were, perhaps, less than those experienced by all the existing courses in gaining approval from regional advisory committees, their own academic boards, and validating bodies. None of the initiators was, however, closely identified with art therapy, nor did the survival of their institution or their jobs seem to depend on it. The expense, in terms of staff and expertise and resources required to mount an art therapy course, was considerable and all the above proposals were made at a time of cutbacks. Both Herts College and Goldsmiths' had initiated training at a time of change in the institution, and the resources had been built up slowly and laboriously. At Birmingham, where an option had started in 1969, it was surprising that a diploma did not emerge given that the college employed art therapists who were active in promoting training, and had already committed resources to the discipline. Reasons for this have already been suggested in Chapter 23.

The insistence by BAAT on either an art degree, or equivalent, or a substantial involvement in the practice of the visual arts prior to training, was felt to be fundamental in defining art therapy as a 'profession' rather than an occupation or a craft. This position has been criticised by Birchnell on many occasions, as 'politically expedient', and he points to the situation in other countries where art therapists come from mainly medical or paramedical backgrounds. However, these countries have no discrete profession of art therapy yet (1989).

As I have tried to show, possession of an art degree with the assumption that this has exposed the graduate to an education in direct contrast to that of doctors, nurses, and OTs, as well as to the in-depth study of media, imagery, symbolism, etc., was seen as crucial in ideological terms. In other words, this foundation would ensure that art therapy offered an 'alternative' view of treatment to the prevailing 'medical' model.

No proposals which challenge this position have to date been presented in Britain, but, with the mutual recognition of higher diplomas under the European directive of 1992, there may well be a further 'struggle' to establish criteria not only for the content and structure of art therapy training itself but for the pre-course requirements.

Scotland, Wales, and Northern Ireland

To this day there are no British art therapy training courses outside England, despite interest on the part of several institutions and obvious need. Rita Simon ran introductory courses at Queen's University, Belfast, but the impetus for starting a training course went when she returned to London. Colleges of art in Glasgow and Edinburgh made preliminary enquiries from BAAT in the late 1970s, but went no further with their

Unresolved training

plans. There have been no formal approaches to training in any Welsh institution, although several art therapists have given lectures and short courses at various art colleges. The lack of training opportunities in these regions obviously means that many suitable applicants for art therapy training are unable to take it up because of financial difficulties or family commitments or both, and that art therapy does not develop at the same pace as in England – and in the south particularly.

To establish the reasons would take a full-scale research project, but tentative thoughts as to the possible main ones suggest that those discussed above may apply, as well as a certain chicken-and-egg situation: there is a shortage of art therapists in all the regions, meaning that there are few suitable placements for potential trainees and little on-the-spot expertise. So colleges would have to build up a network almost from scratch, which would require employing an experienced art therapist in the first instance. However, the lack of a training centre in a region means that there are fewer opportunities to promote art therapy and thus fewer posts get established – unless a regional group is very determined and active in doing this. In the latest Register of Art Therapists (1989) there were nine in Wales, four in West Scotland, and fifteen in East Scotland, not all of whom were employed. There are two in Northern Ireland and three in the Republic. This is hardly a sound basis for extensive campaigning.

The hope, then, is that BAAT, with the help of Manufacturing, Science and Finance (MSF) (once ASTMS) and the DHSS, can try to stimulate employment of art therapists throughout Britain, which in turn will make the establishment of effective, if small-scale, training centres more feasible, and ensure that there is really 'patient choice' concerning access to art therapy.

Part VI

Concluding thoughts

Chapter twenty-six

After 1982: fresh challenges for art therapists

This historical survey has been limited to the period of the 1940s to 1982, during which time art therapists were preoccupied with the struggle for professional recognition. But, of course, things do not stand still. Following the publication of PM(82)6 which recognised the need for art therapists to be trained, and gave them a separate career and salary structure under the Whitley Council, and established them in the National Health Service, there was a long period of consolidation and gathering of energy for the new challenges to be met. In this summary of events post-1982 I cannot do justice to the variety of work and issues which were faced and resolved, and I hope that in due course I, or another 'archaeologist', will dig more deeply. For the time being, I will merely point out some of the most pertinent concerns of the past seven years.

The Joint Grading Committee

One of the first tasks was the establishment of the Joint Staff–Management Whitley Council Grading Committee for Art and Music Therapists, which was to examine and assess the claims for promotion of all therapists to Senior I and above. This committee rarely met, but received the written cases and, on the basis of rather loose criteria, decided whether promotion was in order or not. In the early days post-PM(82)6, the grading committee received hundreds of claims from art therapists who had been stuck on the inadequate 'single-handed' scale for many years, and who saw their salaries and career prospects rapidly enhanced as they gained Senior I status. On the basis of the proposals, the committee gradually built up a set of criteria concerning 'highly skilled and specialised work' as it applied to art therapy.

There were few disagreements between the Staff and Management Sides, and those necessitated meetings, and in four notorious cases took six years to resolve. Generally speaking, though, the committee was useful in allowing both sides to see the scope of an art therapist's work.

Concluding thoughts

Liaison with ASTMS (MSF) and the DHSS: the Pay Review Body

Art therapists' negotiations for a seat on the Whitley Council, following assimilation, were interrupted by the introduction of the Pay Review Body for Nurses and Professions Allied to Medicine (1983). Art therapists had been included as a 'related grade' to occupational therapists, but had not been consulted about this. Alongside the Pay Review Body were proposals to establish a Scientific and Professional Staffs Whitley Council, which both BAAT and ASTMS felt more appropriate, but the DHSS did not agree (letter to myself and Peter Cole, 15 December 1983). Subsequent discussions between BAAT and the DHSS led to the latter agreeing to art therapists (like speech therapists) withdrawing from the PRB, but this did not happen because of the failure of the new Professional Staffs Council to materialise. So art therapists have remained within the PRB, albeit unwillingly, but at the same time seeing their salaries improved as a result.

Regional groups

The idea of forming regional groups throughout Britain had been worked out in the late 1970s by Michael Donnelly, who became chair of BAAT in 1981. To date there are sixteen groups, including Scotland and Wales, and, as mentioned in Chapter 25, they are very uneven in membership with London and the south-east predominating. Each group had its own per capita funding, and was free to draw up its own programme of events. There were two regional conferences each year, with joint meetings with BAAT council. The groups were extremely important to the successful campaigns mounted by BAAT following the publication of the DHSS's Consultative Document, and have remained a valuable source of learning and support for art therapists throughout the country.

After 1982, they played a useful role in identifying problems arising from the Whitley assimilation, and in supporting members seeking promotion. In more recent years, several groups have mounted study days and conferences, which have stimulated publications.

Their other essential function has been to feed members' views into BAAT council via the regional group co-ordinators, thus preserving the 'grass-roots' nature of BAAT's activities.

The training and education sub-committee

This committee continued to meet under the chairmanship of Michael Donnelly, and consisted of two representatives from each training centre and a panel of practising art therapists representing different areas of work. It had the unenviable task of de-accrediting one of the oldest

Art therapy after 1982

approved trainings due to the inability of the host institution to grant a full Diploma in Art Therapy (Waller 1987: 192–3) and the more pleasant one of accrediting a new course at the University of Sheffield (1985). In recent times the Committee has been engaged in redefining the core course requirements for art therapy training and in suggesting improvements to the current structure.

The principles of professional practice

Following an AGM decision, a code of ethics was drawn up by a sub-committee chaired by Joan Woddis, who succeeded Michael Donnelly as chair in 1985. This code gives guidelines for the practice of art therapy, and covers such areas as record keeping, referral system, caseload, minimum conditions, and training. (See Register of BAAT for full account.) Not only did this code provide a model for art therapists themselves, it gave them ammunition in their workplace struggles for professional recognition.

The Registration Board

In the interests of protecting the public, and of making available a list of qualified art therapists for the use of social services departments or other professionals who might seek the advice of an art therapist, a register was compiled and is now published annually. It gives name, home or working address of each member, their qualifications, and area of work (NHS, social services, etc.). It is divided into regional groups, and gives members the chance to communicate easily with each other. The Registration Board, chaired by Joan Woddis, continues to maintain and update the register. At present, registration is synonymous with holding a recognised qualification in art therapy or with full membership of BAAT, whereas in the USA registration follows a period of supervised clinical practice post-training.

The Griffiths Report

The publication of the Griffiths Report (1984), concerning the reorganisation of the NHS and the need to deliver improved services to patients and clients and to give better managerial support to staff, led to considerable anxiety on the part of all health care workers, in that it implied many changes. It was feared that it was really a cost-cutting exercise and that 'competitive' relationships would result (see 'Action Pack for RCN Members', September 1985).

Concluding thoughts

The effects of the reorganisation are, of course, still going on, and have resulted in the need for each profession to justify itself and to assess the level of service being provided. Art therapists have long been accustomed to this process, but are hampered by their lack of clear management structure (often they are managed by OTs and have little say on appropriate committees).

Promotion of art therapy in non-NHS areas

As yet there is no formal establishment for art therapy within the social services and education,[1] although some art therapists have succeeded in negotiating their own terms and conditions, and are employed under the title of 'art therapist', on grades equivalent to a social worker's at various levels. This has the obvious disadvantage of the pre-Whitley days in the NHS, for if an art therapist wishes to move to another social services post, there is no guarantee that the same conditions will prevail. A similar difficulty exists within education services, in that most art therapists who find posts in schools are employed as teachers, giving over part of their timetable to art therapy. As well as having the problem of a split role, they have no guarantee that, for instance, a new headteacher would allow them to continue working as an art therapist. Some therapists work sessionally (in the same way as child psychotherapists), and a few have succeeded in having their job description include almost full-time art therapy, but the position is unsatisfactory for both art therapist and school.

The experience of the training courses has shown that non-NHS institutions often actively seek the services of an art therapist, but do not have the means to employ them in the same way as other staff. They may have a variety of titles – group worker, care officer, day centre worker, instructor – and be performing the duties of an art therapist, but this ultimately has a poor effect on their morale (see Waller 1987: 201–2).

BAAT, then, has two sub-committees (and its council) working consistently on these major problems. Given the reorganisation in health care, the general lack of funding and problems of morale in the 'caring' professions, and the introduction of the 'core curriculum' in education, it could not be a less auspicious time to seek recognition in either the social services or in education. Nevertheless, the will to succeed is there and, unlike in pre-Whitley days, the precedent is already established, as is the training.

The European Community: 1992

It has not been within the scope of this book to deal adequately with the development of art therapy in other countries, including Europe. How-

Art therapy after 1982

ever, with the approach of 1992 and the possibility of art therapists being able to work across the European Community, it is important to be aware of some of the issues which need to be addressed. I believe these are predominantly to do with training and professional status.

As I have tried to show, art therapy in Britain and the USA developed mainly from a synthesis of art education and psychoanalysis, and art therapists come mainly from an art and design background. In other countries this is rarely the case. To illustrate by examples which are most familiar to me: in France, Italy, and Greece, aspiring art therapists come from a psychology or paramedical background. They may have had little or no experience of visual art practice, even at school. In devising training programmes which would approximate to the British model, there would need to be much emphasis on engaging trainees in their own art and media experiences. A similar situation exists in Eastern Europe, as my own work in Jugoslavia and in Bulgaria, through participation in a World Health Organisation sponsored project, has demonstrated (see Waller 1983: 84, 89). In both these countries, and in other places in Eastern Europe, art therapy is seen as a treatment to be carried out by the medical profession, initially at least.

An important development concerning the European Community has been the European Training Initiative, carried out at Herts College of Art, a scheme designed to provide training opportunities for students from the European Community. The participants were funded by scholarships from the European Fund. The scheme ran for a three-year period, until 1987, and provided a nine-month, full-time programme consisting of theoretical studies, experiential workshops, personal experience of media, and a clinical placement. Students came from a variety of backgrounds, including psychology, psychiatry, social work, teaching, occupational therapy. Programmes in both art and drama therapy were provided.

The project provided valuable learning experiences for both students and staff, and led to evaluation of the potential for involvement of British training institutions in assisting the development of courses abroad. For example, Herts College has recently begun to collaborate with Denmark to establish a distance learning model of training, which will consist of units of training that constitute the diploma course at Herts College, taken over three years part time.

Another outcome of the project was the establishment of a database identifying all colleges and institutions within the European Community where courses or options in art therapy were being offered, which gave a picture of the extent of involvement and interest within each member state for the whole area of arts and disability. The computerised database has been widened to include not only programmes of art, music, drama, and dance therapy, but also all organisations and projects where arts are being used with and by disabled people and groups with special needs.

Concluding thoughts

At Goldsmiths' College, plans are well under way to grant external diplomas to those institutions abroad which meet the requirements of the University of London. This development goes alongside research into cross-cultural issues in art therapy and group psychotherapy, which is ongoing in the Art Psychotherapy Unit.

There is emphasis in both these training centres on different countries developing training programmes which are appropriate to their own social and cultural requirements, but at the same time are of an equivalent status to those in Britain, which is the first country to have art therapy State-recognised. Such initiatives will no doubt pave the way for mutual recognition of qualifications after 1992.

Concluding thoughts

In 1989, both art and music therapists experienced a boost to morale, in that, for the first time, the DHSS appointed Advisers in both professions. Despite the many conflicts, which, if we believe in the process model of professions, will continue to exist, training for and practice of art therapy are now firmly established. The number of practitioners is increasing steadily, job opportunities are increasing. There is more opportunity for in-service education and research. The general public seems better informed. Art therapists now must face the massive changes in the organisation of the health service following publication of the government's White Paper. A more competitive working environment and less secure NHS base may be one of the results. Given the challenges ahead, it is to be hoped that we, as art therapists, will continue to do what we seem always to have done, that is to subject ourselves and our profession to self-scrutiny in the interests of providing a genuinely effective alternative treatment to people from all classes and backgrounds (not just those who can afford it) and especially to those who in the past have been considered 'unsuitable' for psychotherapy or 'insight-providing' treatment.

Note

After completion of this manuscript, in August 1990, the National Joint Council approved the postgraduate Diploma in Art Therapy, enabling art therapists to negotiate a career structure in the social sciences.

Appendix: BAAT Registration Advisory Committee

Report and recommendations 1977

Since being formed last year the Registration Advisory Committee has looked at a large number of interconnected questions and issues. The Committee's brief, to make recommendations concerning the registration criteria for practising art therapists, has proved to be both complicated and time consuming. The Committee has in many instances been investigating an enormous body of data and information, clarifying matters endemically resistant to definition, exploring areas where there are few precedents, and attempting to reconcile contradictory requirements. The following is an outline of the Committee's work:

Members of the Committee visited currently functioning art therapy training courses. These were the Postgraduate Diploma in Art Therapy course at the Hertfordshire College of Art and Design in St Albans, the art therapy options of the PGCE and MA courses at the school of Art Education in Birmingham, and the art therapy option of the ATC course at Goldsmiths' College. In addition visits were made to institutions intending to set up courses of training in art therapy; these were at Sunderland Polytechnic and Ilkley College.

The objectives and methods of these different courses were contrasted and compared. By abstracting common ingredients from the courses, particularly those at St Albans, Goldsmiths', and Birmingham, it was possible to obtain a picture of an art therapy 'core' course as it has arisen in current practice.

There was much discussion of the relative advantages and disadvantages of existing courses. Further aspects of the training of art therapists were discussed and evaluated so that any recommended core course would be the result of theoretical as well as pragmatic considerations. The Committee examined the possibility of adapting the American 'credit' system of accumulation registration 'points' to English circumstances. It was concluded that such a system was unnecessarily complicated for the purpose required in this country. It offered no advantages over the simpler procedure whereby intending art therapists have attended one of a small number of well designed courses of training supplemented by high but

Becoming a profession

flexible entrance requirements and a carefully administered probationary system.

Great stress was therefore placed on synthesizing existing and proposed features of training into a core course which would serve as a model against which proposed courses of training for art therapists could be compared and assessed. The Committee's recommendations for a core course are the best balance which its members considered obtainable between, firstly, differing concepts of art therapy training, and secondly, between those requirements which some members found ideal and those which were seen to be practically necessary.

Attention was paid to the entrance requirements of such a course and there was considerable discussion of the differing backgrounds of entrants to art therapy training courses. The need for a probationary period following training was clearly recognised and methods of implementing this were investigated.

As a result of these deliberations the Committee makes the following proposals:

I. The establishment of a Registration Committee

A properly established Registration Committee will perform the task of registering art therapists in accordance with agreed criteria. This Committee, will, in consultation with the Council, be responsible for devising and administering an adequate appeals procedure. The membership of the Registration Committee is to be composed in the first instance of the present members of the Registration Advisory Committee and thereafter to be determined by the Council.

II. Registration criteria

Successful completion of a recognised course of training followed by an appropriate period of probationary work will be essential for intending art therapists to obtain registration. Such registration will be a necessary requirement in order to practice as an art therapist and to join BAAT as a Full Member; such membership should be recognised by employing authorities and by the Whitley Council as signifying the right to practise art therapy.

III. Recommended core course in art therapy

While recognising that colleagues in various institutions will have their own biases and specializations, we recommend that, with regard to a first

Appendix

qualification in art therapy, the following should form the basis of any proposed new course in art therapy:

A. With regard to entry criteria the selection of candidates for art therapy training will depend upon evidence of personal maturity and/or appropriate pre-course experience. Academically, intending students will also normally require a first degree or its equivalent in the visual arts. In cases where applicants have an alternative qualification a substantial and developing experience in art will be expected.
B. There should be a balance between 1 theoretical, 2 clinical, and 3 practical and experiential forms of learning. (See below.)
C. Courses of training should be able to adapt to the changing needs of their students and of their students' prospective clients and employers, and to incorporate theoretical and practical innovations.

Parts 1, 2 and 3 in Section B above to include the following:

1. Theoretical study

Such study will be concerned with the bodies of knowledge which underlie the theory and practice of art therapy. Although it is to be expected that the emphasis will vary according to the therapeutic philosophy of the particular training establishment, it is strongly urged that a catholic selection of fundamental concepts be presented to the student.

(i) An introduction to and study of basic theories and models: psychological, behavioural, medical, psychoanalytical, developmental, educational, biological, anthropological, social, political, philosophical, semiotic, aesthetic, and artistic.
(ii) The adaption of such theories to therapeutic purposes and the historical development of the study of art and psychopathology and of art therapy.
(iii) The manner in which models of art therapy can be derived from the above and consequent methodology.
(iv) Approaches to the questions of the internal coherence and scientific validation of the different forms of art therapy.
(v) The institutional and social contexts for the practice of art therapy.

2. Clinical study

It is recommended that the student spend at least 60 days of placement in appropriate institutions under the supervision of persons with responsibility for the clinical application of art therapy; these may be art therapists, consultants, psychotherapists, psychologists, head occupational therapists, head teachers, or their equivalents in the institutions concerned. Part

Becoming a profession

of this period would naturally be spent in observations but students would also be expected to implement a programme of art therapy and to produce at least one case study. It is hoped that students would have the chance to visit a range of hospitals, clinics, special schools, etc., in connection with their clinical practice.

3. Practical and experimental learning

It is considered essential that students be encouraged to develop their own self-awareness by means of the psychotherapeutic applications of image-making; thus a range of art therapy techniques will be learned at first hand. Investigations will also be made of the appropriateness, possibilities and applications of different media and techniques in art therapy, e.g. gestalt, role-play, dream analysis, projective group techniques. A reassessment of the student's previous art work and of his or her art school training, as well as wider issues in art and aesthetics, will be explored by means of workshops. Students will be required to gain a personal experience of the psychotherapeutic process by means of participation in a training group led by a psychotherapist.

Assessment

Students should be required to provide adequate written and oral evidence of Parts 1 and 2 in Section B. It is recommended that this should include at least one substantial piece of written work. Courses which are submitted to the Registration Committee must have details of internal accountability clearly stated.

Students will be expected to *pass all sections of the course*; i.e. Parts 1, 2, and 3 in Section B above.

IV. Probationary period

It is envisaged that successful completion of a course meeting the requirements set out in III would be followed by one year of probationary work in an approved setting. It will be the responsibility of the student to obtain such employment and to inform the Registration Committee of the probationary employment; to obtain their agreement it must satisfy certain minimum requirements. Exceptionally, a student may propose completion of probation by means of part-time work. The nature of the work, the minimum number of hours per week, and the total length of the probationary period would need to be agreed with the Registration Committee. In most instances 15 hours per week would be taken as a minimum for part-time work. It would, however, be at the Registration Committee's discre-

Appendix

tion to give approval to alternative probationary arrangements. Satisfactory completion of the probationary period together with a good reference from a person clinically or administratively responsible for a probationer's work would be required prior to an art therapist's registration. It is envisaged that the category of Probationary membership of BAAT be created. The regulations governing the probationary period to be decided on by the Registration Committee and the Council by the end of the academic year in 1978.

V. Interim arrangements for registration

As the full registration criteria set out above can only be applied in the first instance to students having commenced recognised courses of training in 1978 and applying for registration in 1980 at the earliest, a set of interim criteria for registration are required in the meantime. These will apply to practising art therapists who are Full Members of BAAT, to student art therapists completing a year's practice after their training, and to students currently attending a course of training. During the interim period it is recommended that BAAT recognises the courses of training at St Albans, Goldsmiths, and Birmingham. The Committee proposes the following interim arrangements for registration:

A. All current Full Members of BAAT will be considered registered art therapists. Former Full Members, whose membership has for one reason or another lapsed, who wish to become registered re-apply for Full Membership by 1.3.78. Membership criteria are as stated in the present BAAT Constitution.

B. Those who have already undergone courses of training in art therapy and are not Full Members of BAAT may apply for registration on completion of a year of full-time work as an art therapist. Exceptionally, applicants for registration may seek the Registration Committee's approval for periods of part-time work equivalent to one year's full-time work. Although such work does not constitute a probationary period as such, proof that the required period of time has been spent working as an art therapist will be required by the Registration Committee. In order to satisfy these requirements the post-training work must begin before the end of the academic year in 1978. Work commenced after that must meet the requirements of the probationary period as in IV above.

C. Students at present undertaking courses of art therapy training finishing in 1978 will be required to satisfy the conditions of the probationary year as in IV above prior to their seeking registration.

271

Becoming a profession

Members of the Registration Advisory Committee are as follows: Diane Waller, John Evans, Pam Gulliver, Michael Edwards, Michael Pope, John Henzel, Robin Holtom, Andrea Gilroy, Shelley Mawbey.

References

Adamson, E. (1970) 'Art for mental health', in J. Creedy (ed.) *The Social Context of Art*, London: Tavistock.

Adamson, E. and Freudenberg, R. K. (1968) *Catalogue* for Art and Mental Health Exhibition, London: Commonwealth Institute.

Agazarian, Y. and Peters, R. (1981) *The Visible and Invisible Group*, London, Routledge.

ASTMS (1980) 'The position of art therapists', in *The Forgotten Professions*, ASTMS submission to the Pay Comparability Committee.

Baly, M. (1980) *Nursing and Social Change*, 2nd edition, London: Heinemann.

Barnard, K. and Lee, K (eds.) (1977) *Conflicts in the NHS*, Bromley, Kent: Croom Helm.

Baron, C. (1987) *Asylum to Anarchy*, London: Free Association Books.

Barton, R. (1959) *Institutional Neurosis*, Bristol: Wright.

Baynes, H. (1940) *Mythology of the Soul*, London: Baillière, Tindall & Cox.

Becker, H. S. (1971) *Sociological Work: Method and Substance*, London: Penguin.

Ben-David, J. and Collins, R. (1966) 'Social factors in the origins of a new science: the case of psychology', *American Journal of Sociology Review* 31 (4): 451–65.

Berman, E. 'Interview', *Another Standard* Summer.

Birtchnell, J. (1976) 'Alternative concepts in art therapy', *Inscape* 1: 15, London: BAAT.

____ (1977) 'Art therapy as psychotherapy', *Inscape* 1 (15).

____ (1984) 'Art therapy as psychotherapy', in T. Dalley (ed.) *Art as Therapy*, London: Tavistock.

Bode, B. H. (1938) 'The concept of needs in education', *Progressive Education* 15 (1).

British Association of Art Therapists (1978) 'Registration and Training Advisory Committee Report', *Inscape* 2 (1).

British Association of Art Therapists (1989) *Artists and Art Therapists: a brief description of their roles within hospitals, clinics, special schools and in the community*, London: BAAT.

Bucher, R. and Strauss, A. (1961) 'Professions in process', *American Journal of Sociology* 66 (January).

Byrne, P. (1980) 'Art therapy training at Birmingham Polytechnic', *Inscape* 4 (1).

References

Cannan, C. (1972) 'Social work: training and professionalism', in T. Pateman (ed.) *Countercourse*, Harmondsworth: Penguin.

Cardinal, R. (1972) *Outsider Art*, London: Studio Vista.

Case, C. (1987) 'A search for meaning: loss and transition in art therapy', in T. Dalley *et al. Images of Art Therapy*, London: Routledge, pp. 36–73.

Champernowne, H. I. (1963) 'Art therapy in the Withymead Centre', *American Bulletin of Art Therapy* spring.

―――― (1971) 'Art and therapy: an uneasy partnership', *Inscape* 1 (3).

Charcot, J. M. and Richer, P. (1887) *Les Demoniaques dans l'art*, Paris.

Churchill, W. (1948) *Painting as Pastime*, London: Odhams Press.

Clegg Commission (1979) *Professions Supplementary to Medicine*, Report No. 4, London: HMSO.

Dalley, T. (ed.) (1984) *Art as Therapy*, London: Tavistock.

Dalley, T. *et al.* (1987) *Images of Art Therapy*, London: Routledge.

Dartington Hall Trustees (1946) *The Visual Arts: Report on the Position of the Visual Arts*, Cumberlege OUP.

Davies, E. (1949) 'Arthur Segal's methods', in 'Report of a one-day conference on art and music therapy', *Rehabilitation* October.

Davis, M. and Wallbridge, D. (1981) *Boundary and Space: An Introduction to the Work of Donald Winnicott*, London: Karnac: Harmondsworth: Penguin (1983).

Dax, E. Cunningham (1949) 'Review of exhibition of patients' art work from Netherne Hospital', *British Medical Journal* 23 July.

―――― (1953) *Experimental Studies in Psychiatric Art*, London: Faber.

Dewey, J. (1934) *Art as Experience*, New York: Minton, Balch & Co.

Doran, L. (1977) 'Ways of working', in *As We See it: Approaches to Art Therapy*, London: students at Goldsmiths' College.

Dyne, D. (1985) 'Questions of training in psychotherapy', *Free Associations*, 3: 92–145, London.

Eisner, E. W. (1972) *Educating Artistic Vision*, New York: Macmillan.

Elston, M. A. (1977) 'Medical autonomy, challenge and response', in K. Barnard and K. Lee (eds) *Conflicts in the NHS*, Bromley, Kent: Croom Helm.

Evans, J. (1979) 'Training in art therapy at Hertfordshire College of Art', *Inscape* 3 (2).

Fairbairn, W. R. D. (1938) 'Prolegomena to a psychology of art', *British Journal of Psychology* 28.

Francis, C. and Warren Piper, D. (1973) 'Some figures about art and design education', in D. Warren Piper (ed.) *After Coldstream: Readings in Art and Design Education 2*, London: Davis Poynter.

Gilroy, A. and Dalley, T. (eds) (1989) *Pictures at an Exhibition: Essays on Art and Art Therapy*, London: Routledge.

Glass, J. (1963) 'Art therapy', *Journal of the National Association for Mental Health* 22: 2.

Goffman, E. (1968) *Asylums: Essays on the Social Situation of Mental Patients and Other Inmates*, Harmondsworth: Penguin.

Goldsmith, A. (1979) 'The St Albans course was the most suitable for me', *Inscape* 3 (2) 8–9.

Goodson, I. (1981) 'Becoming an academic subject: explanation and evolution', *British Journal of the Sociology of Education* 2 (2): 163–79.

References

Gould, S. J. (1981) *The Mismeasure of Man*, Harmondsworth: Pelican.

Gray, J. (1974) *Medicine*, Newton Abbot, Devon: David & Charles.

Griffiths, B. C. and Mullins, N. C. (1972) 'Coherent social groups in scientific change', *Science* 177: 959–64.

Gross, E. (1958) *Work and Society*, New York: Crowell Co.

Gulliver, P. (1976) 'Concepts of work in art therapy', *Inscape* 1: 15.

Guttman, E. and Maclay, W. (1937) 'Clinical observations on schizophrenic drawings', *British Journal of Medical Psychology*.

—— (1941) 'Hallucinations in artists', *Archive of Neurology and Psychology* 45: 130.

Guttman, E., Maclay, W., and Mayer-Gross, W. (1938) 'Spontaneous drawings as an approach to psychotherapy', *British Journal of Medical Psychology* 16 (3–4): 187–205.

Hall, G. S. (1904) *Adolescence: Its Psychology and Its Relation to Physiology, Anthropology, Sex, Crime, Religion and Education*, New York: Appleton.

Halsbury Report (1974) *Review of the Pay and Conditions of the Professions Supplementary to Medicine*, London: HMSO.

Hansen, D. A. and Gerstl, J. E. (1967) *On Education: Sociological Perspectives*, New York: Wiley.

Heard, W. (1986) 'The Ashington miners' art group', Diploma in Art Therapy report, Goldsmiths' College, London.

Henzell, J. (1970) 'On shouting', *Inscape* 2: 15–17.

Herbert, J. (1972) *Note in Catalogue for Exhibition of Art in Hospitals*, BAAT: MIND.

Hill, A. (1943) 'Art as an aid to illness: an experiment in occupational therapy', *Studio Magazine*, August: 125, London.

—— (1945) *Art Versus Illness*, London: George Allen & Unwin.

—— (1947) 'Art in hospitals', *Studio Magazine*, February: 133, London.

—— (1951) *Painting Out Illness*, London: Williams & Norgate.

Hillman, J. (1970) 'An imaginal ego', *Inscape* 2: 2–8.

Hinshelwood, R. (1985) 'Questions of training', *Free Associations* 2.

Hobson, R. (1971) 'The therapeutic community disease', unpublished paper.

—— 'The Messianic community', in R. Hinshelwood and N. Manning (eds) *Therapeutic Communities: Reflections and Progress*, London: Routledge & Kegan Paul.

Holton, R. (1978) *Note in Exhibition Catalogue for Exhibition: The Inner Eye*, Oxford: Museum of Modern Art.

Illich, I. (1975) *Medical Nemesis*, London: Calder & Boyars.

Iveson, J. (1938) *The Occupational Treatment of Mental Illness*, London: Ballière, Tindall & Cox.

Johnson, T. (1972) *Professions and Power*, London: Macmillan.

Jones, K. (1987) 'A little of what you fancy', Diploma in Art Therapy report, Goldsmiths' College.

Jones, M. (1979) 'The therapeutic community: social learning and social change', in R. Hinshelwood and N. Manning (eds) *Therapeutic Communities: Reflections and Progress*, London: Routledge & Kegan Paul.

Kelly, O. (1984) *Community, Art and the State: Storming the Citadels*, Comedia/Minority Press Group Series No. 23, London: Comedia.

References

Khaleelee, O. (1982) *Psychotherapy and the Process of Profession Building*, London: OPUS

Kramer, E. (1958) *Art Therapy in a Children's Community*, Springfield, Ill. : Thomas.

___ (1971) *Art as Therapy with Children*, New York: Schocken Books.

Kris, E. (1932a) *Catalogue* of Postclassical Cameos in the Milton Weil Collection, Vienna.

___ (1932b) 'Ein geisteskranker Bildhauer': *catalogue* of postclassical cameos in the Milton Weil Collection, Vienna.

___ (1952) *Psychoanalytic Explorations in Art*, London: George Allen & Unwin.

___ (1953) 'Psychoanalysis and the study of creative imagination', *Bulletin of the New York Academy of Medicine*, 29: 334–51.

Lacey, C. (1977) *The Socialization of Teachers*, London: Methuen.

Laing, J. (1964) 'Art therapy and expressionism', *Ciba Symposium* 12 (3).

Large, S. E. (1986) *King Edward VII Hospital*, Midhurst, Sussex: Phillimore.

Lemlij, M. Mulvany, S., and Nagle, C. J. (1981) 'A therapeutic community is terminated', *Group Analysis* 19 (3).

Liebmann, M. (1984) 'Art games and art structures', in T. Dalley (ed.) *Art as Therapy*, London: Tavistock.

___ (1986) *Art Therapy for Groups: A Handbook of Themes, Games and Exercises*, Bromley, Kent: Croom Helm.

Littlewood, R. and Lipsedge, M. (1982) *Aliens and Alienists*, Harmondsworth: Pelican.

Lowenfeld, V. (1939) *The Nature of Creative Activity*, London: Kegan Paul, Trench, Trubner & Co.

___ (1970) *Creative and Mental Growth*, New York: Macmillan. First published (1947) New York: Macmillan.

Lyddiatt, E. M. (1971) *Spontaneous Painting and Modelling*, London: Constable.

Macdonald, E. M. (1961) *Occupational Therapy in Rehabilitation*, London, Baillière, Tindall & Cox.

MacDonald, S. (1970) *The History and Philosophy of Art Education*, London: London University Press.

___ (1973) 'Articidal tendencies', in D. Warren Piper (ed.) *After Coldstream: Readings in Art and Design Education 2*, London: Davis Poynter.

MacGregor, J. (1978) 'The discovery of the art of the insane', PhD thesis, Ann Arbor, Mich. : University Microfilms International.

McNeilly, G. (1983) 'Directive and non-directive approaches in art therapy', *The Arts in Psychotherapy* 10 (4).

___ (1987) 'Further contributions to group analytic art therapy', *Inscape* Autumn 1983.

Madge, C. and Weinberger, B. (1973) *Art Students Observed*, London: Faber.

Melia, K. (1983) *Students' Views of Nursing*, 2nd edition, London: Heinemann.

Milner, M. (alias J. Field) (1934) *A Life of One's Own*, London: Chatto & Windus.

Milner, M. (alias J. Field) (1937) *An Experiment in Leisure*, London: Chatto & Windus.

Milner, M. (1938) *The Human Problem in Schools*, edited by S. Isaacs, London: Methuen.

Milner, M. (alias J. Field) (1950) *On Not Being Able to Paint*, London: Heinemann.

References

Milner, M. (1969) *The Hands of the Living God*, London: Hogarth Press.

Molloy, T. (1989) 'Art therapists and psychiatrists', Advanced Diploma study, Goldsmiths' College.

Morgenthaler, W. (1918) 'Übergänge, zwishen Zeichen und Schreiben bei Geisteskranken', in *Schweizer Archiv fur Neurologie und Psychiatrie* 3: 255–305.

____ (1921) 'Ein Geisteskranker als Künstler', : Bern. Translated into French by Henri-Pol Bouché under 'Adolf Wölfli' in *Publications de la Compagnie de l'Art Brut*, Fascicules 2, Paris (1964).

Musgrave, V. and Cardinal, R. (1979) *Outsiders*, Catalogue of Arts Council Exhibition, Hayward Gallery, London.

Naumburg, M. (1947) *Studies of the Free Art Expression of Behaviour Disturbed Children as a Means of Diagnosis and Therapy*, Nervous and Mental Diseases Monographs, New York: Coolidge Foundation.

____ (1950) *Schizophrenic Art: Its Meaning in Psychotherapy*, New York: Grune & Stratton.

____ (1953) *Psychoneurotic Art: Its Function in Psychotherapy*, New York: Grune & Stratton.

____ (1958) 'Art therapy: its scope and function', in E. F. Hammer (ed.) *Clinical Application of Projective Drawings*, Springfield, Ill. : Thomas.

____ (1966) *Dynamically Oriented Art Therapy: Its Principles and Practices*, New York: Grune & Stratton.

Ozga, J. T. and Lawn, M. A. (1981) *Teachers, Professionalism and Class*, London: Falmer Press.

Petrie, M. (1946a) *Art and Regeneration*, London: Elek.

____ (1946b) 'Review of Adrian Hill's *Art Versus Illness*', *Athene* 3 (4): 137.

Pfister, O. (1922) *Expressionism in Art: Its Psychological and Biological Basis*, London: Kegan Paul, Trench, Trubner & Co.

____ (1923) 'Review of Prinzhorn's *Bildernei der Geisteskranken*', *Imago* 9.

Pickford, R. (1967) *Studies in Psychiatric Art: Its Psychodynamics, Therapeutic Value and Relationship to Modern Art*, Springfield, Ill. : Thomas.

Plokker, J. (1964) *Artistic Expression in Mental Illness*, London: Skilton.

Pope, M. (1970) 'Teaching slow learning children', *Special Education* 59 (4).

Prinzhorn, H. (1922) *Bildernei der Geisteskranken*, Berlin: Springer Verlag, translated by E. Von Brockendorff as *Artistry of the Mentally Ill*, Springer, 1972.

____ (1922) and 2nd ed. (1923) *Bildernei der Geisteskranken*, Berlin: Springer Verlag. First English version (1972) translated by E. Von Brockendorff, Berlin/New York: Springer Verlag.

____ (1926) *Bildernei der Gefangenen*, Berlin: Springer Verlag.

Read, H. (1931) *The Meaning of Art*, London: Faber & Faber, reprint (1982).

____ (1943) *Education Through Art*, New York: Pantheon.

____ (1952) *The Philosophy of Modern Art*, London: Faber & Faber.

Reitman, F. (1950) *Psychotic Art*, London: Routledge & Kegan Paul.

Richardson, M. (1948) *Art and the Child*, London: University of London Press.

Ritchie, J. (1972) *Employment of Art College Leavers*, London: HMSO.

Roberts, N. (1967) *Mental Health and Mental Illness*, London: Routledge & Kegan Paul.

References

Roman, S. (1986) 'Art therapy and its relationship to clinical investigations', Diploma in Art Therapy report, Goldsmiths' College.

Roth, G. and Wittick, C. (eds) (1975) *Economy and Society*, Berkeley, USA: University of California Press.

Rumney, R. (1980) 'Art therapy at the Netherne Hospital', Diploma in Art Therapy report, Goldsmiths' College.

Rytovaara, M. (1975) 'A few notes on art therapy', *Inscape* 1: 12.

Salvage, J. (1985) *The Politics of Nursing*, 2nd edition, London: Heinemann.

Sargant, W. (1957) *Battle for the Mind*, London: Heinemann.

Sargant, W. and Craske, N. (1941) 'Modified insulin therapy in war neurosis', *Lancet* 2: 212.

Sargant, W. and Slater, E. (1940) 'Acute war neurosis', *Lancet* 2 (1).

____ (1951) 'Physical methods of treatment in psychiatry', *British Medical Journal* 1: 1315.

Seftel, L. (1987) 'Interview with Edward Adamson', *Journal of Art Therapy* 26 (November).

Segal, A. (1939) *Art as a Test for Normality and its Application for Therapeutical Purposes*, London: Guild of Pastoral Psychology.

____ (1942) *Art and Psychotherapy*, London: Guild of Pastoral Psychology.

Setlogelo, P. (1987) 'Public perceptions of art therapy', Diploma in Art Therapy report, Goldsmiths' College.

Shorske, C. E. (1981) *Fin de Siècle Vienna: Politics and Culture*, Cambridge: Cambridge University Press.

Simon, P.-M. (1988) 'Les écrits et les dessins des alienes', *Archivo di Antropologia Criminelle, Psichiatria e Medicina Legale* 3.

Simon, R. (1970) 'Significance of pictorial styles in art therapy', *American Journal of Art Therapy* 9: 159–76.

____ (1974) 'Pictorial style as a means of communication', *American Journal of Art Therapy* 13: 275–92.

____ (1981) 'Bereavement art' *American Journal of Art Therapy* 20: 135–43.

____ (1985) 'Graphic style and therapeutic change in geriatric patients', *American Journal of Art Therapy* 24 (1): 3–9.

Stanton, A. and Schwartz, M. (1954) *The Mental Hospital*, New York: Basic Books.

Stevens, A. (1986) *The Withymead Centre: A Jungian Community for the Healing Arts*, London: Coventure.

Sully, J. (1895) 'Studies of childhood. XIV. The child as artist', *Popular Science* 48.

Tardieu. A-. A. (1872) *Etudes Medico-Legales sur la Folie*, Paris.

Thevoz, M. (1976) *Art Brut*, London: Academy Editions.

Thompson, M. (1989) *On Art Therapy: An Exploration*, London: Virago.

Timlin, J. (1983) 'An apple for the teacher', in E. Adamson (ed.) *Art as Healing*, London: Coventure.

Timms, N. (1964) *Psychiatric Social Work in Britain*, London: Routledge & Kegan Paul.

Tomlinson, R. (1934) *Catalogue* for Exhibition of Children's Drawings and Paintings at County Hall, London.

References

Tomlinson, R. R. and Mills, J. F. (1966) *The Growth of Children's Art*, London: University of London Press.

Ulman, E. (1963) 'The Withymead Centre', *American Journal of Art Therapy* spring: 96.

—— (1983) 'Obituary of Margaret Naumburg', *American Journal of Art Therapy* 22 (4).

Viola, W. (1942) *Child Art*, London: University of London Press.

Walker, C. (1978) *Note in Catalogue for Exhibition: The Inner Eye*, Oxford: Museum of Modern Art.

Waller, D. E. (1976) 'Myths and reality', *Art Therapy*, London: BAAT.

—— (1979) 'Personal reflections on art therapy training at Goldsmiths' College', *Inscape* 3 (2).

—— (1983) 'Art therapy in Bulgaria, Part I', *Inscape* autumn.

—— (1984a) 'Art therapy in Bulgaria, Part II', *Inscape* spring.

—— (1984b) 'A consideration of the similarities and differences between art teaching and art therapy', in T. Dalley (ed.) *Art as Therapy*, London: Tavistock.

—— (1987) 'Art therapy in adolescence: a metaphorical view of a profession in progress', in T. Dalley *et al. Images of Art Therapy*, London: Routledge.

Waller, D. and Gilroy, A. (1986) 'Art therapy in practice', in D. Steinberg (ed.) *The Adolescent Unit*, Chichester, Sussex: Wiley.

Waller, D. E. and James, A. K. (1984) 'Training in art therapy', in T. Dalley (ed) *Art as Therapy*, London: Tavistock.

Walter, L. (1983) 'Why do so many women become art therapists?', Diploma in Art Therapy report, Goldsmiths' College.

Warsi, B. (1977) 'What is creativity?', unpublished paper *see also* Warsi (1976) 'Alternative concepts in art therapy', *Inscape* 1: (15) London: BAAT.

Weatherson, A. (1962) 'Seeing insanity through art', *New Society* 8: 18.

Wilde, O. (1890) 'The soul of man under socialism', republished 1956 in *Poems and Essays*, London: Collins.

Williams, R. (1958) *Culture and Society 1780–1950*, Harmondsworth: Penguin.

—— (1980) *Problems of Materialism and Culture*, London: Verso.

Wills, D. (1945) *The Barns Experiment*, London: Allen and Unwin.

Winnicott, D. W. (1951) 'Transitional objects and transitional phenomena', in *Collected Papers: Through Paediatrics to Psychoanalysis*, London: Tavistock, 1958.

—— (1971a) *Playing and Reality*, London: Tavistock.

—— (1971b) *Therapeutic Consultations in Child Psychiatry*, London: Hogarth Press.

Yalom, I. (1983) *In-Patient Group Psychotherapy*, New York: Basic Books.

Young, M. (1982) *The Elmhirsts of Dartington: The Creation of a Utopian Community*, London: Routledge & Kegan Paul.

Name index

Adamson, Edward 9–10, 12, 39, 43, 48, 51, 52–3, 59, 82, 87, 99, 102, 109, 111, 112, 116, 225; and St Albans School of Art 137, 139–40, 238; work at Netherne Hospital 30–1, 53–7, 85, 88, 95, 103, 104
Adler, Alfred 62
Agazarian, Y. 140

Bach, Mrs S. 30, 53, 101
Baly, M. 222
Barker, Culver 97, 101
Barnard, K. 41
Baron, C. 69, 235
Barton, R. 65
Baynes, H. G. 25, 63, 66
Becker, H. S. 114
Ben-David, J. 35, 36, 52, 88, 139, 196, 220
Berke, Joe 130
Berman, Ed 49
Bierer, Joshua 58, 60, 100
Birtchnell, John 13, 14, 25, 144, 148, 159, 160, 221, 245, 256
Bode, B. H. 22
Bohm, Hansi 85
Breakwell, Frank 109, 110, 116, 125, 137, 139, 141, 142, 144
Brown, Julienne 227
Bucher, R. xii, 99, 100, 106–7, 108, 117–18, 143, 167, 190, 243, 244
Buller, Dame Georgiana 95
Buller, Millicent 53, 96, 101
Burroughs, Lucy 229

Byrne, Peter 167, 173, 221, 229–30, 232, 234–5, 251

Cable, Graham 116, 119, 142
Cane, Florence 5, 6
Cannon, C. 221
Cant, Julian 29
Cardinal, R. 24
Carstairs, G. M. 103, 110, 112
Case, Caroline 14, 74–5
Catterson-Smith 20
Chalker, Linda 160
Chamberlain, A. F. 19
Champernowne, Gilbert 38, 42, 61–2, 63, 64, 66, 71, 97
Champernowne, Irene 7, 9, 11, 12, 14, 15, 32, 50, 56, 57, 73, 77, 83, 89, 95, 96, 99, 105, 247; and development of the profession 51, 97, 100, 101, 102, 109, 112, 222, 224; work at Withymead Centre 18, 38, 42, 43, 60–72, 222
Chappell, Alex 142
Charcot, J. M. 25
Churchill, Winston 8
Cizek, Franz 16–18, 19, 20, 21, 22, 35, 85
Cole, Peter 262
Collins, R. 35, 36, 52, 88, 139, 196, 220
Cooper, David 130
Coote, Mrs 97
Cornford, Christopher 225
Cracknell, Rupert 136, 137
Craske, N. 41

280

Name index

Dadd, Richard 28
Dalberg 53
Dalley, Tessa 13–14, 76
Davies, Elsie 32, 96, 101, 102
Davis, M. 74
Dax, E. Cunningham 10, 12, 25, 29,
    30, 31, 52, 53–4, 55, 56, 57, 85,
    95, 97, 103
Dewey, John 19, 20, 55
Donnelly, Michael 176, 262
Doran, L. 147
Dubuffet, Jean 24, 25–6
Dyne, D. 219

Eccott, Arthur 20
Eccott, Rosalind 20
Edwards, Michael 82–3, 109, 125,
    126, 137, 142, 143, 155, 156, 160,
    167, 173, 228, 229, 234, 246, 251
Ehrenzweig, Anton, 231
Eisner, E. W. 20, 21–2
Elliot, Lea 229
Elmhirst, Dorothy 38, 51, 60, 61
Elmhirst, Leonard 51, 60, 61
Elston, M. A. 40, 41
Eskow, Lynn 175
Evans, John 112, 160, 167, 191, 221,
    236–7, 239–40, 241, 246

Fairbairn, W. R. D. 25
Foulkes, Janet 210
Francis, C. 138
Freud, Anna 74
Freud, Sigmund 19, 29, 31, 41, 76
Freudenberg, R. K. 10, 53
Froebel, Friedrich 19
Fry, Roger 20–1

Gibb, Evelyn 20
Gilroy, Andrea 4, 49–50, 76, 80, 159,
    164, 166, 171, 172, 183, 184, 185,
    189, 190–5 *passim*, 206, 207, 233,
    251
Glass, Jan 80–1, 82, 85, 109, 111
Godfrey, Norah 95–6
Goffman, E. 65
Goldsmith, Alison 240
Goodson, I. 243

Gould, S. J. 19
Gray, J. 41
Griffiths, Belver 50, 71
Gross, E. 143
Gulliver, Pam 147, 154
Guttmann, Erich 27–9, 30, 32
Guy, Jo 95

Haber, Donna 166, 183, 184, 189, 190,
    193, 204, 207, 209, 212, 213, 214
Hadfield, J. 101
Hall, G. Stanley 19, 20
Halliday, Diana 14, 86–7, 112, 159,
    173
Harris, Anthony 237
Harris, Beryl 58
Heard, W. 40
Henzell, John 84–5, 109, 110, 111,
    116, 117, 133 136, 137, 239
Herbert, J. 147
Hill, Adrian 7, 8, 10, 11, 14, 15, 17,
    36, 40, 43, 45–51, 52, 58, 59, 60,
    66, 73, 84–9 *passim*, 132, 149,
    247; and organisation of the
    profession 51, 57, 94–9, 101, 102,
    105, 109, 112, 116, 117, 125, 171
Hillman, James 132–3
Hinshelwood, R. 243
Hoad, Mary 83
Hobson, R. 68, 70
Hodgkins, Mary 21
Holtom, Robin 148, 173
Huet, Val 14
Hunt, Colin 160
Huxley, Julian 38

Illich, Ivan 49
Isaac, Susan 76
Iveson, J. 46, 100

James, Charity 231
Jarvis, Fred 157, 158, 164
Jenkin, Patrick 209, 210
Jennings, Sue 227
Johnson, T. 169, 181
Jones, K. 47–8, 149
Jones, Maxwell 67
Jowett, P. H. 94

281

Name index

Jung, C. G. 9, 19, 35, 62–3, 66, 76, 83, 87, 133

Kelly, O. 42–3, 48, 146, 149
Kemp, Molly 61
Khaleelee, O. 243
Kimber, W. J. T. 96
Klein, Melanie 14, 74, 76
Klimt, Gustav 16, 17, 18
Knott, Linda 171, 172
Kokoschka, Oscar 18
Kramer, Edith 6–7, 8, 12, 223
Kris, E. 25

Laban, Rudolf 97
Lacey, Colin xiii–xiv
Laing, Joyce 11–12, 77, 84, 115, 137, 139
Large, S. E. 50
Lawn, M. A. 126–7, 136, 169
Lee, K. 41
Lemlij, M. 68
Lewin, Kurt 67
Liebmann, Marion 14
Lipsedge, M. 20
Littlewood, R. 20
Lowenfeld, Margaret 78
Lowenfeld, Viktor 19
Lumley, Dan 159
Lyddiatt, E. M. 10–11, 12, 18, 75, 87–8

Macdonald, E. M. 131–2
MacDonald, S. 16, 22–3, 224–5
MacGregor, John 24, 25
McKinnon, Mr 101
Maclay, Walter 27–9, 30, 32
McMillan, E. L. 151
McNeilly, Gerry 14
Madge, C. 40, 222, 225–6
Main, Tom 30, 67
Mawby, Bernard 137, 142
Maxwell, Frank 142, 151, 153, 155, 157, 160
Mayer-Gross, Walter 27
Melia, K. 222
Metman, Miss 97
Mikardo, Ian 210

Miller, Edmund 126
Mills, J. F. 20
Milner, Marion 73, 75–7
Minsky, Louis 97
Mitchell, R. C. 157
Molloy, Terry 130, 172
Morgenthaler, W. 25
Morris, William 18
Moser 17
Mullins, Nicholas 50, 71
Musgrave, V. 24

Naumberg, Margaret 5–6, 7, 9, 11, 12, 13, 14, 15, 35, 50, 56, 87, 96, 223
Naylor, Besley 116
Neil, A. S. 64
Newton, Mary 142, 159, 160, 171
Nordau, Max 23
North, Marion 227

Olbrich 17
Overend, Nancy 58, 102
Ozga, J. T. 126–7, 136, 169

Payne, Sylvia 76
Penrose, Lionel 29
Penrose, Roland 29, 130
Pestalozzi, Johann Heinrich 19
Peters, R. 140
Petrie, Marie 7–8, 12, 17, 21, 45, 47, 48, 49, 85, 98, 149, 222–3
Pfister, O. 25
Pickersgill, Jill 173
Pickford, Ralph 11, 12, 25, 73, 77–9, 104, 115
Plato 22
Plokker, J. 104
Pope, Michael 81–2, 109, 111, 112, 159, 160
Preston, Gayleen 154, 157, 159, 160
Prinzhorn, Hans 23, 25, 29, 104

Read, Herbert 19, 60, 83, 103, 130
Reitman, Francis 25, 29, 31, 32, 53, 54, 85, 89
Rennie, Andrew 154
Richardson, Marion 20–1
Richer, P. 25

282

Name index

Rickman, Dr 77
Rivett, Miss 97
Robbins, Julia 207
Roberts, N. 41–2
Robertson, Seonaid 231
Robinson, Anna 126
Roman, Stan 29, 30, 53, 54
Romanes, Miss 78
Roth, G. 69
Rousseau, Jean-Jacques 19
Rubenshaw, Mrs 102
Rumney, Rona 55, 56, 57
Rushworth, Dr 78
Rytovaara, M. 148

Salvage, J. 222, 247–8
Sargant, W. 29–30, 41
Schaverien, Joy 228
Schwartz, M. 65
Seftel, L. 112
Segal, Arthur 31–2, 46, 96
Seif, Leonard 62
Setlogelo, P. 4
Shorske, C. E. 17, 18
Simmel, Ernst 31
Simon, P. -M. 25
Simon, Rita 39, 57–9, 60, 88, 102,
 256
Skaife, Sally 14
Slater, E. 41
Sowerby, Miss 101
Stanton, A. 65
Stead, Barry 172
Stevens, Anthony 60, 61, 62, 64, 65,
 67–8, 70, 99
Strauss, A. xii, 99, 100, 106–7, 108,
 117–18, 143, 167, 190, 243, 244
Sully, James 19–20
Summerson, Sir John 138

Tagg, John 154
Tardieu, A. -A. 25
Tarrant, Miss 97, 101
Thevoz, M. 24, 26
Thompson, Martina 88
Timlin, John 82
Tippett, Euanie 61

Todd, Sir Geoffrey 97
Tomlinson, R. 21, 55
Tomlinson, R. R. 20
Trevelyan, John 97, 101, 223–4
Trevelyan, Julian 29

Ulman, Eleanor, 6, 64, 66

Vaughan, Gerard 160, 209, 210, 211
Viola, Wilhelm 17, 19

Wagner, Otto 17
Wain, Louis 28
Walker, C. 147
Walker, Christine 237–8
Wallbridge, D. 74
Waller, D. 4, 14, 44, 49–50, 131, 148,
 156, 158; and BAAT negotiations
 over professional status 142, 159,
 160, 166, 170, 172, 173, 183, 185,
 189, 191, 193, 195, 204, 206, 207,
 210; and training 221, 222, 228,
 231–4, 244, 247, 251, 254, 263,
 264, 265
Walter, L. 70
Warren Piper, D. 138
Warsi, Britta 148, 173
Weatherson, Alexander, 107–8
Webb, Mary 83, 101, 102
Weber, 69
Weinberger, B. 40, 222, 225–6
Wilde, Oscar 48
Williams, Mrs 101
Williams, Raymond 49
Wills, D. 64
Wills, Elizabeth 85–6, 126, 144
Winnicott, Donald 14, 73, 74–5, 76
Wittick, C. 69
Woddis, Joan 14, 263
Wolff, Toni 63
Wolffi, Adolf 25
Wood, Margarita 227

Yalom, I. 65
Yates, Sybil 30, 53
Young, M. 51, 61–2

Subject index

Adamson collection 27, 82
adult education lecturers: BAAT's attempt at comparability with *see under* teachers
aggression and art therapy 11
alcoholics: work with 84, 121
American Art Therapy Association 246
American Bulletin of Art Therapy 9
American Journal of Art Therapy 6
anti-psychiatry movement 130, 141, 237, 247
APMT (Association of Professional Music Therapists) 174, 213, 214
art: in 1940s 38–40; in 1960s 224–6; and emotional development 21–2, 36, 82
art activity and art therapy 4, 6–8, 9, 10, 11, 13, 14, 73, 96
Art and Psychopathology Group 115
art as regeneration movement 17, 47, 149
Art Brut 24, 25–6
art education 38–40, 138–41, 224–5; and art therapy 16–24, 36, 150; child art movement *see* child art movement; *see also individual institutions*
Art Exhibition Bureau 94
art graduates and art therapy 14, 189, 221, 256
art groups 14
Art News 104
art schools *see* art education
art therapist: definitions 3–4, 122,

135; early use of term 36
art therapists: attitude towards NHS 42–4, 51, 69, 102; code of ethics 105, 263; qualifications and training *see* training for art therapy; qualities 98–9, 100–1, 108–9, 111–12, 122–3, 135–6, 242; reflections of pioneers 80–9, 120–2; salaries and conditions of service 117, 119–28 *see also* BAAT; statements about purpose and methods 147–9
art therapy: as a career 80, 225; definition of 3–4, 5, 98, 113, 130; educational v. medical or occupational therapy model 118; as graduate profession 14, 189, 221, 256; medical contributions to 27–32; popular view of 4; professional views 5–15; promotion in non-NHS areas 264; purpose xiii; training *see* training for art therapy; two strands of 73, 96–7, 107–8, 165, 181; working parties and early meetings on 35, 57, 58, 59, 72, 83, 97–9, 100, 101, 102, 103, 105, 107, 109, 112, 223, 224
art therapy panel 102–5
Art Therapy Registration Board 168–9, 171
Artists in Hospitals movement 75
Arts Enquiry 38
Ashington Group 40
Association for Workers with

284

Subject index

Maladjusted Children 144

Association of Professional Movement Therapists 203

Association of Professional Music Therapists of Great Britain 174, 213, 214

ASTMS (Association of Scientific, Technical and Managerial Staff, later MSF) 128, 154, 159, 166, 171, 257, 262; and BAAT's struggle for a Whitley place 212–15; and campaign to establish art therapy in NHS 181–215; campaign with BAAT on DHSS Consultative Document 198–205; and Clegg Commission 206–10 *passim*

ASTMS Research Group 206

ATTI 159

ATTI *Bulletin* 139

Australia: art therapy in 95

Austria: art in 16–18, 35

authority in art therapy 69–70; *see also* leadership

BAAT (British Association of Art Therapists) 82, 84, 85, 86, 88, 98, 230; AGM 1966 116–18, 125; AGMs in late 1960s 130; conflicts of interest in 116, 117; definition of art therapy 3–4; and DHSS *see* DHSS; EGM 1971 140; EGM 1976 168, 169–72, 241, 248; establishment of membership criteria 111–12, 113, 114; first moves towards NHS 151–61; formation of 35, 51, 57, 59, 73, 79, 80, 81, 108, 109–10; inaugural meeting and constitution 113–18, 123; learned society functions 127, 128, 136, 141, 158; as limited company 172–4; negotiations with Whitley Council *see* Whitley Council; and NUT *see under* NUT; Principles of Professional Practice 105, 263; regional groups 262; and St Albans School of Art *see under* Hertfordshire College of Art; struggles for

control of the profession 162–77; and training *see* training for art therapy; and unions 166 *see also* ASTMS, NUT; work on non-NHS areas 264

BAAT Affiliation and Training Sub-Committee 143, 144

BAAT/ASTMS campaign on DHSS Consultative Document 198–205

BAAT/BAOT working party on DHSS Consultative Document 207

BAAT *Newsletter* 125–6, 158, 159, 164

BAAT/NUT campaign on salaries and status 129–50, 151, 152, 154, 227, 238

BAAT Registration Advisory Committee 239; visits 248–52; Report and recommendations (1977) 267–72

BAAT Registration and Training Sub-Committee 176, 177, 196, 198, 221, 233, 239, 241, 242–52

BAAT Registration Board 263

BAAT Training and Education Sub-Committee 221, 227, 262–3

BAAT working party on professional status (1976) 167–9

BAOT (British Association of Occupational Therapists) 191–2, 199–200, 201, 203, 207, 212

Beveridge Report 41

biological determinism 19

Birmingham Polytechnic, School of Art Education *see* School of Art Education, Birmingham

Birmingham prison: art therapy at 21

Brighton School of Art 227, 231

British Association of Occupational Therapists *see* BAOT

British Council for Rehabilitation conference 95–6

British Institute for the Study of the Arts in Therapy (BISAT) 127, 174–6, 201

British Journal of Medical Psychology 77

British Medical Association 40

285

Subject index

British Medical Journal 57, 103
British Psycho-Analytical Society 76, 77, 86
British Red Cross 48, 50, 52, 53, 58, 80, 96
Bulgaria: art therapy in 265

Canada: art therapy in 95
Cassel Hospital, Surrey 67
Central Youth Employment Executive 237
charisma 69
child art movement 6, 16–24, 32, 36, 99, 111–12
child psychology and development 19–20, 76, 223
children: psychoanalysis and 73, 74–5; work with 14, 78, 81, 82, 86, 87, 222–3, 264
Clegg Commission 205, 206–15
Coldstream Report 138–40, 224
colleagueship 143
commercial art 39, 52, 85
community artists 146, 149
Confederation of Health Service Employees (COHSE) 166
Conference of Art Therapists in Hospitals and Clinics (1950) 101, 223–4
Council for National Academic Awards (CNAA) 200, 234, 235, 239, 252, 254, 255
Council for the Professions Supplementary to Medicine 127, 191, 192, 203–4, 219
counter-transference 13
creativity 75; and madness 26, 110
cultural imperialism 48–9
Current Opinion 23

Dadaism 104
Dartington Hall 60, 61
Dartington Hall Trustees 38–40; *see also* Elmhirst, Dorothy; Elmhirst, Leonard *in Name Index*
Denmark: links with Herts College 265
Department of Education and Science

see DES
Department of Health and Social Security *see* DHSS
depersonalisation 28
depression and art therapy 132
DES 136, 137, 152, 154, 157, 158, 160, 164, 232, 233, 234, 236, 238, 251
DHSS 119, 120, 122–4, 129–30, 136, 137, 144, 145, 152, 162–5 *passim*, 173, 238, 247, 251, 257;
definition of art therapist 3; linkage of art therapy with occupational therapy 96, 103, 151, 152–3, 163, 210–11; and training 141, 153, 170, 183, 211–12, 236, 238, 240, 242, 244, 250, 251
DHSS Advisers in art and music therapy 266
DHSS Circular HC(77)33 Amended 187
DHSS Consultative Document on Art, Music, Drama, etc. Therapy 190, 195, 196, 197–205, 207, 234, 239, 262
DHSS Personnel Memorandum (80)17 211–12
DHSS Personnel Memorandum (1981) 3
DHSS Personnel Memorandum (82)6 214–15, 251, 261
DHSS Working Party Report on the Remedial Professions (1973) 151, 198
diagnosis and art work 5, 32, 36, 54, 55, 95, 96, 98, 110, 165, 223
diversion: art therapy as 7, 8, 96, 99, 123, 132, 165, 195
doodling 28–9, 76, 77
Dutch Art Therapists Committee 95

Eastern Europe: art therapy in 265
Eastern Regional Hospital Board 130, 153
education: art therapy as 130; employment in 120; promotion of art therapy in 264

286

Subject index

emotional development and art 21–2, 36, 82

encounter group movement 68

European Community 1992 256, 264–6

European Training Initiative 265

Evening Standard doodle competition 28

exhibitions 57, 94, 103–5, 108, 109, 110, 144, 225

Expressionism 31, 104

France: art therapy in 265

free expression 5, 50, 96, 132 *see also* spontaneous art

fringe therapists 112

Gilbert and Irene Champernowne Trust 61, 83, 86, 175

Goldsmiths College 156–7, 165, 166, 167, 185, 186, 190, 211, 212, 214, 221, 227, 228, 235, 236, 239, 244–5, 250, 251, 252, 256, 266; case study 231–4

Greece: art therapy in 265

Griffiths Report (1984) 263–4

group dynamics and interaction 14, 140

group psychotherapy 14, 58, 266

groups; influence on art therapy 100; work with 14, 53

Guardian 209

Halsbury Committee 152, 155, 156, 164, 206

Hay MSL Ltd 206, 207, 208, 211

Hertfordshire College of Art: European contacts 265; relations with BAAT 128, 139–40, 144, 153–5, 159, 160, 167, 171, 183, 199, 241; training courses 137–8, 141, 142, 145, 156, 157, 165, 166, 167–8, 185, 186, 190, 200, 211, 212, 214, 221, 232, 235, 236–41, 244–6, 250–1, 252, 256

Hornsey School of Art 227, 230, 231

hospitals 58, 65, 87–9, 97–8, 106, 112, 119, 120, 121, 122, 131, 135, 136, 162, 223

Hougton Committee on teachers' pay 154, 155, 164

image-making and art therapy 3, 5–6, 7, 9, 10, 14, 18, 35, 66, 73, 75, 96, 99

industrial therapy 131, 132

inner symbol: art and 95

insane art 22–4

Inscape 12, 60, 79, 80, 130, 132, 144, 147, 148, 159, 221, 231, 240, 250

Institute of Contemporary Art 103, 105, 108, 109, 110

Institute of Education, London University 134, 157, 227, 242, 253

International Society for Art and Psychopathology 117

International Society for Education through Art (INSEA) 126, 144

Ireland: art therapy in 256–7

Italy: art therapy in 265

Joint Secretaries' Report 164–6, 183, 186, 189–91, 198, 199, 205, 211, 212, 239

Joint Staff–Management Whitley Council Grading Committee for Art and Music Therapists 261

Jugoslavia: art therapy in 265

King Edward VII Sanatorium, Midhurst 45–6, 49, 84, 96

leadership 68–9, 71–2; of art therapy movement 50–1, 71, 73, 77, 96, 116

leucotomy, lobotomy 29–30, 54

local education authorities 120, 185; campaign for the employment of art therapists under *see* teachers

McLellan Galleries 105

McMillan Report 165

Manufacturing, Science and Finance (MSF formerly ASTMS) *see* ASTMS

Maudsley Hospital 27–9, 67

medical model of illness 131, 141,

287

Subject index

248, 256
medicine and art therapy 27–32, 132, 187–8
mental illness: and art 25–32, 52, 53–7, 85; treatment 1940–63 41–2; treatment 1963 onwards 130–3, 141, 147–9, 154, 247
mescaline intoxication 28, 29
Ministry of Health *see* DHSS
modern art 23
MSF (formerly ASTMS) *see* ASTMS
music therapy, therapists 95, 127–8, 266

National Association for Mental Health 117; art therapy working parties under sponsorship of *see under* art therapy
National Association for the Prevention of Tuberculosis 94–5
National Association of Local Government Officers (NALGO) 166
National Council for Diplomas in Art and Design (NCDAD) 224–5
Netherne Hospital 29, 31, 53–7, 82, 103, 116
neuro-psychiatry 28
New Society 107–8
NHS 4, 12, 37, 40–4, 53, 69, 83, 100, 106, 110, 128, 133, 135, 149; Adrian Hill and 43, 51, 102; BAAT and first moves towards 151–61; BAAT/ASTMS campaign to establish art therapy in 181–215; changes in organisation and art therapy 266; Irene Champernowne and 18, 42, 43, 69; Whitley Council *see* Whitley Council
non-directive therapy 18, 20, 36
Northern Ireland: art therapy in 256–7
Northfield Military Hospital, Birmingham 30, 53, 67
nurses, nursing 138, 139, 152, 156, 212, 222, 247–8
Nursing Mirror 94
NUT: BAAT as a Central

Association of 16, 118, 119–28, 237; campaign with BAAT on salaries and status 129–50, 151, 152, 154, 227, 238; withdrawal of BAAT from 155–61, 164, 235, 239

object-relations theory 14, 74–5
occupational therapy 7–8, 42, 46, 49, 56, 84, 85, 86, 89, 99, 100–1, 123, 129–33, 145, 223; art therapy officially linked profession with 96, 103, 151–3, 154, 163, 166, 187–8, 191–2, 194–5, 198, 199–201, 202, 203, 210–11, 212, 213, 215, 262; and St Albans course 156; training 222
Outsider Art 24, 25–7

Paddington Centre for Psychotherapy 135, 152, 231, 235, 236
Paddington Day Hospital 69
Paddington Institute 135, 142
paramedical professions: art therapists compared with 123, 141, 155, 162; *see also under* occupational therapy
Parliamentary involvement with art therapy 125, 137, 142, 155, 156, 157–8, 160–1; and Clegg Commission 209, 210; and DHSS Consultative Document 198, 200 202
passive role of artist 54–5, 56, 95
patients and art therapy 132, 135, 147–8, 188
Patients First 208, 210, 211
patronage of the arts 60
Pay Review Body for Nurses and Professions Allied to Medicine (1983) 262
physical disease: art therapy and 12, 58, 84, 86, 131
play therapy 103
preventive medicine: art therapy as 12
primitive art 20, 22–4
prisons 21, 135, 184–5
Professional Nurses' Conference 94

Subject index

professionalism v. unionism 124–8, 136–7, 141, 158–9

profession(s): art therapy and xii–xiii, 99, 100, 106, 117–18, 181, 190, 243 *see also* BAAT; DHSS and 202; statutory control 219

Professions Supplementary to Medicine Act (1960) 204

psychiatric patients 135, 147–8

psychiatric treatment *see* mental illness

psychiatrist and art therapy 5

psychiatry: anti-psychiatry movement 130, 141, 237, 257; and art 25–32, 53–7

psychoanalysis 54, 77,; art therapy as 6; Freudian 7, 11, 73, 74, 76, 77, 78, 86, 87; influence on art therapy 73–9; Irene Champernowne and 62–3, 224; Jungian 62–3, 67, 71, 86, 87; and Withymead 67, 71

psychology 36, 52–3, 139; of art 77; of children *see* child psychology and development

psychotherapy 9–10, 13, 41, 78, 100, 266; art therapy as 11, 13, 98, 99, 106, 123, 235; for children *see* children, work with; for ethnic groups 20; as qualification for art therapy 125; training for 219, 222, 243

psychotic art 28, 52, 85 *see also under* psychiatry

Queen's University, Belfast 256

recapitulation theory 19–20

regeneration movement 17, 47, 149

Regional Advisory Council 232, 233, 253, 254, 255

Register of Art Therapists 257, 263

rehabilitation 42, 45, 58, 100, 132; art therapy as 7, 12, 46, 95–8, 165

Rehabilitation Journal 95

remedial art teaching distinguished from art therapy 237–8

remedial professions: DHSS working

party on 151, 198

research 12

role conflict, hybridisation 52–3, 88–9, 196

Royal College of Art 38, 39

Royal College of Psychiatrists 159, 199, 207

St Albans School of Art *see* Hertfordshire College of Art

schizophrenia 23, 28, 30, 56, 110

Schizophrenic Art Exhibition 103–5

School of Art Education, Birmingham 12, 134, 137, 144, 156, 167, 190, 211, 212, 214, 221, 228, 229–31, 234, 236, 237, 242, 244–5, 250, 251, 252, 256

Scientific and Professional Staffs Whitley Council 262

SCOPE 200–1

Scotland: art therapy in 256–7, 262

Scottish Department 130

Scottish Society for the Study of Art and Psychopathology 73, 77, 84, 116

Scottish Society for Study of the Psychopathology of Expression 79

Secession movement 16–17, 31

Segal school, London 85, 86

servicemen: rehabilitation of 30, 53, 58, 67

SESAME 173–4

sexuality and art therapy 11

Sheffield University 252, 263

shock therapy 100

Slade 38, 39

Social Psychiatry Centre, Hampstead 58, 59

social psychiatry clubs 58, 60, 65

social services: promotion of art therapy in 264, 266

Society for Art Education 144

Society of Music Therapy 127

South West Metropolitan Regional Hospital Board art therapy committee 97

Special Education 81

speech therapists 154, 187, 204, 210,

289

Subject index

213, 262
spontaneous art 10–11, 82, 87; *see
    also* free expression
strike action 209
Studio Magazine 45, 49
sublimation of feelings: art and 7, 11
Summerson Committee 138, 141
Sunday Times 110
Surrealism 29, 104
Switzerland 35
symbolism 97, 99, 100 *see also*
    unconscious, the

Tavistock Clinic 62
teachers: BAAT's campaign for
    comparability with 123–4, 128,
    129–50, 151, 152, 154, 227, 238,
    242
therapeutic communities 30, 122;
    Withymead 67–70
therapeutic value of art 96, 98, 221
Times, The 11, 23, 49, 96
training for art therapy 93, 101–2,
    103, 113, 117, 122–3, 125, 134,
    143, 144, 145, 156–7, 159, 182,
    212, 219–57; attempts which
    failed 253–7; early lack of 27;
    early views on 221–8; of
    graduates 14, 189, 221, 256; post
    1982 262–3; within European

Community 265–6; Withymead
    and 61, 71, 101
transference relationship between
    patient and therapist 6, 7, 10, 12,
    13, 14, 56, 63

unconscious, the : art therapy and 3, 4,
    5, 9, 10–11, 73, 96, 99
University of Birmingham School of
    Art Education *see* School of Art
    Education, Birmingham
USA: art education 20; art therapy in
    5–7, 16, 35, 87, 149, 246, 263,
    265; definitions of art therapy 3,
    5; fringe therapy 112

visual arts *see* art
voluntary service 149, 195

Wales: art therapy in 256–7, 262
Whitley Council 151, 153, 154, 156,
    162–6; Clegg Commission 205,
    206–15; negotiations with 142,
    145, 183–96, 212–15, 251, 261,
    262
Withymead Centre 38, 42, 43, 60–72,
    83, 86, 89, 95, 96, 98, 99, 101,
    106, 109, 131, 222
work, workshops 131, 132
World Health Organisation 265

290